# ON VIRTUE ETHICS

Virtue ethics is perhaps the most important development within late twentieth-century moral philosophy. Rosalind Hursthouse, who has made notable contributions to this development, now presents a full exposition and defence of her neo-Aristotelian version of virtue ethics. She shows how virtue ethics can provide guidance for action, illuminate moral dilemmas, and bring out the moral significance of the emotions. Deliberately avoiding a combative stance, she finds less disagreement between Kantian and neo-Aristotelian approaches than is usual, and she offers the first account from a virtue ethics perspective of action 'from a sense of duty'. She considers the question which character traits are virtues, and explores how answers to this question can be justified by appeal to facts about human nature. Written in a clear, engaging style which makes it accessible to non-specialists, *On Virtue Ethics* will appeal to anyone with an interest in moral philosophy.

# On Virtue Ethics

ROSALIND HURSTHOUSE

OXFORD
UNIVERSITY PRESS

*This book has been printed digitally and produced in a standard specification
in order to ensure its continuing availability*

# OXFORD
UNIVERSITY PRESS

Great Clarendon Street, Oxford OX2 6DP

Oxford University Press is a department of the University of Oxford.
It furthers the University's objective of excellence in research, scholarship,
and education by publishing worldwide in

Oxford  New York

Auckland  Bangkok  Buenos Aires  Cape Town  Chennai
Dar es Salaam  Delhi  Hong Kong  Istanbul  Karachi  Kolkata
Kuala Lumpur  Madrid  Melbourne  Mexico City  Mumbai  Nairobi
São Paulo  Shanghai  Singapore  Taipei  Tokyo  Toronto

Oxford is a registered trade mark of Oxford University Press
in the UK and in certain other countries

Published in the United States
by Oxford University Press Inc., New York

© Rosalind Hursthouse 1999

The moral rights of the author have been asserted

Database right Oxford University Press (maker)

Reprinted 2002

ISBN 0-19-823818-5

*To*
*Elizabeth Anscombe and Philippa Foot*

# Acknowledgements

My first thanks must go to the many Open University students to whom I have taught virtue ethics at their summer schools over the last ten years, for the experience and moral wisdom they brought to bear on our discussions.

The first three chapters are based on previously published articles, now recast, but Chapters 4–5 are little changed from 'Virtue Ethics and the Emotions' (in Daniel Statman (ed.), *Virtue Ethics*, Edinburgh: Edinburgh University Press, 1997).

I am rather embarrassed to reveal how many people have been kind enough to help me by reading the entire manuscript of the penultimate draft—how could it all have been commented on by so many and still contain so many flaws? But it would be churlish in the extreme not to thank my two 'anonymous' readers for Oxford University Press (one of whom, as I should have guessed from the penetration of the comments, turned out to be Michael Slote), and also Simon Blackburn, William Charlton, Roger Crisp, Thorsteinn Gylfason, Anselm Müller, Tom Sorell, Christine Swanton, Rebecca Walker, Stephen Watt, Sue Weir, and, most especially, Carol Voeller, who generously spent hours of international telephone calls going through the whole thing with me in painstaking detail. A shocking number of typographical errors remained, many of which, at least, have been removed by the expert editing of Angela Blackburn, for which I am most grateful.

The penultimate draft was written in New Zealand, where I was sustained, guided, and corrected by many conversations with Christine Swanton, as, indeed, I have been for years. I can only hope that I may contribute as much to her forthcoming book on virtue ethics as she has contributed to this one.

When, having finished a book, one comes to write the acknowledgements, it sometimes strikes one that the footnote references and bibliography do not entirely capture one's philosophical debts. I think the quantity of footnotes to John McDowell and Gary Watson are just about right, but the extent to which I have benefited from reading, in particular, Julia Annas and Stephen Hudson, is, somehow, not properly represented and so I would like to record my indebtedness here.

Finally, no quantity of footnotes, nor anything else, could adequately register my debt to Elizabeth Anscombe and Philippa Foot. But I am grateful to them for giving me permission to dedicate this book to them, thereby enabling me at least to acknowledge it.

# Contents

# Introduction

'Virtue ethics' is a term of art, initially introduced to distinguish an approach in normative ethics which emphasizes the virtues, or moral character, in contrast to an approach which emphasizes duties or rules (deontology) or one which emphasizes the consequences of actions (utilitarianism). Imagine a case in which it is obvious that I should, say, help someone in need. A utilitarian will emphasize the fact that the consequences of doing so will maximize well-being, a deontologist will emphasize the fact that, in doing so, I will be acting in accordance with a moral rule such as 'Do unto others as you would be done by' , and a virtue ethicist will emphasize the fact that helping the person would be charitable or benevolent. Virtue ethics is both an old and a new approach to ethics, old in so far as it dates back to the writings of Plato and, more particularly, Aristotle, new in that, as a revival of this ancient approach, it is a fairly recent addition to contemporary moral theory.

Up until about thirty years ago, normative ethics was dominated by just two theories: deontology, which took its inspiration from the eighteenth-century philosopher Immanuel Kant, and utilitarianism, which derives, in its modern incarnations, from the eighteenth- and nineteenth-century philosophers Jeremy Bentham and J. S. Mill. In the hundreds of books and articles on normative ethics published during the sixties and seventies, it was common to find versions of one or both of these theories outlined, discussed, amended, applied, compared, and criticized—but no mention made of any third possibility which harked back to the ancient Greeks.

Gradually, a change was observable. In some books designed as undergraduate texts in normative ethics, various articles critical of the prevailing orthodoxy were cited as calling for a recognition of the importance of the virtues, and a few paragraphs on 'what a virtue ethicist would say' inserted. At first, the mentions tended to

2 *Introduction*

be short and dismissive. Virtue ethics was regarded not as a third approach in its own right, but as emphasizing a few interesting points—such as the motives and character of moral agents—that deontologists and utilitarians could usefully incorporate into their approaches. Then, as more articles were written in its defence, it acquired the status of 'the new kid on the block'—yet to establish its right to run with the big boys, but not to be dismissed out of hand. And now in the latest collections (as I write, in 1998), it has acquired full status, recognized as a rival to deontological and utilitarian approaches, as interestingly and challengingly different from either as they are from each other.

Why has modern moral philosophy revived the ancient approach of virtue ethics? On the face of it, it does seem odd that, armed with two theories derived from philosophers of the 'modern world', any moral philosopher, let alone a whole movement of them, should have felt it necessary to go all the way back to Plato and Aristotle. Given how long ago they wrote, given how different our world is from that of their Athens, given, moreover, Aristotle's (at least) deplorable views on both slavery and women, is it not absurd to turn to them for inspiration on ethics? 'On the face of it' perhaps, yes, but in practice and in detail, no.

For a start, it must be emphasized that those who espouse virtue ethics nowadays do not regard themselves as committed to any of the lamentable, parochial details of Aristotle's moral philosophy, any more than many deontologists inspired by Kant think they are committed to his views on, for example, animals.[1] What each has done is provide Western moral philosophy with a distinctive approach, an approach that, its proponents think, can fruitfully be adapted to yield what we now recognize as moral truth.

There are a number of different stories to be told about why an increasing dissatisfaction with deontology and utilitarianism should have resulted in the revival of virtue ethics (and no way of determining which is the most accurate), but certainly part of any story seems to be that the prevailing literature ignored or sidelined a number of topics that any adequate moral philosophy should

---

[1] Kant himself denied that we had any duties to any animals, on the grounds that they were not persons but things. However, Tom Regan, one of the two most famous defenders of 'animal liberation', is a deontologist and moreover one who employs Kantian ideas: see his *The Case for Animal Rights* (1983).

address. Two I mentioned above—motives and moral character; others were moral education, moral wisdom or discernment, friendship and family relationships, a deep concept of happiness, the role of the emotions in our moral life, and the questions of what sort of person I should be, and of how we should live. And where do we find these topics discussed? Lo and behold, in Plato and Aristotle.

Now of course, this is not just a coincidence. The modern philosophers whom we think of as having put virtue ethics on the map—Anscombe, Foot, Murdoch, Williams, MacIntyre, McDowell, Nussbaum, Slote[2]—had all absorbed Plato and Aristotle, and in some cases also Aquinas. Their criticisms of 'modern moral philosophy' were no doubt shaped by what they had found insightful in those earlier writers and then found lacking in the moderns. But the fact remains that, once they are pointed out, many people, not just those who have read the ancient Greeks, immediately recognize the topics as important ones in moral philosophy.

Indeed, one interesting upshot of the emergence of virtue ethics is that some deontologists and utilitarians have reacted to it by recognizing its importance and seeking to address it within the terms of their own theories. Hence, for example, the revived interest in Kant's Doctrine of Virtue, the elaboration of character-based versions of Kantianism and utilitarianism, and the utilitarian Peter Singer's latest book on 'How are we to live?'.[3] This is currently resulting in some very exciting work, particularly in the area of Aristotelian and Kantian scholarship. A recent collection has McDowell bringing Aristotle closer to Kant, and Herman and Korsgaard bringing Kant closer to Aristotle.[4] I have not yet come

---

[2] It seems to be just an accident that N. J. H. Dent's *The Moral Psychology of the Virtues* (1984), S. Hudson's *Human Character and Morality* (1986), and E. Pincoffs's *Quandaries and Virtues* (1986) have not been quite as influential as the writings of the authors mentioned here.

[3] O. O'Neill, 'Kant After Virtue' (1984); R. B. Louden, 'Kant's Virtue Ethics' (1986); R. Crisp, 'Utilitarianism and the Life of Virtue' (1992); J. Driver, 'The Virtues and Human Nature' (1996); B. Herman, *The Practice of Moral Judgement* (1993); M. Baron, *Kantian Ethics Almost Without Apology* (1995); Peter Singer, *How Are We to Live?* (1996).

[4] J. McDowell, 'Deliberation and Moral Development in Aristotle's Ethics'; B. Herman, 'Making Room for Character'; Christine Korsgaard, 'From Duty and for the Sake of the Noble: Kant and Aristotle on Morally Good Action', all in S. Engstrom and J. Whiting (eds.), *Aristotle, Kant and the Stoics* (1996). See also Stephen Hudson, 'What is Morality all About?' (1990).

across an attempt to interpret Mill in Aristotelian ways but I suspect it will happen any day.[5]

This has meant that the lines of demarcation between the three approaches have become blurred. Describing virtue ethics loosely as an approach which 'emphasizes the virtues' will no longer serve to distinguish it. By the same token, of course, deontology and utilitarianism are no longer perspicuously identified by describing them as emphasizing rules or consequences in contrast to character.[6] No one, as far as I know, is bothered by the fact that there are no longer satisfactory short answers to the questions 'What is deontology?' and 'What is utilitarianism?', but currently, at least some philosophers seem bothered by the fact that we virtue ethicists cannot come up with one to answer 'What is virtue ethics?'. The demand that virtue ethics, unlike the other two approaches, should be able to state its position succinctly, in terms both sufficiently broad (or disjunctive?) to get all virtue ethicists in and sufficiently tight to keep all deontologists and utilitarians out, seems a bit excessive. Why should anyone expect us, uniquely, to be able to do it?

One reason I think people want us to do it is simply unfamiliarity. No one actually in moral philosophy, as I am and the complainants are, minds deontology and utilitarianism being introduced by loose slogans because we all learnt the terms when we were students and have been familiar with them ever since, like 'rationalism' and 'empiricism'. We use the slogans in our lectures but we know how to go beyond them, introducing the next philosophical generation of students to, for example, rule and 'government house' variants once we have told them about act utilitarianism. Armed with a sense of the difference between the two familiar approaches, we confidently identify utilitarian strands in a particular deontologist's thought and vice versa. But, apart from the people who actually espouse virtue ethics, as I do, only a few can do the same with a virtue approach.

I doubt that any short answer to 'What is virtue ethics?' would provide a satisfactory solution. What is needed is a familiarity with

---

[5] See the notes to ch. 2 of R. Crisp (ed.), *Utilitarianism* (1998).

[6] Three excellent recent survey articles on modern virtue ethics all constantly qualify the usual slogans, pointing out ways in which new developments in utilitarianism and deontology have subverted them. See G. V. Trianosky, 'What is Virtue Ethics all About?' (1990), Justin Oakley, 'Varieties of Virtue Ethics' (1996); and Daniel Statman, 'Introduction to Virtue Ethics' (1997).

virtue ethics comparable to that which everyone in the profession has with deontology and utilitarianism. But this is not easy to acquire from the existing literature. Although there are lots of articles, there is, as I write, only one book which explores virtue ethics systematically and at length, namely Michael Slote's *From Morality to Virtue* (1992). What I offer is another one, which addresses different issues, in different ways. My approach is more concerned with details, examples, and qualifications than Slote's, and, in being thereby less abstract, is more committed to exploring a particular version of virtue ethics. Books espousing other versions are doubtless in the pipeline[7] and pretty soon it ought to be the case that everyone in moral philosophy is as familiar with 'the' virtue ethics approach as they are with the other two and stops worrying about definitions.

In saying this, I do not mean to claim, in advance of future developments, that virtue ethics, in contrast to deontology and utilitarianism, is bound to survive, as Oakley puts it, 'as an enduring feature of the ethical landscape'.[8] Indeed, I rather hope that future generations of moral philosophers, brought up on all three approaches, will lose interest in classifying themselves as following one approach rather than another; in which case all three labels might become of merely historical interest. But that is still over the horizon, for much of what those future generations could be taught under the label 'virtue ethics' still needs to be provided.

An obvious gap is the topic of justice, both as a personal virtue and as the central topic in political philosophy, and I should say straight out that this book makes no attempt at all to fill that gap. In common with nearly all other existing virtue ethics literature, I take it as obvious that justice is a personal virtue, and am happy to use it as an occasional illustration, but I usually find any of the other virtues more hospitable to the detailed elaboration of points. But, in a book of this length, I do not regard this as a fault. I am writing about normative ethics, not political philosophy, and even when regarded solely as a personal virtue (if it can be), justice is so contested and (I would say) corrupted a topic that it would need a book on its own.

---

[7] Indeed, just as I was writing this introduction, I found Linda Zagzebski's *Virtues of the Mind* (1996), whose second part is substantial enough to count as a book on virtue ethics in its own right.
[8] Oakley, 'Varieties of Virtue Ethics', 152.

I say 'corrupted' because it has become all too common to allow
a vague concept of justice and rights to encompass large areas of
morality that virtue ethicists believe are better dealt with in terms
of other, more concrete, virtues. According to virtue ethics—and in
this book—what is wrong with lying, when it is wrong, is not that
it is unjust (because it violates someone's 'right to the truth' or their
'right to be treated with respect') but that it is *dishonest*, and dishonesty is a vice. What is wrong with killing, when it is wrong, may
be not so much that it is unjust, violating the right to life, but, frequently, that it is callous and contrary to the virtue of charity. Nor
do I subscribe to the view that, if some action is 'absolutely
required', it thereby falls into the province of justice rather than one
of the other virtues. From the perspective of virtue ethics, one can
say that it is 'absolutely required' that one does not 'pass by on the
other side' when one sees a wounded stranger lying by the roadside,
but the requirement comes from charity rather than justice.

Although I acknowledge the existence of the gap, it would be
premature to assume that this gap cannot be filled. In their introduction to *Virtue Ethics*, Crisp and Slote, admitting that virtue
ethics needs to meet the challenge, cite several virtue ethicists who
are beginning to do so[9] and look forward to the day when there will
be an 'Oxford Readings in Virtue Politics'. There certainly seems to
be a growing concern over whether justice is the only virtue which
should figure in discussions of political morality. Could human
beings even sustain social union, let alone a just one, if parents did
not love their children, and if there were no such thing as what
Aristotle describes as 'civic friendship'? Statman, admitting that
'the whole issue concerning VE and political theory . . . has only just
started to be explored' suggests that communitarianism 'might turn
out to be the political aspect of VE'.[10] Who knows. But while we do
not know, we should keep an open mind, not waste our time trying

---

[9] R. Crisp and M. Slote (eds.), *Virtue Ethics* (1997). They cite the articles by Baier
and Slote included in their collection and also Martha Nussbaum's 'Aristotelian
Social Democracy' (1990) and my own 'After Hume's Justice' (1990–1). In the bibliography they also give William Galston's *Liberal Purposes: Goods, Virtues and
Diversity in the Liberal State* (1991), but omit to mention what Statman rightly
describes as Slote's 'pioneering discussion', in 'Virtue Ethics and Democratic Values'
(1993).
[10] Statman, 'Introduction to Virtue Ethics', 18.

to show in advance that since virtue ethics is to be specified in such and such a way, it is bound to be unable to give an account of justice or political morality.

A deeper reason for the demand that we should come up with a crisp answer to 'What is virtue ethics?', I suspect, is the persistence of the belief that virtue ethics is not, as I claimed above, 'a rival to deontological and utilitarian approaches, as interestingly and challengingly different from either as they are from each other'. The suspicion is that, if only the virtue ethicists could be induced to state their position baldly, in a short list of theses, it would become clear that any of the theses that were not obviously and ludicrously false or indefensible could be accommodated by deontology or utilitarianism. But trying to make out that virtue ethics does have a distinctively different approach by listing putatively distinctive and plausible claims it subscribes to, seems to me a needlessly combative task. As things are now, the approach is still new enough to be distinctive, and the aim of this book is to explore what insights can be gained into moral philosophy when it is spelt out in a really detailed and comprehensive way. If utilitarians and deontologists disagree with what I say then of course I shall want to argue with them, and maybe some of our sticking points will be disagreements over particular theses that, typically, though by no means universally, they espouse and virtue ethicists reject, or vice versa. But maybe not. And if they were to agree, and their only protest was 'But we can say that too—that's a utilitarian (or a deontological) thesis', I should not be inclined to argue at all; I should be delighted. Let us by all means stop caring about how we distinguish ourselves and welcome our agreements.

I used to be much more combative and eager to argue that virtue ethics was not only a rival to the other two approaches but the best, and was able to solve or avoid problems that the other two were committed to finding intractable. While virtue ethics was not generally recognized and was being dismissed, I think that was the right tactic, and one powerfully pursued in Slote's *From Morality to Virtue*. But the reaction to virtue ethics' emergence that I mentioned above has been so sudden and so fruitful that, only six years after that book's publication, I find it reasonable to hope that the combative stance is no longer necessary. Hence, though I contrast virtue ethics with simple versions of deontology and utilitarianism in the early chapters, I do so only to aid initial comprehension rather than to deny the possibility of sophisticated developments, and references to them fade away as the book progresses.

Up until now my use of 'we' has mostly been limited to 'myself and other virtue ethicists or moral philosophers'. From now on, unless context clearly indicates otherwise, I shall be using it to mean 'me and you, my readers', and I am making certain assumptions about my readership. It is not possible to write a book in moral philosophy without taking a fair amount of common ground for granted, and I am assuming that anyone who is interested enough in the area to read such a book shares my own ethical outlook to a fair extent. We may have lots of detailed disagreements but, I assume, we all think that ethics matters, and that (broadly speaking and allowing for all the detailed disagreements) we are against murder, dishonesty, cruelty, and so on and in favour of benevolence, honesty, justice, and so on. Hence, I assume, we would fill out those 'and so ons' in the same way.

## NEO-ARISTOTELIANISM

The particular version of virtue ethics I detail and discuss in this book is of a more general kind known as 'neo-Aristotelian'. The general kind is 'neo' for at least the reason I noted above, that its proponents allow themselves to regard Aristotle as just plain wrong on slaves and women, and also because we do not restrict ourselves to Aristotle's list of virtues. (Charity or benevolence, for example, is not an Aristotelian virtue, but all virtue ethicists assume it is on the list now.) It is 'Aristotelian' in so far as it aims to stick pretty close to his ethical writings wherever else it can. Hence what I present here is only one version of virtue ethics amongst many possible ones.

For one thing, virtue ethics does not have to be Aristotelian in the sense just given. Michael Slote's recent 'agent-based' version of virtue ethics is not at all, he thinks, Aristotelian, but is to be found in the nineteenth-century ethicist Martineau,[11] and some of Christine Swanton's work pays more attention to Nietzsche than to Aristotle.[12] For another, any virtue ethics which is 'Aristotelian' as

---

[11] Michael Slote, 'Agent-Based Virtue Ethics' (1995).
[12] C. Swanton, 'The Supposed Tension Between "Strength" and "Gentleness" Conceptions of the Virtues' (1997).

described inevitably aims to stick close to the author's interpretation of Aristotle, and interpretations of Aristotle, on many of the relevant issues, vary. (Thus, to cite one example amongst many, there is a debate over whether Aristotle is intrinsically elitist. To some readers,[13] this aspect of his thought seems ineliminable. To others, myself included, this is not so. We agree that the elitism, like the sexism, is present, but we do not think it is built into the very structure of his thought.) And finally, as I first discovered when I tried to apply neo-Aristotelianism to abortion,[14] and later to the question of moral dilemmas, there are all sorts of specific areas that come up in contemporary moral philosophy about which Aristotle said little or nothing. When this happens, the neo-Aristotelian virtue ethicist has to launch out on her own, perhaps, as often in my case, feeling that she is pursuing a line of thought which is a natural development of his (albeit conscious of the fact that it would make him rotate in his grave); or perhaps self-consciously moving away from him. But either way, there are lots of different directions to go, so in launching out on our own we may come up with different versions.

Indeed, for all my claims to being 'Aristotelian', most of this book must be described, in a way, as 'launching out on my own', because I have tried to write it without presupposing that my readers have read Aristotle's *Nicomachean Ethics*. And, consistently with that presupposition, I must say something here about what I import from him. In fact, just how much is imported, straight over the gap of two thousand years, how much has dropped out of our thought only recently, and how much is still around, needing only to be brought to the surface and acknowledged again, would be a delicate question in the history of ideas. But, for whatever reason, there are certainly some familiar stumbling blocks for many people who are unacquainted with Aristotle's ethics, and they should be addressed straight away.

The first is the concept of *eudaimonia*, usually translated as 'happiness' or 'flourishing' and occasionally as 'well-being'. Each translation has its disadvantages. The trouble with 'flourishing' is that animals and even plants can flourish, but *eudaimonia* is only possible for rational beings. The trouble with 'happiness', on any

---

[13] See Peter Simpson, 'Contemporary Virtue Ethics and Aristotle' (1992).
[14] *Beginning Lives* (1987) and 'Virtue Theory and Abortion' (1991).

contemporary understanding of it uninfluenced by classically trained writers, is that it connotes something subjective. It is for me, not for you, to pronounce on whether or not I am happy, or on whether my life, as a whole, has been a happy one, and barring, perhaps, cases of advanced self-deception and the suppression of unconscious misery, if I think I am happy, then I am—it is not something I can be wrong about. Contrast my being healthy, or flourishing. Here we have no difficulty in recognizing that I might think that I was healthy, either physically or psychologically, or think that I was flourishing, and just be mistaken. In this respect, 'flourishing' is a better translation of *eudaimonia* than 'happiness' . It is all too easy for me to be mistaken about whether or not my life is *eudaimon*, not simply because it is easy to deceive oneself, but because it is easy to have the wrong conception of *eudaimonia*, believing it to consist largely in pleasure, for example. 'Well-being' is also a better translation than 'happiness' in this respect, but its disadvantages are that it is not an everyday term and that it lacks a corresponding adjective, which makes for clumsiness.

However, despite the undoubted fact that 'happiness' can have this subjective connotation, it does seem that we also have a more objective notion much closer to that of *eudaimonia*, a notion of 'true (or real) happiness', or 'the sort of happiness worth having'. We tend to say that someone may be happy, though not truly happy, if they are living in a fool's paradise, or engaged in what we know is pointless activity, or brain-damaged and leading the life of a happy child. When we hope that our children will grow up to be happy and have happy lives, we hope for more than that they will lie around all day in a drug-induced haze of contentment.[15]

The second is the concept of a virtue (or vice) itself. Suppose someone were described as having the virtue of honesty. What would we expect them to be like?

Most obviously we expect a reliability in their actions; they do not lie or cheat or plagiarize or casually pocket other people's possessions. You can rely on them to tell you the truth, to give sincere references, to own up to their mistakes, not to pretend to be more knowledgeable than they are; you can buy a used car from them or ask for their opinion with confidence. In thinking about the virtues,

---

[15] For an authoritative discussion of tensions between modern conceptions of happiness and ancient ideas of *eudaimonia* see Julia Annas, 'Virtue and Eudaimonism' (1998).

many people stop here—or indeed, rather earlier, with just a couple of examples—and are thereby led to describe the virtues as no more than mere tendencies to act in certain ways, perhaps in accordance with a rule.

But this is not the Aristotelian concept. Despite a few awkward exceptions (friendship, gratitude), a virtue is generally held to be a character trait, a state of one's character. If you have the virtues of, say, generosity, honesty, and justice, generous, honest, and just is the sort of person you are. Clearly, one can give the appearance of being a generous, honest, and just person without being one, by making sure one acts in certain ways . And that is enough to show that there is more to the possession of a virtue than being disposed to act in certain ways; at the very least, one has to act in those ways for certain sorts of reasons. But, in fact, we think of such character traits as involving much more than tendencies or dispositions to act, even for certain reasons.

For example, we think of honest people as people who tend to avoid the dishonest deeds and do the honest ones in a certain manner—readily, eagerly, unhesitatingly, scrupulously, as appropriate. They hasten to correct a false impression their words have led you into which would be to their advantage; they own up immediately without waiting to see if they are going to be found out, they give voice to the truth everyone else fears to utter; they are concerned to make sure you understand what you are signing or agreeing to do for them.

We expect a reliability in the actions that reflect their attitude to honesty, too. We expect them to disapprove of, to dislike, and to deplore dishonesty, to approve of, like, and admire honesty, and so we expect them in conversation to praise or defend people, real or fictitious, for their honesty, to avoid consorting with the dishonest, to choose, where possible, to work with honest people and have honest friends, to be bringing up their children to be honest. Where relevant, we expect them to uphold the ideals of truth and honesty in their jobs; if they are academics, to be resistant to fashion and scrupulous in their research; if they are teachers, to resist pressure to teach what they do not believe, or if doctors to defend the importance of trust between doctor and patient, or if in business, to resist sharp practice and argue for honesty as the best policy.

And this spills over into the emotions we expect from them. We expect them to be distressed when those near and dear to them are dishonest, to be unresentful of honest criticism, to be surprised, shocked, angered (as appropriate) by flagrant acts of dishonesty, not to be amused by certain tales of chicanery, to despise rather than to envy those who succeed by dishonest means, to be unsurprised, or pleased, or delighted (as appropriate) when honesty triumphs.

Finally, we may not actually expect, but may notice, if we are fortunate enough to come across someone thoroughly honest, that they are particularly acute about occasions when honesty is at issue. If we are less than thoroughly honest ourselves, they put us to shame, noticing, as we have failed to do, that someone is obviously not to be trusted, or that we are all about to connive at dishonesty, or that we are all allowing someone to be misled. As Stephen Hudson has rightly remarked: 'The unity of character is extremely labyrinthine. It couples systematically a person's values, choices, desires, strength or weakness of will, emotions, feelings, perceptions, interests, expectations and sensibilities.'[16]

One important fact about people's virtues and vices is that, once acquired, they are strongly entrenched, precisely because they involve so much more than mere tendencies to act in certain ways. A change in such character traits is a profound change, one that goes, as we say, 'all the way down'. Such a change can happen slowly, but on the rare occasions when it happens suddenly, the change calls for special explanations—religious conversion, an experience that changes the person's whole outlook on life, brain damage, or drugs. It is certainly not a change that one can just decide to bring about oneself overnight, as one might decide to break the habit of a lifetime and cease to have coffee for breakfast.

That the virtues are not merely tendencies to act in certain ways is not an unfamiliar thought. What is more unfamiliar is the Aristotelian idea that they are not only character traits but excellences of character. Each of the virtues involves getting things right, for each involves *phronesis*, or practical wisdom, which is the ability to reason correctly about practical matters. In the case of generosity this involves giving the right amount of the right sort of thing, for the right reasons, to the right people, on the right occasions. 'The right amount' in many cases is 'the amount I can afford' or 'the amount I can give without depriving someone else'. So, for instance, I do not count as mean or even ungenerous when, being

---

[16]   Hudson, *Human Character and Morality* (1986).

relatively poor, or fairly well off but with a large and demanding family, I do not give lavish presents to richer friends at Christmas. Nor do I count as mean or even ungenerous if I refuse to let people exploit me; generosity does not require me to help support someone who is simply bone idle, nor to finance the self-indulgence of a spendthrift. Any virtue may contrast with several vices or failings, and generosity contrasts not only with meanness or selfishness but also with being prodigal, too open-handed, a sucker.

When we think of the virtues in general, or 'virtue' *tout court*, it seems that we think in the Aristotelian way. The concept of a virtue is the concept of something that makes its possessor good; a virtuous person is a morally good, excellent, or admirable person who acts and reacts well, rightly, as she should—she gets things right. These seem obvious truisms. But when we think of particular examples of virtues, we sometimes give these truisms up. We may say of someone that he is too generous or honest, generous or honest 'to a fault'. It is commonly asserted that someone's benevolence might lead them to act wrongly, to break a promise they should have kept, for example, in their desire to prevent someone else's hurt feelings. Or we may think of the 'virtue' of courage as something that, in a desperado, enables them to do far more wicked things than they would be able to do if they were timid. So, it would appear, being generous, honest, benevolent, or courageous, despite their being virtues, can also be faults; or they are not always virtues, but sometimes faults. Someone who is generous, honest, benevolent, or courageous might not be a morally good, admirable person—or, if it is still a truism that they are, then morally good people may be led or enabled by what makes them morally good to act wrongly! Which all sounds very odd.

Odd as it is, it would be futile to insist that it was wrong. As far as my own linguistic intuitions go, the only virtue term we have which is guaranteed to operate as a virtue term—that is, to pick out something that always makes its possessor good—is 'wisdom'. (Perhaps also 'just'—I am not certain.) People can be 'too clever by half' but not too wise. But all the other candidates seem to accept 'too' or 'what a pity he is so . . .'. However, we do not have to talk this way, and we have various circumlocutions that enable us to hang on to the truisms that a virtue is a good way to be; that it makes its possessor good and enables her to act well. We can make sense of the claim that it is impossible to be too generous or too honest. Someone initially described that way can be redescribed as not quite having the virtue of generosity but a misguided form of it, as not so much honest as candid or outspoken. Instead of saying, without qualification, that someone's benevolence led them to act wrongly on a particular occasion, we might say, again, that they had, not the virtue, but a misguided form of it, or (depending on the nature of the case) a perverted form of it, or that they were on the right path but did not possess the virtue yet, or possessed it to a very imperfect degree. And we may say that the desperado is daring but does not possess the virtue of courage.

The third thing I import from Aristotle is a pair of interrelated distinctions.

(1) There is a distinction between acting from reason, which we, typically, do, and what the other animals and small children do when they 'act'.

(2) There is a distinction between rational wanting or desire, which we, typically, have, and the mere passion or desire that impels the other animals and small children.

The distinctions derive, I think myself, from a specially realistic feature of Aristotle's thought—that he never forgets the fact that we were all once children. To read almost any other famous moral philosopher is to receive the impression that we, the intelligent adult readers addressed, sprang fully formed from our father's brow. That children form part of the furniture of the world occasionally comes up in passing (about as often as the mention of non-human animals), but the utterly basic fact that we were once as they are, and that whatever we are now is continuous with how we were then, is completely ignored.

We all know that there is a difference between being a child and being an adult—and we all know that the difference is not merely physical. 'When I was a child', says St Paul, 'I spake as a child, I understood as a child, I thought as a child: but when I became a man, I put away childish things.' We manifest that knowledge in our ascriptions of moral responsibility—albeit often with great difficulty—regarding intentional homicide committed by eight-year-olds, or those with a 'mental age' of eight, differently from when it is committed by those who have 'reached the age of reason'. So in the moral sphere we do assume there is a distinction between being mentally a child and mentally an adult. But what is it? Most moral philosophers have nothing to say relevant to this question because, having overlooked the fact that the rational adult moral agents they are addressing were children, they do not see it as a problem. But Aristotle does—and hence the distinctions.

Neither distinction is entirely unfamiliar in modern philosophy. Many philosophers have wanted to distinguish acting from reason from acting from desire, and many have given accounts of special forms of rational wanting which contrast with non-rational or 'basic' wanting. But the distinctions, as thus drawn, are both technical and highly contentious, whereas the distinction between being mentally an adult and mentally a child is neither. Moreover, they tend to be presented as hard and fast, whereas, as we know, the transition from childhood to adulthood is a continuum; there is no precise point at which the change occurs. Although I would not stake my life on the impossibility of someone's coming up with the necessary and sufficient conditions for 'acting from reason' in the way we, typically, do, and animals and small children do not, I am quite certain that any such analysis would have to embody, somehow, that continuum. Further, mental maturity is made up of many factors. 'Has a mental age of five' is often a gross judgement which, perforce, ignores ways in which the subject has mental attributes that no ordinary five-year-old has. (This fact is no doubt connected to the fact that the distinction between the mental and the physical is often shaky. Is the desire to have sexual intercourse, or children, a mental attribute or a physical one?) Conversely, rational adults are of course not immune to childish or animal impulses or passions, but we are not thereby 'in the same state' as children or animals. We know, dispositionally if not occurrently, that the impulse or passion is innocent or deplorable, unduly strong or weak, justifiable or unjustifiable, only to be expected under the circumstances or calling for justification, and so on, and that knowledge is part of the state we are in but not of whatever states animals and small children are ever in.

This brings me to a fourth thing I do not so much import from Aristotle as find him hospitable to, namely a philosophical psychology which runs counter to the prevailing contemporary view. In contemporary philosophy of action, there is a fervid debate about whether any intentional action must be prompted in part by a desire, or whether it is possible to be moved to action by a belief—such as the belief that doing so-and-so is morally required—alone. The debate all takes place against the background of the assumption that beliefs and desires are as different as gold and oxygen, and usually also the assumption that the distinction between the rational and the non-rational is equally hard and fast. But Aristotle is happy to describe 'choice' (*prohairesis*) as either desiderative intellect or intellectual desire; it belongs to both the cognitive and the conative faculties and is not to be broken down into two bits, a belief and a desire. Moreover, when he describes the soul as 'part rational, part irrational', he does not think it matters to which part we assign the desiderative. The 'vegetative' part (the cause of nutrition and growth in living things) is definitely irrational; and the theoretical is definitely rational. But the desiderative can be regarded as irrational, because it can run counter to reason, or as rational, because it is receptive to reason. There is no answer to the question 'Is it rational or irrational *tout court*?'; all there is to be said is that it is irrational in this way and rational in that.

To anyone sympathetic to the writings of the later Wittgenstein, such rejections of clear-cut distinctions in philosophical psychology are as natural and necessary as breathing. Such philosophers are in a minority at the moment, and it is no part of my brief in this book to try to convert the philosophical world to the minority view, much as I would like to do so. But it is still worth coming clean about it at the outset, to remove one further stumbling block. I have found when teaching virtue ethics to graduate students, or discussing papers by, in particular, Anscombe, Foot, and McDowell with fellow philosophers, that what often blocks understanding is the unconscious assumption that everyone shares the view that, for example, beliefs and desires are natural kinds, or that a reason is a belief/desire pair that causes an action, or that all mental states are brain states—or, more generally, that philosophy is supposed to uncover or construct the foundations of our thought. Struggling to square these assumptions with what is said, the audience finds what is said deliberately obscure or wilfully incomplete, or inconsistent, or open to such blindingly obvious objections that they think they cannot have understood. Sometimes—not always, of course—the cloud lifts if one says, 'But you don't believe that so-and-so if you're a Wittgensteinian.' What follows then is not necessarily agreement, but at least an understanding of just where the disagreement lies.

## THE PLAN OF THE BOOK

My hope is that this book will be used as a textbook, helping to familiarize up-and-coming students with virtue ethics' distinctive approach to a variety of problems and issues in moral philosophy. Bearing in mind that different teachers want to stress different things in their courses, I have divided it into three relatively independent parts, whose constituent chapters are much more closely related, and the parts increase in difficulty as the book progresses. Also bearing in mind that different teachers have their own views about what they want to cover in the way of associated material, I have mostly aimed to keep extended discussion of other authors' writings to a minimum; though the topic of Part II does necessitate some detailed attention to Aristotle and Kant, and Part III presupposes knowledge of some of the literature relevant to the issue of objectivity in ethics.

*Part I. Action*

*Chapter 1. Right action.* Virtue ethics has been characterized, *inter alia*, (1) as an ethics which is 'agent-centred' rather than 'act-centred'; (2) as addressing itself to the question 'What sort of person should I be?' rather than to the question 'What sorts of action should I do?'; (3) as taking certain areteic concepts (*good [well]*, *virtue*) as basic rather than deontic concepts (*right, duty, obligation*); and as (4) rejecting the idea that ethics is codifiable in rules or principles that can provide specific action guidance. Although there is some truth in all these, they tend to foster a common misconception, namely, that virtue ethics does not, and cannot, provide action guidance, the way utilitarianism and deontology do.

But this is a misconception: virtue ethics can provide a specification of 'right action'—as 'what a virtuous agent would, characteristically, do in the circumstances'—and such a specification can be regarded as generating a number of moral rules or principles (contrary to the usual claim that virtue ethics does not come up with rules or principles). Each virtue generates an instruction—'Do what is honest', 'Do what is charitable'; and each vice a prohibition—'Do not act, do what is dishonest, uncharitable.'

*Chapter 2. Resolvable Dilemmas.* Such rules may seem to fall foul of the 'conflict problem', failing to give us action guidance when the requirements of different virtues conflict. But deontology, notoriously, is subject to the same problem when its rules conflict, and many regard the way act utilitarianism resolves hard cases by applying its single maximizing rule as a disadvantage rather than an advantage of its approach. Where hard cases or dilemmas are, *ex hypothesi*, resolvable, virtue ethics in fact employs a strategy similar to that of some forms of deontology; it argues that the putative conflicts are merely apparent. That recognizing a conflict as merely apparent may call for moral wisdom or discernment is explicitly acknowledged in virtue ethics, which takes seriously Aristotle's point that moral knowledge, unlike mathematical knowledge, cannot be acquired merely by attending lectures and is not characteristically to be found in people too young to have much experience of life. A normative ethics should not aim to provide a decision procedure which any reasonably clever adolescent could apply. (This is one aspect of the rejection of the claim that ethics is codifiable.)

*Chapter 3. Irresolvable and Tragic Dilemmas.* In particular a normative ethics should not aim to provide a decision procedure which resolves every dilemma in advance of deciding whether or not there are any irresolvable dilemmas. If there are any, then action guidance, in such cases, is not possible. However, action assessment is still not only possible, but needed—and virtue ethics can provide a particularly satisfying account of the differences between unworrying, distressing, and genuinely tragic dilemmas, the latter being those from which even the most virtuous agent cannot emerge with her life unmarred.

These three chapters are all concerned with virtue ethics in relation to action, and I conclude them by reconsidering some of the standard theses used to sum up virtue ethics' position in this area.

*Part II. Emotion and Motivation*

*Chapter 4. Aristotle and Kant.* The discussion of dilemmas brought in mention of the emotions the virtuous would feel on certain occasions, in particular, regret and even extreme grief as reactions to what 'had to be done'. Virtue ethics is often praised, especially at the expense of Kant's deontology, for giving a better account of the moral significance of the emotions than the other ethical approaches, and, in particular, for giving a more attractive account than Kant of 'moral motivation'. However, a careful consideration of Aristotle's *enkrateia/arete* distinction (the distinction between strength of will or 'continence' and full virtue) and the famous passage in Kant's *Groundwork* in which he discusses moral worth, reveals that, in many ways, Aristotle and Kant are much closer than is usually supposed. Insofar as Aristotle has a notion of 'motivation', the continent and the fully virtuous agent have the same motivation—they both act from reason (*logos*) in the form of 'choice' (*prohairesis*).

*Chapter 5. Virtue and the Emotions.* Where Aristotle is arguably superior is in his account of human rationality, an account that allows the emotions to participate in reason, rather than being mere animal, non-rational, impulses, and thereby play their proper role in the specification of full virtue. The virtues are concerned with actions and feelings, and the moral education needed to develop them involves the education of the emotions. The full significance of this fact can be fruitfully illustrated through an example of moral miseducation, namely, the inculcation of racism.

*Chapter 6. The Virtuous Agent's Reasons for Action.* We noted in Chapter 4 that the fully virtuous act from reason, in the form of 'choice'. Do they, thereby, act 'out of a sense of duty' or 'because they think it's right'? When we consider carefully what is involved in the attribution of such a reason, we can see that the answer is 'Yes' (thus bringing Kant and Aristotle even closer together). The virtuous, when acting virtuously, act for a great variety of different reasons. These form certain ranges, characteristic of particular virtues such as honesty, friendship, justice, courage, temperance, etc. When children and people who are in a transitory emotional state act for such reasons, they do not count as 'acting out of a sense of duty', but when the virtuous, who act from a settled state of character, act for such reasons, they do. Acting from virtue is sufficient for acting from duty.

*Chapter 7. Moral Motivation.* Moreover, acting from virtue, from a settled state of character, sets the standard for acting from duty, or because one thinks it's right. Whatever their sincerely avowed reasons for acting, people act 'from duty' to the extent that their character resembles that of the ideally virtuous agent. Hence moral motivation can be a matter of degree, and is not introspectible.

## Part III. Rationality

The final section of the book is on the 'rationality of morality' in relation to virtue ethics, the question of whether there is any 'objective' criterion for a certain character trait's being a virtue. The standard neo-Aristotelian premise that 'A virtue is a character trait a human being needs for *eudaimonia*, to flourish or live well' should be regarded as encapsulating two interrelated claims, namely, that the virtues benefit their possessor, and that the virtues make their possessor good *qua* human being (human beings need the virtues in order to live a characteristically good human life). These are separately discussed in the first three chapters of this part, and eventually brought together at the end of the final one.

In these chapters I express disagreement with two main schools of thought. I assume, rather than argue for, the view that it is a mistake to suppose that ethics can be given any sort of foundation 'from the neutral point of view'. I assume that ethical thought has to take place within an acquired ethical outlook. However, despite disagreeing with those who seek to provide such a foundation, I do not take up the other familiar position which locates all fundamental ethical disagreements in disagreements about values, which I also deny. Ethical disagreements can be seen to lie in disagreements about facts, albeit, frequently, rather odd facts.

*Chapter 8. The Virtues Benefit their Possessor.* Some familiar objections to the very idea that the virtues on the standard list benefit their possessor can quickly be cleared away. We may also note that, when we consider the claim in the context of bringing up our own children or reflection on our own lives, rather than in the context of trying to convince the wicked or the moral sceptic, we believe it. According to Phillips and McDowell, we believe it in so far as we are virtuous, because we have special conceptions of *eudaimonia*, benefit, harm, and loss, which guarantee its truth. Hence any appeal to the sort of facts that Hare and Foot give in support of the claim are irrelevant. I agree with them that there is no discerning the truth of 'the virtues benefit their possessor' from a neutral or wicked standpoint, but not with their explanation. The sorts of facts that Hare and Foot give form essential support for the claim, and are essential to our inculcating virtue in our children. However, they are odd facts, which philosophy has, as yet, no easy way to classify.

*Chapter 9. Naturalism.* There is another way of interpreting the premise that the virtues are those character traits a human being needs for *eudaimonia*, to flourish or live well, which has it expressing a form of naturalism. We interpret it as saying that the virtues are those character traits that make a human being a good human being—are those traits that human beings need to live well as human beings, to live a good, characteristically human, life. Ethical evaluations of human beings as good or bad are taken to be analogous to evaluations of other living things as good or bad specimens of their kind. The analogy is instructive, because it reveals that several features of ethical evaluation thought to be peculiar to it, and inimical to its objectivity, are present in the quasi-scientific evaluation even of plants.

*Chapter 10. Naturalism for Rational Animals.* However, the analogy can only be pushed so far. Ethics is not a branch of biology. Other living things have characteristic ways of going on that they cannot choose to change, against the background of which they can be evaluated as good or bad specimens. But in so far as we have characteristic ways of going on, we can intelligibly ask 'Is that a good way to go on?' of almost any of them and look for ways of changing it if we think the answer is 'No'. Hence it can be rightly claimed that ethical naturalism, construed as the attempt to ground ethical evaluation in a scientific account of human nature, is a misconceived enterprise. But that is a far cry from claiming that no account of human nature can be objectively well-founded and moving straight to the idea that any conception of it is as good as any other.

*Chapter 11. Objectivity.* The two different interpretations of the premise that 'a virtue is a character trait a human being needs for *eudaimonia*' can ultimately be seen as interrelated, for both rely on the idea that our nature is such that the virtues, as we know them, suit human beings. This fact, if it is a fact, is a highly contingent one. It is a contingent fact that we can, individually, flourish or achieve *eudaimonia*, contingent that we can do so in the same way as each other, and contingent that we can do so all together, not at each other's expense. If things had been otherwise then, according to the version of virtue ethics presented here, morality would not exist, or would be unimaginably different.

PART I

# ACTION

# I

# Right Action

Virtue ethics has been characterized in a number of ways. It is described (1) as an ethics which is 'agent-centred' rather than 'act-centred'; (2) as concerned with Being rather than Doing; (3) as addressing itself to the question, 'What sort of person should I be?' rather than to the question, 'What sorts of action should I do?'; (4) as taking certain areteic concepts (*good*, *excellence*, *virtue*) as basic rather than deontic ones (*right*, *duty*, *obligation*); (5) as rejecting the idea that ethics is codifiable in rules or principles that can provide specific action guidance.

I give this list because these descriptions of virtue ethics are so commonly encountered, not because I think they are good ones. On the contrary, I think that all of them, in their crude brevity, are seriously misleading. Of course, there is some truth in each of them, which is why they are so common, and I shall return to them as we proceed, to note what truth, with what qualifications, they may be seen as containing. Readers familiar with the recent literature I mentioned in the Introduction, which has blurred the lines of demarcation between the three approaches in normative ethics, will no doubt have discarded or qualified them long since. But here, at the outset, it seems best to begin at a simple level, with the descriptions most readers will recognize, and work our way through to some of the complications and subtleties that are not so well known.

## RIGHT ACTION

The descriptions, especially when encountered for the first time, can easily be read as all making roughly the same point, and one way in which they are all misleading is that they encourage the thought that virtue ethics cannot be a genuine rival to utilitarianism and deontology. The thought goes like this:

> If virtue ethics is 'agent-centred rather than act-centred', con-cerned with 'What sort of person should I be?' rather than 'What sorts of action should I do?' (with 'Being rather than Doing'), if it concentrates on the *good* or *virtuous* agent rather than on *right* action and on what anyone, virtuous or not, has an *obligation* to do; how can it be a genuine rival to utilitari-anism and deontology? Surely ethical theories are supposed to tell us about right action, i.e. about what sorts of act we should do. Utilitarianism and deontology certainly do that; if virtue ethics does not, it cannot be a genuine rival to them.

Now the descriptions do not actually say that virtue ethics does not concern itself at all with right action, or what we should do; it is in so far as it is easy to take them that way they are misleading. For virtue ethics can provide action guidance. The way it does this can most helpfully be shown by comparing it with the guidance given by some versions of utilitarianism and deontology, all laid out in a similar way.

Suppose an act utilitarian began her account of right action as follows:

P.1. An action is right iff it promotes the best consequences.

This premise provides a specification of right action, forging the familiar act-utilitarian link between the concepts of right action and *best consequences*, but gives one no guidance about how to act until one knows what to count as the best consequences. So these must be specified in a second premise, for example:

P.2. The best consequences are those in which happiness is maximized—which forges the familiar utilitarian link between the concepts of *best consequences* and *happiness*.

Many simple versions of deontology can be laid out in a way that displays the same basic structure.They begin with a premise pro-viding a specification of right action:

P.1. An action is right iff it is in accordance with a correct moral rule or principle.

Like the first premise of act utilitarianism, this gives one no guidance about how to act until, in this case, one knows what to count
as a correct moral rule (or principle). So this must be specified in a
second premise, which begins

P.2. A correct moral rule (principle) is one that . . .

and this may be completed in a variety of ways, for example,

(1) . . . is on the following list — (and then a list follows, perhaps completed with an 'etc.'), or
(2) . . . is laid down for us by God, or
(3) . . . is universalizable/a categorical imperative, or
(4) . . . would be the object of choice of all rational beings,

and so on.

Although this way of laying out fairly familiar versions of utilitarianism and deontology is hardly controversial, it shows that
there is something wrong with an over-used description of them,
namely the slogan, 'Utilitarianism begins with' (or 'takes as its fundamental concept' etc.) 'the Good, whereas deontology begins with
the Right.'[1] If the concept a normative ethics 'begins with' is the one
it uses to specify right action, then utilitarianism might indeed be
said to begin with the Good (taking this to be the same concept as
that of the best), but we should surely hasten to add, 'but only in
relation to consequences or states of affairs, not, for instance, in
relation to *good* agents, or living *well*'. And even then, we shall not
be able to go on to say that most versions of deontology 'begin with'
the Right, for they use the concept of moral rule or principle to specify right action. The only versions which, in this sense, 'begin with'
the Right would have to be versions of what Frankena calls
'extreme act-deontology'[2] which (I suppose) specify a right action
as one which just *is* right.

And if the slogan is supposed to single out, rather vaguely, the
concept which is 'most important', then the concepts of *consequences* or *happiness* seem as deserving of mention as the concept

[1] For a particularly illuminating critique of Rawls's distinction, see G. Watson,
'On the Primacy of Character' (1990). See also Hudson, 'What is Morality all
About?', (1990) and Herman, *The Practice of Moral Judgement*, ch. 10, who both
challenge the slogan in relation to Kant's deontology.
[2] W. Frankena, *Ethics* (1973).

of the Good for utilitarianism, and what counts as most important for deontologists (if any one concept does) would surely vary from case to case. For some it would be God, for others universalizability, for others the Categorical Imperative, for others rational acceptance, and so on. (Should we say that for Kant it is the good will, or the Categorical Imperative, or both?)

It is possible that too slavish a reliance on this slogan contributes to the belief that virtue ethics cannot provide its own specification of right action. For many who rely on it go on to say, 'Utilitarianism derives the concept of the Right from that of the Good, and deontology derives the Good from the Right; but how can virtue ethics possibly derive the Good and the Right from the concept of the Virtuous Agent, which it begins with?' Now indeed, with no answer forthcoming to the questions 'Good *what*? Right *what*?', I have no idea. But if the question is, 'How can virtue ethics give an account of right action in such a way as to provide action guidance?' the answer is easy. Here is its first premise.

P.1.  An action is right iff it is what a virtuous agent would characteristically (i.e. acting in character) do in the circumstances.

This specification rarely, if ever, silences those who maintain that virtue ethics cannot tell us what we should do. On the contrary, it tends to provoke irritable laughter and scorn. 'That's no use', the objectors say. 'It gives us no guidance whatsoever. Who are the virtuous agents?'

But if the failure of the first premise of an account of right action, the premise which forges a link between the concept of right action and a concept distinctive of a particular normative ethics, may provoke scorn because it provides no practical guidance, why not direct similar scorn at the first premises of act utilitarianism and deontology in the form in which I have given them? Of each of them I remarked, apparently in passing, but really with a view to this point, that they gave us no guidance. Act utilitarianism must specify what are to count as the best consequences, and deontology what is to count as a correct moral rule, producing a second premise, before any guidance is given. And, similarly, virtue ethics must specify who is to count as a virtuous agent. So far, the three are all in the same position.

Of course, if the virtuous agent can be specified only as an agent disposed to act in accordance with correct moral rules, as is sometimes assumed, then virtue ethics collapses back into deontology and is no rival to it. So let us add a subsidiary premise to this skeletal outline, intended to show that virtue ethics aims to provide a non-deontological specification of the virtuous agent *via* a specification of the virtues, which will be given in its second premise.

P.1a. A virtuous agent is one who has, and exercises, certain character traits, namely, the virtues.

P.2. A virtue is a character trait that . . .

This second premise of virtue ethics, like the second premise of some versions of deontology, might be completed simply by enumeration—'is on the following list'—and then a list is given, perhaps completed with 'etc.'. Or we might interpret the Hume of the second *Enquiry* as espousing virtue ethics. According to Hume, we might say, a virtue is a character trait (of human beings) that is useful or agreeable to its possessor or to others (inclusive 'or' both times). Or we might give the standard neo-Aristotelian completion, which claims that a virtue is a character trait a human being needs for *eudaimonia*, to flourish or live well.

Here, then, we have a specification of right action, whose structure closely resembles those of act utilitarianism and many simple forms of deontology. Comparing the three, we see that we could say, 'Virtue ethics (in its account of right action) is agent-centred rather than consequences- or rules-centred. It is agent-centred in that it introduces the concept of the virtuous *agent* in the first premise of its account of right action, where utilitarianism and deontology introduce the concepts of *consequences* and *moral rule* respectively.' That's true; it does. But note that it is not thereby 'agent-centred *rather than* act-centred'. It has an aswer to 'How shall I decide what to do?'

So there is the first misunderstanding cleared away. Virtue ethics does have something to say about right action. But this is only a first step in dealing with the misunderstanding, for many people find what it has to say unsatisfactory. The reasons for their dissatisfaction are so varied that they will occupy us for several chapters; in this one, I shall concentrate on some that are naturally expressed in the complaint that virtue ethics does not and cannot tell us what to do; the complaint that it does not and cannot provide moral guidance.

'Virtue ethics does not provide us with moral guidance'—how can it fail to, when it has provided a specification of right action? Sometimes people suspect that it has provided only a circular specification, not a specification that we could use to guide us. 'It has told us that the right action is what a virtuous agent would do. But that's a truism. Of course the virtuous agent "does what is right"; if she didn't, she wouldn't be virtuous; we are just going round in circles.'

Now it is true that the first premise of virtue ethics' account of right action has the air of being a truism. For although act utilitarians will want to deny the deontologists' first premise ('No! We should break the rule if the consequences of doing so would be better than those of keeping it'), and deontologists will deny the utilitarian one ('No! We must stick to the rules regardless of the consequences'), it is quite likely that both of them would accept what virtue ethics says: 'An action is right iff it is what a virtuous agent would do.' But, if they did, they would each be assuming that they had settled what right action was already, using their first and second premises, and were then using the truism to specify what, for them, counted as a virtuous agent: 'A virtuous agent is one who does what is right (in my sense of "right").'[3]

What I need to emphasize is that the apparent truism, 'An action is right iff it is what a virtuous agent would characteristically do in the circumstances', is not figuring as a truism in virtue ethics' account of right action. It is figuring as the first premise of that account, a premise that, like the first premises of the other two accounts, awaits filling out in the second premise. Perhaps I could make this clearer by restating the first premise, and its supplement, in a way that made the necessity for filling them out glaringly obvious, thus:

P.1.  An action is right iff it is what an X agent would characteristically do in the circumstances, and

P.1a. An X agent is one who has and exercises certain character traits, namely the Xs.

[3] Cf. Watson's opening paragraphs in 'On the Primacy of Character'.

And put that way, P.1 does not look at all like a truism.

Unfortunately, it now looks uninformative, once again, apparently, contrasting unfavourably with the first premises of act utilitarianism and deontology: 'We all have some idea about what best consequences might be and of what correct moral rules or principles are, but what on earth is an X agent?' But now I must repeat the point made earlier. The other first premises, taken strictly, are equally uninformative. We overlook this point because the utilitarian specifications of best consequences are so familiar, and all the deontologists we know cite familiar moral rules. But, for all that is said in the first premise of either, strange things might emerge in the second.

Someone might specify the 'best consequences' as those in which the number of Roman Catholics was maximized (and the number of non-Catholics minimized). It would be a very odd view to hold; no proper Catholic could hold it, but some madman brought up in the Catholic faith might. Or someone might specify the 'best consequences' as those in which certain moral rules were adhered to. 'We all have some idea of what best consequences might be', not because this is *given* in the first premise of the act utilitarian account, but because we are all familiar with the idea that, by and large, if an action has, as a consequence, that many people are made happy, or much suffering is relieved, this counts as a good consequence.

Similarly, when we read the deontologist's first premise, we suppose that 'we all have some idea of what correct moral rules or principles are'. We expect (something like) 'Do not kill' and 'Keep promises'. We do not expect 'Purify the Aryan race', 'Keep women in their proper place, subordinate to men', 'Kill the infidel'. But we know only too well that these not only might be specified, but have been specified, as correct moral rules. As far as the first premise of the deontological account of right action goes, we do not, in fact, have any idea, given by that premise, of what correct moral rules or principles are; we bring our own ideas to it.

So, understood as a first premise comparable to those of act utilitarianism and deontology, 'An action is right iff it is what a virtuous agent would, characteristically, do in the circumstances', far from being a truism, is, *like* the first premises of the others, uninformative. All three start to be informative only when the second premise is added.

### EPISTEMOLOGICAL PROBLEMS

At this stage we may notice an interesting division in the three accounts, a division which puts act utilitarianism on one side, and deontology and virtue ethics on the other. As soon as act utilitarianism produces its second premise, saying that the best consequences are those in which happiness is maximized, we seem to know where the act utilitarian stands. (I shall question below whether we really do, but we certainly seem to.) We can work out that the act utilitarian will say, for example, that it is right to tell a lie when telling the truth would make no one happy and someone very unhappy. But whether we know what a deontologist and a virtue ethicist will say about such a case after they have produced their second premises depends on the form they take.

If a list of correct moral rules or virtues is given, we have something fairly concrete. If one list contains 'Do not lie' and the other 'Honesty', we can work out that the deontologist and virtue ethicist are probably not going to agree with the act utilitarian about the rightness of telling the lie. But what if the deontologist's second premise is one of the others I gave? We all know that there has been, and is, much dispute about what God has laid down, and about what it is rational to accept, and so on—in short, much dispute about which moral rules or principles are the correct ones. When a deontologist produces one of her abstract tests for the correctness of a moral rule, we may be sure that she will defend and justify the rules she believes are correct in terms of it—but what these will be we do not know. Will she defend rules prohibiting suicide or abortion or rules permitting them? Will she turn out to be a pacifist or a supporter of killing in self-defence? We do not know.

Virtue ethics is similarly non-committal. We all know, it is said, that there has been, and is, much dispute about which character traits are the virtues. When a virtue ethicist produces one of her abstract tests, we may be sure that she will defend the character traits she believes are the virtues in terms of it, and dismiss the ones she does not accept—but what these will be we do not know. Will she defend humility, modesty, and compassion or (like Hume, Aristotle, and Nietzsche, respectively) will she dismiss them? Will she defend impartiality or friendship? We do not know.

So here we have an interesting contrast between act utilitarianism on the one hand, and deontology and virtue ethics on the other.

The latter look as though they are bound to land us with a huge problem about how we can *know* that a particular action is right, for whatever either says, we can ask 'But how do we know *which* moral rules or principles are the correct ones, *which* character traits are the virtues?' If they each just produce their list we can worry whether it is the right list. If they produce one of their abstract tests we can worry about the fact that, with sufficient ingenuity, or different further premises, these can be got to yield different results. So both lay themselves open to the threat of moral cultural relativism or, even worse, moral scepticism. Maybe we can do no more than list the rules, or character traits, accepted by our own culture or society and just have to accept that all we can know is what is right according to us, which might be wrong according to some other culture. Or, even worse, when we remember how much moral disagreement there is between 'us', maybe we cannot even do that. Maybe we have to accept that there isn't anything that counts as knowing that a particular action is right; all there is, is feeling convinced that it is because it is in accordance with a certain rule one personally wants to adhere to, or because it is what would be done by the sort of person one personally wants to be.

Act utilitarianism is not, or not immediately, open to the same threat. True, it may be hard, on occasion, to predict the consequences of an action, but this is a practical problem in life which all three accounts have to take on board. Though it is sometimes said that deontologists 'take no account of consequences', this is manifestly false, for many actions we deliberate about only fall under rules or principles when we bring in their predicted consequences. A deontological surgeon wondering whether she should perform a particular operation on a patient may be in doubt, not because she has any doubts about the correctness of her principles, but because it is so hard for her to predict whether the consequences of the operation will be that the patient enjoys several more years of life or is finished off. A surgeon who subscribes to virtue ethics has the same problem: she may not doubt that charity, which is concerned with others' good, is a virtue; her doubt is over whether the consequences of the operation will be that her patient is benefited or harmed.

The difficulty of being able to predict the consequences of one's actions does not bring with it the threat of moral relativism or moral scepticism; it is just a general problem in life. However, if the consequences concern *happiness*, as in the utilitarian account, doesn't the threat come in there? Different cultures, different individuals, have different ideas of happiness. How can we know that a particular action is right if we cannot define precisely and correctly that 'happiness' we are supposed to be maximizing?

I think that one might well press something along these lines as a problem for utilitarianism, and this is a point to which I shall return below. But it is hardly plausible to say it shows that act utilitarianism is *immediately* open to the threat of moral relativism and scepticism. Suppose people's ideas of happiness do vary; why should that matter, for practical purposes? This person will be happy if I give her a book on religious contemplation and upset if I give her a sexy novel, someone else will delight in the novel but be bored to tears by the other. If I can afford both books, act utilitarianism makes it perfectly clear what I should do, without having to define happiness or worry about the fact that these two people doubtless have very different ideas of it. As Jonathan Glover robustly remarks, 'most of us, whether utilitarians or not, take some account of the likely effects of our actions on people's happiness, and we should all be in a mess if there was no correspondence between trying to make someone happier and succeeding'.[4]

So let us say, for the moment, that act utilitarianism is not immediately threatened by the spectre of moral relativism or scepticism, but that virtue ethics, in company with deontology, is. And, having said it and acknowledged the problem, let us put it to one side for later chapters.[5] For the moment I shall assume that both deontology and virtue ethics give an open-ended, and familiar, list in their second premises. Deontology, we may suppose, lists such familiar rules as 'Do not kill', 'Tell the truth', 'Keep promises', 'Do no evil or harm to others', 'Help others/promote their well-being', etc.; virtue ethics lists such familiar character traits as justice, honesty, charity, courage, practical wisdom, generosity, loyalty, etc. And, having assumed that, we can return to the question of whether virtue ethics, even given such a list, somehow fails to provide guidance in the way that act utilitarianism and deontology do.

[4] J. Glover, *Causing Death and Saving Lives*, 3.
[5] Indeed, given the size of the problem, one might say 'for a later book'. But I do return to it in Chapters 8–11.

## MORAL RULES

A common objection goes as follows.

Deontology gives a set of clear prescriptions which are readily applicable. But virtue ethics yields only the prescription, 'Do what the virtuous agent—the one who is just, honest, charitable etc.—would do in these circumstances.' And this gives me no guidance unless I am (and know I am) a virtuous agent myself—in which case I am hardly in need of it. If I am less than fully virtuous, I shall have no idea what a virtuous agent would do, and hence cannot apply the only prescription virtue ethics has given me. True, act utilitarianism also yields only a single prescription ('Do what maximizes happiness'), but there are no parallel difficulties in applying that; it too is readily applicable. So there is the way in which virtue ethics' account of right action fails to be action guiding where deontology and utilitarianism succeed.

In response, it is worth pointing out that, if I know that I am far from perfect, and am quite unclear what a virtuous agent would do in the circumstances in which I find myself, the obvious thing to do is to go and ask one, should this be possible. This is far from being a trivial point, for it gives a straightforward explanation of an important aspect of our moral life, namely the fact that we do not always act as 'autonomous', utterly self-determining agents, but quite often seek moral guidance from people we think are morally better than ourselves. When I am looking for an excuse to do something I have a horrid suspicion is wrong, I ask my moral inferiors (or peers if I am bad enough), 'Wouldn't you do such-and-such if you were in my shoes?' But when I am anxious to do what is right, and do not see my way clear, I go to people I respect and admire: people who I think are kinder, more honest, more just, wiser, than I am myself, and ask them what they would do in my circumstances. How, or indeed whether, utilitarianism and deontology can explain this fact, I do not know, but, as I said, the explanation within the terms of virtue ethics is straightforward. If you want to do what is right, and doing what is right is doing what the virtuous agent would do in the circumstances, then you should find out what she would do if you do not already know.

Moreover, seeking advice from virtuous people is not the only thing an imperfect agent trying to apply the 'single prescription' of virtue ethics can do. For it is simply false that, in general, 'if I am less than fully virtuous, then I shall have no idea what a virtuous agent would do', as the objection claims. Recall that we are assuming that the virtues have been enumerated as, say, honesty, charity, fidelity, etc. So, *ex hypothesi*, a virtuous agent is one who is honest, charitable, true to her word, etc. So what she characteristically does is what is honest, charitable, true to her word, etc. and not what would be dishonest, uncharitable, untrue to her word. So, given such an enumeration of the virtues, I may well have a perfectly good idea of what the virtuous person would do in my circumstances, despite my own imperfection. Would she lie in her teeth to acquire an unmerited advantage? No, for that would be both dishonest and unjust. Would she help the wounded stranger by the roadside even though he had no right to her help, or pass by on the other side? The former, for that is charitable and the latter callous. Might she keep a death-bed promise even though living people would benefit from its being broken? Yes, for she is true to her word. And so on.[6]

This second response to the objection that virtue ethics' account of right action fails to be action guiding amounts to a denial of the oft-repeated claim that 'virtue ethics does not come up with any rules', (which is another version of the thought that it is concerned with Being rather than Doing), and needs to be supplemented with rules. We can now see that it comes up with a large number of rules. Not only does each virtue generate a prescription—do what is honest, charitable, generous—but each vice a prohibition—do not do what is dishonest, uncharitable, mean.[7]

Once this point about virtue ethics is grasped (and it is remarkable how often it is overlooked), can there remain any reason for thinking that virtue ethics cannot tell us what we should do? Yes,

---

[6] Cf. Anscombe: 'It would be a great improvement if, instead of "morally wrong" one always named a genus such as "untruthful", "unchaste", "unjust". . . the answer would sometimes be clear at once.' 'Modern Moral Philosophy' (1958, repr. 1981), 33.

[7] Making this point in earlier articles, I expressed the generated rules adverbially—act honestly, charitably, generously; do not act dishonestly, etc. But the adverbs connote not only doing what the virtuous agent would do, but also doing it 'in the way' she would do it, which includes 'for the same sort(s) of reason(s)', and it has seemed to me better here to separate out the issue of the virtuous agent's reasons for a later chapter.

there is one. The reason given is, roughly, that rules such as 'Do what is honest, do not do what is uncharitable', are, like the rule 'Do what the virtuous agent would do', still the wrong sort of rule, still somehow doomed to fail to provide the action guidance supplied by the rules (or rule) of deontology and act utilitarianism.

But how so? It is true that these rules of virtue ethics (henceforth 'v-rules') are couched in terms, or concepts, that are certainly 'evaluative' in *some* sense, or senses, of that difficult word. Is it this which dooms them to failure? Surely not, unless many forms of utilitarianism and deontology fail for this reason too.

There are, indeed, some forms of utilitarianism which aim to be entirely 'value-free' or empirical, such as those which define happiness in terms of the satisfaction of actual desires or preferences, regardless of their content, or as a mental state whose presence is definitively established by introspection. Such forms run into well-known problems, and have always seemed to me the least plausible, but I accept that anyone who embraces them may consistently complain that v-rules give inferior action guidance in virtue of containing 'evaluative' terms. But a utilitarian who wishes to employ any distinction between the higher and lower pleasures, or pronounce on what rational preferences would be, or rely on some list of goods (such as autonomy, friendship, or knowledge of important matters) in defining happiness, must grant that even her single rule is implicitly 'evaluative'. (This is why, briefly, I think that utilitarianism is not generally immune to the threat of moral relativism or scepticism, as I mentioned above.)

What about deontology? If we concentrate on the single example of lying, defining lying to be 'asserting what you believe to be untrue, with the intention of deceiving your hearer(s)', then we might, for a moment, preserve the illusion that a deontologist's rules do not contain 'evaluative' terms. But as soon as we remember that few deontologists will want to forego principles of non-maleficence and (or) beneficence, the illusion vanishes. For these principles, and their corresponding rules (do no evil or harm to others, help others, promote their well-being), rely on terms or concepts which are at least as 'evaluative' as those employed in the v-rules.

We see revealed here a further inadequacy in the slogan 'Utilitarianism begins with the Good, deontology with the Right' when this is taken as committing deontology to making the concept of the Good (and, presumably, the Bad or Evil) somehow derivative from the concept of the Right (and Wrong). A 'utilitarian' who relied on the concept of right, or virtuous, action in specifying his concept of happiness would find it hard to shrug off the scare quotes, but no one expects a deontologist to be able to state each of her rules without ever employing a concept of *good* which is not simply the concept of *right action for its own sake*, or without any mention of *evil* or *harm*.

We might also note that few deontologists will rest content with the simple, quasi-biological 'Do not kill', but more refined versions of that rule such as 'Do not murder', or 'Do not kill the innocent', once again employ 'evaluative' terms, and 'Do not kill unjustly' is itself a particular instantiation of a v-rule.

Supposing this point were granted, a deontologist might still claim that the v-rules are markedly inferior to deontological rules as far as providing guidance for children is concerned. Granted, adult deontologists must think hard about what really constitutes harming someone, or promoting their well-being, or respecting their autonomy, or murder, but surely the simple rules we learnt at our mother's knee are indispensable. How could virtue ethics plausibly seek to dispense with these and expect toddlers to grasp 'act charitably, honestly, and kindly, don't act unjustly', and so on? Rightly are these concepts described as 'thick'! Far too thick for a child to grasp.

Strictly speaking, this objection is rather different from the *general* objection that v-rules fail to provide action guidance, but it arises naturally in the context of the general one and I am more than happy to address it. For it pinpoints a condition of adequacy that any normative ethics must meet, namely that such an ethics must not only come up with action guidance for a clever rational adult, but also generate some account of moral education, of how one generation teaches the next what they should do. But an ethics inspired by Aristotle is unlikely to have forgotten the question of moral education, and the objection fails to hit home. Firstly, the implicit empirical claim that toddlers are taught only the deontologist's rules, not the 'thick' concepts, is surely false. Sentences such as 'Don't do that, it hurts the cat, you mustn't be cruel', 'Be kind to your brother, he's only little', 'Don't be so mean, so greedy', are commonly addressed to toddlers. For some reason, we do not seem to teach 'just' and 'unjust' early on, but we certainly teach 'fair' and 'unfair'.

Secondly, why should a proponent of virtue ethics deny the significance of such mother's-knee rules as 'Don't lie', 'Keep promises', 'Help others'? Although it is a mistake (I have claimed) to define a virtuous agent simply as one disposed to act in accordance with deontologist's moral rules, it is a very understandable mistake, given the obvious connection between, for example, the exercise of the virtue of honesty and refraining from lying. Virtue ethicists want to emphasize the fact that, if children are to be taught to be honest, they must be taught to love and prize the truth, and that *merely* teaching them not to lie will not achieve this end. But they need not deny that, to achieve this end, teaching them not to lie is useful, or even indispensable.

So we can see that virtue ethics not only comes up with rules (the v-rules, couched in terms derived from the virtues and vices) but, further, does not exclude the more familiar deontologists' rules. The theoretical distinction between the two is that the familiar rules, and their applications in particular cases, are given entirely different backings. According to deontology, I must not tell this lie because, applying the (correct) rule 'Do not lie' to this case, I find that lying is prohibited. According to virtue ethics, I must not tell this lie because it would be dishonest to do so, and dishonesty is a vice.[8]

## UNCODIFIABILITY

What then of the claim that virtue ethics, typically, rejects the idea that ethics is codifiable in rules or principles that can provide specific action guidance? It now stands revealed as a claim that invites the rather tiresome response, 'Well, it all depends on what you mean by "codifiable".'

It used to be quite commonly held that the task of normative ethics was to come up with a set (possibly one-membered, as in the case of act utilitarianism) of universal rules or principles which would have two significant features: (a) they would amount to a decision procedure for determining what the right action was in any

---

[8] This clear distinction (between deontology and virtue ethics) is just one of the many things that has been blurred by the recent happy convergence of Kantians and virtue ethicists.

particular case; (b) they would be stated in such terms that any non-virtuous person could understand and apply them correctly.[9] Call this the 'strong codifiability thesis'. And it was, and is, indeed typical of virtue ethicists to reject that thesis.[10] But, for at least two, no doubt related, reasons, the idea is now much less common.

One reason has been the increasing sense that the enterprise of coming up with such a set of rules or principles has failed. In the early, heady days of applied ethics, it looked feasible, but as more philosophers relying on the same abstract principles applied them in such a way as to produce different conclusions, as different modifications or exclusion clauses were put on the general principles to yield different conclusions, as more philosophers trying to resolve real-life hard cases in medical ethics found themselves compelled to say that there were good arguments on both sides—as, quite generally, the gap between the abstract principles and the complex particularity of concrete moral situations became more obvious, so the idea that the rules should have both the features mentioned began to lose its appeal.

The concurrent emergence of virtue ethics articulated at least one way in which the original idea needed to be modified. It became increasingly obvious, when one considered whether doctors needed to be virtuous, that arrogant, uncaring, dishonest, and self-centred ones could not be guaranteed to do what they should merely by requiring that they acted in accordance with certain rules. The Devil, after all, can quote scripture to serve his own purposes; one can conform to the letter of a rule while violating its spirit. Hence it was recognized that a certain amount of virtue and corresponding moral or practical wisdom (*phronesis*) might be required both to interpret the rules and to determine *which* rule was most appropriately to be applied in a particular case.[11]

Of course, I am not claiming that this is now universally recog-

---

[9] E. Pincoffs, 'Quandary Ethics' (1971), identified this as the dominant view of the task of normative ethics at the time, beginning his article with a number of illustrative quotes from contemporary authors.

[10] Most notably, J. McDowell in 'Virtue and Reason' (1979).

[11] 'It is true that principles underdetermine decisions. This is hardly news for those who have advocated ethical theories that makes principles or rules central. Kant, for example, insisted that we can have no algorithm for judgement, since every application of a rule would itself need supplementing by further rules.' O'Neill, 'Abstraction, Idealization and Ideology in Ethics', (1987), 58.

nized, only that it is much more common than it used to be, particularly in books *of* applied ethics as opposed to books about what normative ethics is or should be. So should we say that those who have given up the original idea 'reject the idea that ethics is codifiable' as, it is said, virtue ethicists do? Clearly, they share with virtue ethicists the view that ethics is not *as* codifiable as used to be commonly supposed, but there is still, I think, a lingering view that it is, or ought to be, more codifiable than virtue ethics makes it out to be.

Sometimes this amounts to no more than the mistake I noted earlier, namely the view that virtue ethics does not come up with any rules or principles, combined, I suspect, with a gut unwillingness to join the virtue ethics camp. Beauchamp and Childress, whose *Principles of Medical Ethics*, from being initially dismissive, has become increasingly friendly to virtue ethics in its successive editions, are still to be found insisting that virtue ethics needs to be *supplemented* by a list of principles, which they give. They do not say, but they might well, that it doesn't *codify* enough. But the list looks like this:

| *Principles* | *Corresponding Virtues* |
|---|---|
| Respect for autonomy | Respectfulness |
| Nonmaleficence | Nonmalevolence |
| Beneficence | Benevolence |
| Justice | Justice or fairness |

| *Rules* | |
|---|---|
| Veracity | Truthfulness |
| etc.[12] | |

Now if this is all that is at issue, let us by all means say that virtue ethics does *not* reject the idea that ethics is codifiable. It does not need to be supplemented by such principles; it embodies them already—and many many more besides. (It is a noteworthy feature of our virtue and vice vocabulary that, although our list of generally recognized virtue terms is, I think, quite short, our list of vice terms is remarkably—and usefully—long, far exceeding anything that anyone who thinks in terms of standard deontological rules has

---

[12] T. L. Beauchamp and J. F. Childress, (eds.). *Principles of Biomedical Ethics*, 4th edn. (1994), 67.

ever come up with. Much invaluable action guidance comes from avoiding courses of action that are irresponsible, feckless, lazy, inconsiderate, uncooperative, harsh, intolerant, indiscreet, incautious, unenterprising, pusillanimous, feeble, hypocritical, self-indulgent, materialistic, grasping, short-sighted, . . . and on and on.)[13]

What else might still be at issue? A prevailing criticism of virtue ethics, related to the idea that it gives up on codifiability too soon, that it does not codify enough, is that it fails to provide action guidance when we come to hard cases or dilemmas. So it is to a consideration of virtue ethics in relation to hard cases—a surprisingly large topic—that we now turn.

---

[13] Some virtue ethicists might want to insist on a strong correspondence between the virtues and the vices; not only that to each virtue there corresponds at least one particular vice but also that every vice is opposed to some particular virtue. Of course one can, formally, insist that to laziness there corresponds the virtue of being the opposite of lazy, which happens to lack a word in English ('industriousness' doesn't really work); more plausibly one could claim that describing someone as 'responsible' in a character reference describes them as having a particular virtue for which we have the adjective but not the noun. But I do not myself believe that things are that tidy.

2

# Resolvable Dilemmas

Still considering the reasons people have for finding virtue ethics' account of right action unsatisfactory, that it somehow fails to provide us with action guidance, we come to the 'conflict problem'. 'The requirements of different virtues,' it is said, 'can point us in conflicting directions. Charity prompts me to kill the person who would (truly) be better off dead, but justice forbids it; so virtue ethics fails to give me any guidance over the rightness or wrongness of euthanasia. Honesty points to telling the hurtful, even devastating, truth, kindness and compassion to remaining silent or even lying; so virtue ethics fails to give any guidance to, for example, doctors, over whether they should or should not sometimes lie to their patients. And so on. So virtue ethics lets us down just at the point where we need it most, where we are faced with the really difficult moral quandaries and do not know what to do.'

In the mouth of a hard-line act utilitarian, this is a comprehensible criticism, for, as is well known, almost the only conflict that classical utilitarianism's one rule can generate is the tiresome logical one between the two occurrences of 'greatest' in 'the greatest happiness for the greatest number'. But it is strange to find the very same criticism coming from deontologists, since they are, notoriously, faced with the same problem. Indeed, moral quandaries or dilemmas are usually defined in deontological terms, as created by conflicting moral principles or rules that generate conflicting requirements in the situation at issue. So is it being assumed that deontology can solve the conflict problem in a way that virtue ethics cannot? Or does the objection reveal (rather early in the day!) that it is only utilitarianism that gives us adequate action guidance and that the other two should be abandoned forthwith? Before tackling these questions I must spend some time discussing the topic of dilemmas itself, for this turns out to be surprisingly complicated. I shall also find it necessary to say some more about the phrase 'right action'.

## DILEMMAS AND REMAINDER

In current philosophical literature on the topic of dilemmas we find an odd split. There is, on the one hand, a large body of literature disputing the theoretical question of whether there are, or even could be, 'irresolvable' moral dilemmas. (An irresolvable moral dilemma is usually specified as a situation where doing $x$ and doing $y$ are equally wrong, but one has to do $x$ or $y$, or one in which two moral requirements conflict but neither overrides the other (roughly).) Contained within the literature are related disputes about what the existence of irresolvable dilemmas does, or would, entail, such as the falsity of moral realism or cognitivism (or, alternatively, their truth!), the failure of moral absolutism, the impossibility of a moral theory's providing a decision procedure, and so on.

Embedded in this literature is the important idea of 'remainder' or 'residue'. Suppose there are irresolvable dilemmas and someone is faced with one. Then, whatever they do, they violate a moral requirement, and we expect them (especially when we think in terms of real examples) to register this in some way—by feeling distress or regret or remorse or guilt, or, in some cases, by recognizing that some apology or restitution or compensation is called for. This—the remorse or regret, or the new requirement to apologize or whatever—is called the (moral) 'remainder' or 'residue'. Even when a dilemma is resolvable, one moral requirement clearly overriding the other, many writers want to insist that it is resolvable only 'with remainder'; the overridden requirement retains its force in some way, so regret, or perhaps the recognition of a new requirement, are still appropriate.

On the other hand, there is an even larger body of literature in applied ethics on 'hard cases' (which are also called 'dilemmas') such as infanticide in the case of handicap, or abortion in the case of rape, or lying to the person in intensive care about the fact that she is the only member of her family to have survived the car accident, and so on. And a remarkable fact about this second body of literature is that it rarely, if ever, takes any notice of the first. Those who contribute to it (a) rarely even entertain the possibility that the dilemma they are discussing is irresolvable; on the contrary, they assume that there must be one, correct, decision to be made about it which it is the business of their moral theory—usually utilitarianism or deontology—to reveal or discover. And (b), concentrating exclusively on the question 'Which is *the right* act in this case, *x* or *y*?', they fail to say anything about 'remainder' or 'residue'. Both (a) and (b) require discussion, and I shall begin with (b), leaving (a) until the next chapter.

The failure to mention remainder in debates in applied ethics is, I think, usually a deplorable oversight, the result of the writers' having committed at least one of several fallacies.

Sometimes it results from simply committing the fallacy of the false dilemma. The writers (frequently unconsciously) take the dilemma to be '*either x* is the morally right act to do here (without qualification) and *y* is the one that's morally wrong *or y* is the morally right act (without qualification), etc.' They simply overlook the third possibility of, for example, 'Well, they are both pretty awful, but (supposing the dilemma is resolvable) *x* isn't quite as bad as *y*.'

The unconscious assumption that, in any case of moral dilemma or conflict, one side must be unqualifiedly morally right and the other plain wrong runs very deep in everyday thought, extending even to the cases in which the moral conflict is between two different agents. I find it noteworthy (and deplorable) that, in some theatres where David Mamet's *Oleanna* was performed,[1] a noticeboard in the foyer invited those who had seen the play to answer the question, 'Who is right? Her or Him?', and *thousands* of people signed up saying 'Her' or 'Him'. How could they have failed to see that the alternatives presented—she is right/morally justified *or* he is right/morally justified—so signally fail to exhaust the possibilities? Rejecting the forced choice offered by the noticeboards, I wanted to say that *neither* was right, nor morally justified; I thought that they both behaved badly (though, marginally, he was even worse than her).

Now it may be easier to see the fallacy in the *Oleanna* case because the forced choice (Which is the morally right one?) is

---

[1] In the first act, She, a student, comes to see Him, a professor, about the fact that she is failing his class. He is too busy with his own concerns to hear her problem, though not too busy to make various unacceptable, sexist, pronouncements. In the second act she returns, in a more assertive mode, to tell him that she has brought charges of sexual harrassment against him; he stands to lose not only his tenure but his beloved house; he gets very angry.

between two people, not two courses of action. My bet is that, if the noticeboards had asked 'Who would you like as a friend, Her or Him?', many more people would have slipped between the horns of the dilemma and roundly said 'neither'. (Moreover, my guess, borne out by conversations I have had with people about my rejection of the forced choice, is that those who signed up implicitly took themselves to be answering a question about a course of action: 'If you *had* to back one of them, whom would you back, Her or Him?')

Why is the fallacy harder to see when the choice is between two courses of action? At least in part because it is very easy to confound two different senses of the phrases 'morally right decision', or 'right moral decision'.

Suppose we have a moral dilemma which is resolvable—$x$ is worse than $y$. Then the decision to do $y$ rather than $x$ is, in the circumstances, the *right* decision. Moreover (supposing the decision to have been made on the moral grounds that $x$ is worse than $y$), it is a moral decision, or one that has been made morally. So it is the 'morally right decision' or the 'right moral decision', and this is one way in which we use those phrases.

Now suppose we have a morally right act—a good deed. As such, it is an act that merits praise rather than blame, an act that an agent can take pride in doing rather than feeling unhappy about, the sort of act that decent, virtuous agents do and seek out occasions for doing (given the truism that 'the virtuous agent does what is right'.) Moreover, agents can take pride in deciding to do such actions— they are the sorts of decision that decent virtuous agents make— and are praised for thus deciding, whether or not the act comes off. Suppose it does not come off, well, that is a pity, but still, we say, they made the 'morally right decision', the 'right moral decision'; good for them. And here, we use those phrases in a second, different, way.

The difference can be brought out by considering the claim: 'When morally right decisions come off—when the agent succeeds in doing what she intended to do—we get morally right action.' So we may truly, indeed, trivially, say when using 'morally right decision' in the second way. But if we are using 'morally right decision' in the first way, we cannot say this truly, for it is obviously false. The man who has induced two women to bear a child of his by promising marriage, can only marry one, but he may not be in an irresolvable dilemma; it may be worse to abandon A than B, and let us suppose he makes 'the morally right decision' and marries A, perforce breaking his promise to B and condemning her child to illegitimacy. He merits not praise, but blame, for having created the circumstances that made it necessary for him to abandon B; he should be feeling ashamed of himself, not proud, and so on. And even when the agent is faced with a resolvable moral dilemma through no fault of her own, the lesser of the two great evils that she (*ex hypothesi* rightly) decides to opt for will still not be a morally right or good act, not one that leaves her with those 'circumstances [so] requisite to happiness', namely 'inward peace of mind, consciousness of integrity, [and] a satisfactory review of [her] own conduct' as Hume so nicely puts it. On the contrary, it will, or should, leave her with some sort of 'remainder'.

So my claim is that many philosophers who resolve hard cases in applied ethics debates but fail to mention 'remainder', frequently (of course not always) equivocate on 'morally right decision', and are thence readily led to accepting a false dilemma. The question, 'Which is the morally right decision, to do $x$ or to do $y$?', is confounded with the very different question, 'Which is the morally right action (with no qualification about remainder, the good action about which the agent need feel no regret), $x$ or $y$?' *If* there are no irresolvable dilemmas, the first question does not pose a false dilemma, but even if every moral dilemma is resolvable, the second certainly does, for the correct answer may well be 'Neither'.

This tendency to overlook remainder is, I think, actively encouraged by demanding at the outset that a normative ethics should 'give an account of right action'; that this is what is required for it to be 'action guiding'. In order to dispel the prevailing illusion that virtue ethics, in being 'agent-centred rather than act-centred', does not even pretend to give any action guidance, I began by yielding to this demand, and stressing the point that virtue ethics can be regarded as supplying a whole lot of rules—the v-rules. But we can now see some point in pulling back a bit, in re-introducing the idea that virtue ethics concentrates on the *agent* rather than the *act*. 'Utilitarianism and deontology are act-centred'; thereby, when their proponents consider hard-case dilemmas, they concentrate exclusively on the question, 'Which is the right act, $x$ or $y$?' And since one cannot decide to feel regret, and feeling regret is not an *act* in the required sense, they thereby cut themselves off from thinking of bringing in that sort of 'remainder'. A proponent of virtue ethics, concentrating on the question, 'What would a virtuous agent do in this situation?', is, given the concentration on the agent and the wider scope of 'do', all set up to answer (for example), '*x*, after much hesitation and consideration of possible alternatives, feeling deep regret, and doing such-and-such by way of restitution'.

Although I am, personally, sympathetic to doctors rather than otherwise, one does hear occasional hair-raising stories about the arrogance and callousness of some. What people often complain about is not whatever decision the doctors made, but the manner in which they delivered it or acted on it. No expressions of regret, no expression of concern over whether anything could be done to make it less likely that such decisions would have to be made in the future; having made (what they take to be) the morally right decision, they seem to think that they can review their own conduct with complete satisfaction. But if someone dies, or suffers, or undergoes frightful humiliation as a result of their decision, even supposing it is unquestionably correct, surely regret is called for. A dose of virtue ethics might make them concentrate more on how they should respond, rather than resting content with the thought that they have made the right decision.

I do not make these remarks in a combative spirit; as I said in the Introduction, my aim is not to do utilitarianism and deontology down. I did once think that, in being 'act-centred rather than agent-centred', they were theoretically disarmed from being able to do justice to moral dilemmas with remainder, but I thereby failed to anticipate the exciting and creative reaction to the emergence of virtue ethics that I also mentioned in the Introduction. There is, now, neo-Kantian interest in what agents should feel (as part of virtue), and some utilitarian concern with the necessity of cultivating certain character traits, namely, virtuous ones, in agents. When this is carried over to the treatment of dilemmas in applied ethics, we shall, I hope and expect, find that the discussions change for the better. After all, once one has noticed the possibility of giving the virtue ethicist's answer, one will be more ready to remember about regret, and then, thinking of how the regret might be expressed, come up with richer answers such as '*x*-and-apologize-or-make-restitution-as-soon-as-possible' or '*x*, after a long, patient, sensitive discussion with those involved'. Deontologists and utilitarians are not cut off from doing this in virtue of being 'act-centred'.

## RIGHT ACTION AGAIN

Bearing the above in mind, let us look again at virtue ethics' 'account' of right action. 'An action is right iff it is what a virtuous agent would, characteristically, do in the circumstances'— and we are supposing that we have a standard list of virtues and vices. Does this 'account', we might now ask, provide action *guidance*, or action *assessment*, or both? The significance of the distinction between these two did not surface in the first chapter, but we now need to look at it.

When I seek action guidance, I am asking, 'What shall I do (in this situation in which I am, or with which I shall shortly be confronted)?' A normative ethics is supposed to provide me with the wherewithal to find the answer (unless I am faced with an irresolvable dilemma).

'The' answer may take many different grammatical forms. Having worked 'it' out for myself I may conclude 'I must/should/ought to do *x*', or '*x* is/would be the right thing to do/the right action to take', or 'I'll do *x*'. A person advising me may say, 'You must/should/ought to do *x*' or '*x* is/would be the right thing to do' or 'Do *x*'. Writers in applied ethics rarely issue imperatives to their readers in the form of 'If you are in such-and-such a situation, do *x*'; they sometimes have 'If you are in . . . then you must/should/ought to[2] . . .', but more often the pronoun is impersonal ('Anyone who is in . . . must/should/ought to . . .') or first or third person. And often they have '*x* is/would be the right thing to do/the right action'.

In the context of seeking and finding action guidance from normative ethics, all these grammatically different forms may readily be regarded as saying the same thing, as giving the same answer. It doesn't matter whether I express an intention ('I'll do *x*') or receive what is beyond doubt a directive ('do *x*'), whether I work out or am told something about myself, or give myself (or am given) an implicit directive ('I/You must/should/ought to do *x*'), or whether I work out, or find out something about an action ('*x* is/would be right'). For the context is, after all, supposed to be one in which my

---

[2] I am not unaware of the fact that some writers have drawn subtle distinctions between these three auxiliary verbs; I ignore them because I do not think they are relevant in this context.

aim is practical and, moreover, proper. I am hoping to be able to form an intention, and, seeking directives, I have turned to normative *ethics* for guidance. I have not turned to an examination of my personal preferences, or the law, or a Machiavellian acquaintance, for I want to do what can truly be assessed as *right*. And, in many cases, we can regard the grammatically different answers as providing, simultaneously, action guidance and the reassuring action assessment. Deciding to do *x* is the morally correct decision and *x* is the morally right action.

But dilemmas which are resolvable only with remainder show how these two may come apart. Suppose I have, through previous wrongdoing, landed myself in a situation in which I am forced to choose between two evils. Ashamed of the previous wrongdoing, I turn to normative ethics for guidance—what shall I do? Supposing that the dilemma is resolvable, since *x* is worse than *y*, many of the answers remain appropriate—I'll do *y*, Do *y*, I/you must/ought to do *y*, anyone who is in this situation ought to do *y*. But '*y* is the right action' is now inappropriate; *y* is *not* right. It involves, say, causing a terrible amount of suffering, breaking a promise, or doing what is shabby. In vain do I protest that now 'I want to do what is right', to undo past wrongdoing and start afresh with a clean slate. I should have thought of that before. The 'satisfactory review of my own conduct' is not for me, or at least, not yet; remorse and guilt are my portion.

Here we see action guidance and action assessment distinguished. The explicit directives and the oughts, shoulds, and musts give the guidance, but '*y* is the right action' assesses the action and gives it a tick of approval. And in some cases, the tick is not warranted. So '*y* is the right action' is not true.

How does this point fare in relation to the virtue ethics account? Consider again the distinctly non-virtuous man who has induced two women to bear a child of his by convincing each that he intends to marry her, under the assumption that it would be worse to abandon A than B. (I am taking it as obvious that we are not imagining a case in which the double commitment has come about through an innocent mistake; he thought A had been killed in a car crash, say, and only then turned to B's arms.) The virtue ethics account refuses to assure him that in marrying A he would be doing 'a morally right act—a good deed'. He will not, in marrying A, be 'doing what a virtuous agent would, characteristically, do in the circumstances', because no virtuous agent would have *got* himself into these circumstances in the first place. An interesting further point is that that claim remains true even if, by extraordinary luck, everything works out as well as it possibly could. (Suppose that he does not even have to break his promise to B nor condemn her child to illegitimacy because she is glad to release him from it and marry a previous lover who is delighted to adopt the child.) The consequences of his marrying A are just fine, he does not violate any moral rule in doing so—but on the virtue ethics account, although he can congratulate himself on his good luck, he cannot congratulate himself on having done what is right. Some people may find this counter-intuitive, but I myself find it an attractive feature of the account.

And, given the availability of the v-rules (particularly the vice-rules), the specification still provides action guidance. Perhaps it would be callous to abandon A, but not to abandon B. Perhaps it would be more irresponsible to abandon A than to abandon B. Perhaps, when she finds out about it all, B, unlike A, loses any desire to marry the swine; then it would be plain folly, and arrogant into the bargain, to try to force her into marriage rather than the still compliant and loving A. Then marrying A would be the morally right decision.

So is the virtue ethics account of right action only providing action guidance, yielding answers to the question, 'What is the morally right decision for me to make here?', or is it also providing action assessment, yielding answers to the question, 'What is the morally right thing for me to do here?' Well, given that 'There isn't one' is *an* answer to the latter question, albeit not an answer we usually expect, I think we should say that it is doing both. Given the sorts of cases considered so far, a resolvable dilemma which arises in circumstances in which a virtuous agent might well find herself will be resolvable by a morally right decision, and what is *done*, such as '*x*, after much painful thought, feeling deep regret, and doing such-and-such by way of restitution' will be assessed as morally right. Resolvable dilemmas which no virtuous agent would ever be faced with will also be resolvable by a morally right decision, but what is done will not be assessed as morally right. (This will be explored further in the next chapter in relation to rather different sorts of cases.)

## THE CONFLICT PROBLEM:
## RESOLVABLE DILEMMAS

Still leaving the question of irresolvable dilemmas to one side, let us
return to the 'conflict problem'. Can deontology solve it, in resolvable cases, in a way that virtue ethics cannot?

With respect to resolvable dilemmas, the deontologist's strategy
is to argue that the 'conflict' between the two rules which has generated the dilemma is merely apparent or *prima facie*. But the proponent of virtue ethics may employ the same strategy. According to
her, too, many of the putative quandaries are merely apparent,
resulting not from a conflict of deontological rules but from too
clumsy an application of the virtue or vice terms. Does kindness
require not telling hurtful truths? Sometimes, but in this case, what
has to be understood is that one does people no kindness by concealing this sort of truth from them, hurtful as it may be. (An example might be a teacher's telling a dedicated, mature student that,
contrary to his hopes and dreams, he was not capable of postgrad-
uate work in philosophy.) Or, in a different case, the nature or
importance of the truth in question puts the consideration of hurt
feelings out of court, and it is not unkind, or callous, to speak out.
(No one thinks a doctor unkind or callous because she tells her
patients the shattering truth that they have only six months to live,
though obviously it could be done in an unkind or callous way.)
Does charity require that I kill the person who would be better off
dead but who wants to stay alive, thereby conflicting with justice?
Not if, in Foot's words, 'a man does not lack charity because he
refrains from an act of injustice which would have been for someone's good'.[3] It is important to note here that none of these judgements amounts to a judgement about the comparative importance
of the virtues in question; it is not being said that, for example, the
virtue of honesty is more important than, or outranks, the virtue of
kindness, nor that justice outranks charity. (I shall say more about
this later.)

One does not have to agree with the three views expressed here
to recognize this as a *strategy* available to virtue ethics, any more
than one has to agree with the particular views of deontologists

³ P. Foot, 'Euthanasia' (1977; repr. 1978), 60.

who, for example, may claim that a certain rule outranks or over-rides another, or that a certain rule has a certain exception clause built in, or is to be interpreted in a certain way, when they argue that a putative case of conflict is resolvable.[4] Whether an individual moral philosopher has resolved a putative moral dilemma correctly is one question: whether the normative ethics she espouses has the wherewithal to resolve it is an entirely different question, and it is the latter with which we are concerned here.

Given the similarity of their strategies, it is not surprising that, at this point, both deontologists and virtue ethicists may find them-selves subject to the same objection. Do not their resolutions of dilemmas both depend, at bottom, on an entirely unsatisfactory notion, that of intuition (or 'insight' or 'perception' or 'the exercise of judgement')? How is one supposed to tell that this rule outranks that, or that this rule has a certain exception built in; how is one supposed to tell that 'one does people no kindness by concealing this sort of truth from them' except by intuition? Those philoso-phers who resolve the dilemmas in particular ways may say that, in this case, it is necessary to 'exercise judgement'. But if both deon-tology and virtue ethics are going to wind up depending on some mysterious 'exercise of judgement' whenever they turn their atten-tion to difficult cases, then it surely is only utilitarianism that can pretend to give us adequate action guidance.

To this possible objection at least some deontologists respond by denying the necessity for the dependence. These are the deontolo-gists who still subscribe to the strong codifiability thesis that I men-tioned at the end of the last chapter. They suppose (a) that they have (or will be able to formulate in time) a complete and consistent set of rules in which second-order ranking rules or principles settle any conflicts among first-order rules, which have been formed with much more precision than the 'mother's-knee' versions, and which may also be supposed to have had many necessary exception clauses built into them. Such a system would determine what was required

---

[4] Judith Jarvis Thomson's deservedly famous article on abortion, 'A Defense of Abortion' (1971), illustrates this. The conflict between the foetus's (putative) right to life and the mother's right to determine what happens to her own body is in part resolved by a particular interpretation of what the right to life involves, namely the right not to be killed unjustly. The strategy is fine; what many people disagree with is Thomson's resolution of the conflict.

in every situation and (b) would not rely on intuition or insight to resolve conflicts. It would, in Onora O'Neill's nice description, 'be an algorithm not just for some situations but for life'.[5] So it seems that, at least in theory, deontology can solve the conflict problem in a way that virtue ethics cannot, without dependence on the dubious notion of 'intuition', or 'exercise of judgement'.

Such deontologists presumably have a certain picture of what would count as an adequate normative ethics. According to this picture, an adequate normative ethics, one that is adequately action guiding, must be one that yields a decision procedure which can be used to resolve conflicts or settle moral quandaries without recourse to moral wisdom. Such a picture implicitly appeals to a certain test of adequacy of normative ethics which, at least on the face of it, act utilitarianism passes with flying colours, for it does indeed yield such a decision procedure. But, for several reasons, not all deontologists accept the production of an 'algorithm for life' independent of the exercise of judgement, as a suitable test of adequacy. Those who regard Kant's ethics as 'adequate' may well reject it, for, as O'Neill notes, Kant himself insists that we can have no algorithm for judgement, since every application of a rule would itself need supplementing with further rules.[6] More generally, many deontologists insist that recognizing what the 'morally salient' features of a particular situation are, applying certain rules rather than others and weighing and balancing competing considerations correctly, requires exercising not merely judgement, but also the faculties of 'moral sensitivity, perception, [and] imagination'[7]—moral wisdom or *phronesis*, in short.

So we get a division of opinion about what counts as adequate action guidance. Utilitarians still, perhaps, tend to the view that a normative ethics is inadequate unless it can provide a decision procedure; deontologists are simply divided, and virtue ethics, like some forms of deontology, does not even aim to produce an 'algorithm for life' independent of judgement. Those of its proponents who follow Aristotle closely always quote him with approval on ethics not being definable by rules but resting in some cases on a decision based on 'perception'. But, one might say, what rea-

---

[5] 'Abstraction, Idealization and Ideology in Ethics'.          [6] Ibid.
[7] S. Scheffler, *Human Morality* (1992), 43.

sons have we for believing this, beyond the fact that Aristotle says so?

Well, we might appeal to the reasons some deontologists give—that when we think realistically about some hard cases we just do find the rules, in one way or another, underdetermining decisions. Whether this rule applies to, or can be rightly extended to cover, this case; whether, given it applies, a higher-order rule which determines its outranking another rule also applies—these are sometimes questions whose answers we can 'justify' only by saying, 'It *does*—can't you see?'

This could be seen as a particular version of a standard objection to utilitarianism made by non-utilitarians. A standard objection is that it misrepresents the texture of our moral experience, making it out to be much simpler than it really is. In this particular version, the objection is to the very fact that utilitarianism does (so nearly) come up with a decision procedure independent of judgement. It is bound to say that ethical decisions hardly ever 'rest with perception', since there is no question as to whether its single rule applies to a particular case, no problems about its extension, and no higher-order rules. *But* it thereby misrepresents our moral experience, failing to capture the number of occasions where we want to say, 'This other (non-utilitarian) rule or consideration just *does* apply here, and it is not simply obvious that it is outranked by the rule about minimizing suffering, though I agree it sometimes is—don't you see?'

It is, inevitably, difficult to distinguish this objection from the even more standard one—that, according to non-utilitarians, utilitarianism so frequently yields the wrong resolutions of hard cases. But it is possible. Take the cases where the deontologists and virtue ethicists agree with the utilitarian judgement about which act is right—we have to do this thing that prevents suffering. They may still object that *getting* to this resolution is not the simple matter that the act utilitarian's crisp decision procedure has represented it as being. That, for example, in order to avoid a great amount of suffering that would be brought about by keeping it, a promise had to be broken, is something that has to be taken into account; judgement has to be exercised to determine whether this was the sort of promise that could be broken and whether the good effects of doing so are sufficient to justify it, and so on. It is a mistake, according to this objection, to represent our deliberations on such matters as the straightforward application of the utilitarian calculation.

## CODIFIABILITY AGAIN

So, from the point of view of those who think a normative ethics should produce a decision procedure, virtue ethics does reject codifiability and thereby provides inadequate action guidance. But one might expect that those who agree with virtue ethicists that normative ethics should not aspire to produce such a decision procedure but must recognize the need for moral wisdom, particularly in the resolution of hard (but, *ex hypothesi*, resolvable) cases, would not make the same criticism. However, as I noted at the end of the last chapter, it still persists in coming up; there is still, on the part of non-virtue ethicists, the suspicion that a bit more in the way of rules or general principles—a bit more codification—is called for than virtue ethics admits.

One form the criticism persists in is the claim that virtue ethics lamentably fails to come up with a priority ranking of the virtues. Just appealing to them is not enough; they, and the corresponding v-rules, must be supplemented by rules or principles to the effect that, say, honesty outranks kindness; without this, its action guidance is inadequate. This criticism reveals a possible ambiguity in the concession that moral wisdom is necessary to resolve hard (albeit resolvable) cases.

When I originally outlined the strong codifiability thesis, I said that it required (a) that the rules should provide a decision procedure and (b) that they should be applicable by the non-virtuous as well as the virtuous, applicable, that is, without recourse to any moral wisdom. Now it may be that those who accept the necessity for moral wisdom, but think that virtue ethics needs to come up with a priority ranking of the virtues, take themselves to have rejected only (b). That is, they still aspire to a set of rules which would determine what it was right to do in every case, but they accept that such a set could only be applied correctly and efficaciously by someone with a certain amount of moral wisdom; it could not be applied just mechanically.

I do not know of anyone who has explicitly articulated such a position, but I cannot see what else could lie behind the complaint that virtue ethics does not come up with a priority ranking of the virtues. Given that this is offered as a criticism directed at virtue ethics, it must surely stem from the belief that, in failing to do this, virtue ethics compares unfavourably with some envisaged normative ethics which does better. But given the close association I noted between virtues such as charity (or benevolence) and honesty, and rules such as 'Help others, do not harm them' and 'Do not lie', what could be envisaged but a system that explicitly ranks some version (perhaps very subtle) of those two rules, or provides some algorithm (albeit one that only the wise could understand and apply) about how they are to be weighted in every relevant circumstance?

Following McDowell, I certainly want to reject not only (b) but also (a). The very idea that even the ideally morally wise could rank the virtues, or the deontologists' rules, or grasp an algorithm for their weighting, just seems to me to be giving up on the insights gained from considering what can actually be said about the resolutions of real-life hard cases. When we look at their resolutions, we see that we bring a variety of considerations to bear on different cases; sometimes one consideration is centrally, even overridingly, important; on other occasions we just put it to one side, on others we do not worry about how important it is because it is combined with others in such a way as to settle the issue; on others it is important but nevertheless outweighed, in these circumstances, by a combination of others, and so on. That is just how things are. Any codification ranking the virtues, like any codification ranking the rules, is bound to come up against cases where we will want to change the rankings.

Or so I and other anti-codifiers assert, and I will leave this particular argument here. It has been, at least, worth getting out into the open what is at issue when virtue ethics is criticized for not providing a priority ranking of the virtues, but the idea that normative ethics consists of a decision procedure, even if only in the form of a decision procedure that the fully virtuous and wise agent ideally employs, dies hard, and I do not pretend to be able to kill it off.

However, the rejection of the idea of (even an ideal and morally nuanced) decision procedure does not amount to the claim that there are no true generalizations or general principles in ethics, and this does not seem to me to be obviously true. The view is commonly attributed to the McDowell of 'Virtue and Reason',[8] but I don't think this can be right. Citing Aristotle as his authority, McDowell says that 'the best generalisations about how one should

---

[8] e.g. by Crisp and Slote in their introduction to *Virtue Ethics* (1997),14.

behave hold only for the most part',⁹ and I have always taken him
to mean by 'the best generalisations' something like the v-rules,
rules or principles which have a pretty *general* application and the
*best* blend of specificity and flexibility, but which nevertheless do
not hold in every conceivable case. I never took him to be saying
that, for example, 'do not sexually abuse children for pleasure' held
'only for the most part'. Indeed, no one can cite Aristotle as their
authority for denying that there are any such exceptionless or 'absolute' rules, because Aristotle himself says firmly that some actions
'have names that directly connote depravity', citing (what is standardly translated as) 'adultery', theft, and murder.¹⁰ As we shall see
in the next chapter, committing virtue ethics, in advance, to an outright denial of any form of absolutism, would have some odd
results. The rejection of codification, I take it, involves not the blanket rejection of any absolute prohibitions, but the recognition that,
whatever they may be, they provide very little in the way of general
action-guidance, certainly not a code in accordance with which one
can live and act well.

A second form in which the criticism of virtue ethics as insufficiently codified persists is the claim that the v-rules are not specific
enough; they need to be supplemented by (replaced by, analysed
into?) proper deontological rules (whatever they may be).

With respect to *one* pair of v-rules, namely, 'Do what is just; do
not do what is unjust', I accept at least the first part of this criticism;
I agree they are 'not specific enough', and that they await the virtue
ethics' account of justice whose non-existence I acknowledged in
the introduction. But, I want to insist, they thereby contrast strik-
ingly with all the others. Recall the long list of things that I said we
would expect of someone who was thoroughly honest (pp. 11–12
above). I do not suppose that anything I mentioned struck my readers as untoward or even particularly insightful; it was just a list that
anyone with a reasonable grasp of what is involved in honesty could
come up with. But it was long, could have been a lot longer—and
*specific*, packed with details.

True, some of the details can be enshrined in non-v-rules; we can
say, 'Do not lie, do not cheat.' But that still allows being 'econom-

---

⁹ McDowell, 'Virtue and Reason', 337.
¹⁰ *Nicomachean Ethics*, 1107a10–11.

ical with the truth' in the way that dishonest, cunning people are; we have set the standards too low. So should we add, 'Do not be economical with the truth, always tell it'? But now we have gone too far, specifying not honesty, but brutal frankness or candour or ingenuousness. Though the latter two have their charm in youth, they connote insensitivity, thoughtlessness, and plain folly in people old enough to know better, unlike honesty, which does not. (How one dreads those frank, candid, people who begin, 'I hope you won't mind my saying this but . . . ') So should we say, 'Eschew being economical with the truth, tell it not always but when . . . '? But when what? There is no better way to capture when one should speak out and when one should remain discreetly silent, when one should tell the whole truth and when one should tell only part of it, than by saying, 'When the honest person would.'

We could all come up with a similar list of what we might expect of someone who was dishonest. And the same goes for charity, generosity, loyalty, friendship, temperance, courage, kindness, integrity, self-respect . . . and their corresponding vices. How sensible of Beauchamp and Childress to use the virtue words to state their principles! They are *much* more specific than 'Promote others' good' or 'Do no harm'.


## MORAL WISDOM

The effort of trying to imagine someone reaching correct moral decisions about what to do by cranking through a decision procedure without exercising judgement (which really does call for a great stretch of the imagination) may bring one to another (insufficiently acknowledged) insight of Aristotle's—namely that moral knowledge, unlike mathematical knowledge, cannot be acquired merely by attending lectures, and is not characteristically to be found in people too young to have much experience of life.[11] We do not think of moral or practical wisdom—of knowledge of what one should do—as easily come by, as something that an adolescent is likely to have, even if the adolescent is a genius at mathematics or

---

[11] Ibid. 1142a12–16.

science or the stock market and has been to lectures on normative ethics.[12]

With respect to resolvable dilemmas, virtue ethics, as I noted above, employs a strategy similar to that of some forms of deontology. It argues that the putative 'conflicts' are merely apparent, but does not suppose that their resolution can be found independently of the exercise of judgement. And the form the strategy takes within virtue ethics provides an immediate explanation, in some cases, of why agents do not know the answer to 'What should I do in these circumstances?' despite the fact that there *is* an answer. Trivially, the explanation is that they lack moral knowledge of what to do in this situation, but why? In what way? The lack, according to virtue ethics' strategy, arises from an inadequate grasp of what is involved in doing what is *kind* or *unkind*, in being *honest*, or *just* or *lacking charity* or, in general, of how the virtue (and vice) terms are to be correctly applied.

Here we come to an interesting defence of the v-rules, often criticized as being too difficult to apply. I rejected earlier the idea that, in virtue of employing 'thick' concepts, the v-rules were too difficult to teach to children at all, but I did not attempt to deny that they are difficult to apply correctly; they are. While we were thinking that an adequate normative ethics must come up with clear

---

[12] From the moment that I first read it, this has struck me as one of Aristotle's most profound insights. (True only 'for the most part' of course, since adolescents are often notable for an idealism that can serve as a needed corrective to the corrupted 'realism' of their elders. Sometimes the latter say, 'Oh, things are much more complicated than you think; you will learn the necessity of compromise', and the former say, rightly, 'No, in this case it's very simple; we just have to go for such-and-such and we'll work out where to go from there.')

I have noted that it is an insight that deontologists can readily take on board. Wondering, in a non-combative spirit, whether utilitarians could similarly take on board the idea that adolescents tend to lack moral knowledge, however well provided with utilitarian theory, I discovered, rather to my surprise, that I thought they could. In so far as they go for a rich, objective conception of happiness or well-being, they can share with the virtue ethicists the idea that few adolescents have an adequate grasp of such a conception. More concretely, they can note the fact that adolescents tend to be much more gormless about consequences than they are about ideals. Think of all those innocent young optimists who say, confidently, 'I can handle drugs', 'Our relationship is a serious commitment but we don't get bothered about casual sex on the side', 'We won't have any serious difficulties in standing together, because we're all committed to the same ideals', 'I don't need my parents' love and approval; I can cut myself off from them without any hang-ups'. And then reap the whirlwind.

guidance about what ought and ought not to be done which any reasonably clever adolescent could follow if she chose, we might well suppose that this was an unsatisfactory feature of the v-rules. But now we have discussed dilemmas and recognized that knowledge of what one should do in a particular hard case is not knowledge that we expect adolescents, however clever, and however well armed with a normative ethics they have been given in a book, to have, it should no longer seem an unsatisfactory feature. It can be seen, on the contrary, as a particularly desirable one. If the rules that determine right action are, as the v-rules are, very difficult to apply correctly, involving for instance, a grasp of 'the *sort* of truth that one does people no kindness in concealing' or 'the *sort* of truth that puts consideration of hurt feelings out of court', then the explanation of why adolescents so often do not know what they should do (even if they think they do) is readily to hand. Adolescents do not, in general, have a good grasp of that sort of thing, however clever they are. And *of course* I have to say 'the sort of truth that . . . ' and 'that sort of thing', relying on my readers' knowledgeable uptake. For if I could neatly define the sorts then, once again, clever adolescents could acquire moral wisdom from textbooks.

Indeed, most, if not all, of us have an imperfect grasp of these 'sorts', which is why we should sometimes seek advice over dilemmas, sometimes take heed when people we respect for their wisdom disagree with us about what we are proposing to do or have done, and sometimes simply defer to their judgement at least *pro tem* and try to acquire their understanding of things in a particular area.

Although I am aiming to be non-combative I must at this point say something somewhat combative about simple deontology's rules, namely that I am prepared to defend the thesis that, in practice, few, if any, of them are simpler, or clearer, or easier to apply correctly, than the v-rules of virtue ethics. I am not going to embark on doing this example by example, since that would be an endless task. Instead, I note two points. One I made earlier: that mature deontologists undoubtedly have to think hard about what really constitutes harming someone, or promoting their well-being, or respecting their autonomy. I made this point originally in connection with the 'evaluative' terms involved; I now make it in the context of the necessity for exercising judgement. Anyone who has had difficulties with their adolescent children knows what sort of grasp

of those terms the children have and how one has to strive to bring
them to a better understanding.

The second point involves the apparently simple 'mother's-knee'
rules. When the cases are clear and unproblematic, so is the
application of, for example, 'Keep promises', 'Don't lie', 'Tell the
truth'. But as soon as the cases become 'hard cases', the understanding and application of even these rules becomes a difficult and
delicate matter, once again involving judgement and a grasp of such
things as 'the sort of promise that may be broken, or need not be
kept, or (even) should not be kept and should never have been
made'.

So I conclude, *pro tem*, that, given certain premises, virtue ethics
has as much codification as an adequate normative ethics needs,
and that the 'conflict problem' does not constitute a particular
problem for it as far as resolvable dilemmas are concerned. What
about irresolvable ones?

# 3

# Irresolvable and Tragic
# Dilemmas

I take an irresolvable dilemma to be a situation in which the agent's moral choice lies between $x$ and $y$ and there are no moral grounds for favouring doing $x$ over doing $y$.[1] We could also describe it as a situation in which the agent's choice lies between $x$ and $y$ and nothing would count as *the* reasonable practical answer to 'Should I do $x$ or $y$?'[2] Any putative example I gave at the outset would be bound to be controversial, for any particular situation I thought constituted an irresolvable dilemma could be one that someone else thought was to be resolved in a particular way, and some people think that there just aren't any irresolvable dilemmas anyhow.

## ARE THERE ANY IRRESOLVABLE DILEMMAS?

I mentioned at the beginning of the last chapter that the contributors to the prevailing literature on hard cases in applied ethics 'rarely even entertain the possibility that the dilemma they are discussing is irresolvable; on the contrary, they assume that there must be one, correct, decision to be made about it which it is the business of their moral theory . . . to reveal or discover'. Are there any irresolvable dilemmas? Are they justified in making this assumption? Well, there is justifiability according to one's own lights, and justifiability *tout court*. I begin with the former.

Act utilitarians are, by and large, justified in making the assumption, according to their own lights. For, in so far as their theory basically eliminates the conflict problem, it eliminates irresolvable

---

[1] R. B. Marcus, 'Moral Dilemmas and Consistency' (1980).
[2] David Wiggins, 'Truth, Invention and the Meaning of Life' (1976).

conflicts. It is true that the classical statement of the supreme utilitarian value, 'the *greatest* happiness for the *greatest* number', can be made to generate an irresolvable dilemma when each 'greatest' directs one differently and incompatibly. It is also true that A's happiness and B's happiness or suffering may be incommensurable, creating an irresolvable dilemma, and that a third sort may be presented by a case in which $x$ and $y$ are the only alternatives and each will produce exactly the same amount of suffering. But the fact is that the hard cases that are discussed in applied ethics are not, by and large, of any of these sorts; when they are not, the act utilitarian is, by her own lights, justified in her assumption that she can find the one right decision to be made about them. She thinks that, excepting a few arcane cases, moral life is pretty straightforward. However, the same is not true of deontologists.

One might think that deontologists would have been attracted to deontology (as opposed to utilitarianism) with its plurality of rules or principles precisely because that plurality could represent life as full of irresolvable conflict in a way that utilitarianism does not. Utilitarianism is all geared up to resolve dilemmas right, left, and centre; those who think that life is much more complicated and difficult than utilitarianism makes out turn to deontology. But people do not, in general, seem to be attracted to, and espouse, deontology because they think that life is full of irresolvable dilemmas; rather they turn to it as a system of ethical thought which, like utilitarianism, resolves them, but in a different way. Deontologists are indeed to be found characteristically maintaining that utilitarians have made out a particular putative hard case to be too simple—they have concentrated merely on the consequences of killing someone or refusing to (in which case many others die), of keeping the promise or breaking it, of telling the truth or telling a lie, and so on—and neglected to consider the nature of the act itself. But this introduction of further considerations, with its implication that utilitarianism has overlooked genuine moral complexity, does not, in general, lead on to the conclusion that the putative dilemmas are irresolvable. Standardly, in the literature, it leads on to the conclusion that the putative dilemma *is* resolvable—but in the opposite way to that which the utilitarians gave.

So it looks as though deontologists espouse deontology because they think it comes up with better resolutions of dilemmas than utilitarianism, but tend to share the utilitarians' view that there are very few, if any, irresolvable ones. But given they think moral life is complex and difficult, the question remains *why*?

I can think of a possible explanation, but it is far from providing a justification. The possible explanation is to be found in deontology's religious ancestry, in the fact that past deontologists, and some contemporary ones, believe that we are living in a world shaped by the omniscient, omnipotent, and perfectly good God, who gave us reason that we might know, and obey, His commands. And it is certainly true that God's Providence would be incompatible with the existence of some irresolvable dilemmas. As Geach rightly remarks, we may be sure, given God's Providence, that none of His faithful servants will be faced with the desperate choice between sin and sin[3]—to be damned if he does and damned if he doesn't, as Ruth Barcan Marcus puts it.[4]

But even the assumption of God's Providence does not guarantee that there are no irresolvable dilemmas. For one thing, the qualification 'none of His faithful servants' is so important. God's Providence may indeed be expected to preserve the innocent from inescapable sin but no such guarantee extends to the wicked, nor even to those who, while not actually wicked, have sinned. I take it that the adage 'one sin leads to another' is supposed to refer not only to the Aristotelian point about habituation, but also to this pitfall: that if I disobey one of God's commands, I step outside the protection of his Providence and lay myself open to the possibility of being forced to sin again, faced with a desperate choice that does lie between sin and sin. God's Providence is no guarantee of a right answer to 'Should I marry A or B?' in the case considered before.

Secondly, even God's Providence does not guarantee that any dilemma, or moral quandary, confronting an agent through no fault of her own is resolvable, only that it may be got through without *sin*, without, that is, violating an absolute prohibition. Within Roman Catholic teaching, lying is absolutely prohibited but deception is not. (Of course that does not mean that deception is generally OK, only that it is sometimes permissible whereas lying never is.) So one might, through no fault of one's own, be faced with the choice between telling the truth and deception, and that might be irresolvable since it is not a choice between sin and sin. Murder is

---

[3] P. T. Geach, *The Virtues* (1977), 155.
[4] Marcus, 'Moral Dilemmas and Consistency'.

absolutely prohibited but not using extraordinary means to preserve life is not; so, through no fault of one's own, one might be
faced with the choice between using extraordinary means on one's
child for another six months or stopping the treatment now, and
that might be irresolvable since it is not a choice between sin and
sin.

I can quite readily imagine situations in which these decisions
would be very painful, situations in which one would agonize over
'what is the *right* thing to do?' passionately concerned to find a
determinate answer to that question, but not even Roman Catholic
doctrine supports the idea that we can always find such an answer
(notwithstanding the not uncommon claim that Aquinas's natural
law doctrine precludes irresolvable dilemmas.)

So I think I can see how it might be that an assumption about
there being no irresolvable dilemmas crept in to deontology, namely
through an inadequately explored view about what God's Providence would guarantee. But this explanation leaves the assumption
without a shred of justification. And what about those deontologists, whether theists or not, who believe that their moral theory is
independent of any theistic presuppositions? How can they justify
the assumption? It seems to embody the conviction that practical
rationality *cannot* run out of determining moral grounds, but why
should anyone be convinced of that—unless they thought that God
had guaranteed it?

In fact, if the claim is put in a different, unexpected, context, few
people are convinced of it. In the context of applied ethics, we
always think of dilemmas as being a forced choice between evils,
something we agonize over. But, in the context of the abstract discussion of whether there are such things as irresolvable dilemmas,
Foot has nicely raised the possibility that there may be positively
pleasant ones. We may be faced with a choice between goods where
not having either is no loss, and 'there are no moral grounds for
favouring doing *x* over *y*'.[5] She does not give examples, but here is
one. Suppose I must give my daughter a birthday present; it would

---

[5] P. Foot, 'Moral Realism and Moral Dilemma' (1983). Simon Blackburn vigorously defends the view that irresolvable dilemmas ('stable agent's quandaries') are
commonly encountered in any sort of practical reasoning, and (as I do in relation to
resolvable but tragic ones) questions the common assumption that appropriate
regret necessarily exhibits the agent's recognition that he has failed to fulfil a requirement. See Blackburn, 'Dilemmas: Dithering, Plumping, and Grief' (1996).

certainly be very mean not to, given our relationship, her age and hopes, my financial circumstances, and so on. But I am faced with an *embarras de richesse*; giving any one of a whole range of things is equally desirable and acceptable. So there is an irresolvable dilemma—not one that worries us, not one where the final decision matters, but there all the same—providing a clear case where practical rationality simply runs out of determining moral grounds.

So does the conviction that practical rationality *cannot* run out hold only of the distressing dilemmas? That does look very odd. We have this rational faculty; we know that it sometimes runs out of determining grounds when the decision does not worry or distress us, but we supposedly have a guarantee that this will not happen when we find the decision painful. That does seem to express an optimism that nothing but the existence of a (vaguely conceived) nurturing deity could possibly justify.

It is indeed true that a deontologist might also subscribe to a form of realism (in Dummett's sense of 'realism')[6] and thereby believe that, even in Foot's sort of case, there must be something that truly is *the* right action. But far from justifying the assumption that we can find out what it is, this form of realism insists on the possibility of truth beyond our capacity to discover or recognize it.

So I conclude that deontologists, according to their own lights, are not justified in the assumption that they can resolve every distressing hard case. What about justifiability *tout court*? Should we accept that life sometimes just does face us with distressing dilemmas to which we cannot, and could not, find *the* right answer? If so, then once again we have a particular version of a standard objection to utilitarianism (cf. p. 55 above)—that it misrepresents the texture of our moral experience. As before, it is difficult, but not impossible, to distinguish the objection from the common one that it resolves hard cases in the wrong direction. The objection is not that one, but rather, with respect to some hard cases, that it aspires to resolve them at all. Given some of the terrible dilemmas that life sometimes presents, the objection goes, an adequate normative ethics—one that adequately captures our moral experience—would embody the fact that we really cannot resolve some of them, not aim to show us how to do it.

---

[6] M. Dummett, *Truth and Other Enigmas* (1978), 102–4 and 145–65. For a brief but helpful discussion of the distinction between Dummett-type realism and cognitivism in ethics, see Foot, 'Moral Realism and Moral Dilemmas'.

From now on, I shall take it as a premise that there are irresolvable distressing dilemmas, and that it is a test of the adequacy of a normative ethics that it allows for this possibility. The question then is what it can find to say about them. What does virtue ethics say?

## IRRESOLVABLE DILEMMAS IN VIRTUE ETHICS

For a start, proponents of virtue ethics can readily admit the possibility of irresolvable dilemmas as even quite common, because they are relaxed about not providing a decision procedure, not even one that only those with moral wisdom can understand and apply. Far from supposing that it is the business of their approach to show us the way out of any and every dilemma, they deny that normative ethics should be conceived of as providing a decision procedure.

What is it for a dilemma to be irresolvable, in terms of virtue ethics, bearing in mind what it said about right action? Basically this: two genuinely virtuous agents are faced with the same moral choice, between *x* and *y*, in the same circumstances. And, acting characteristically, one does *x* and the other does *y*. (I was careful to specify right action as what *a* virtuous agent would do, not what *the* virtuous one would do; this is the stage at which the indefinite article really matters.)

Apply this to the example of the pleasant irresolvable dilemma discussed earlier. My guidance-seeking question is: 'Shall I give my daughter *a* or *b*?' Virtue ethics directs me to find the answer to this question by finding the answer to another:'What would a virtuous agent characteristically do in my circumstances?' But the supposition that the dilemma is truly irresolvable is tantamount to supposing the possibility of the following. We have two virtuous agents, each of whom (let us suppose, rather unrealistically) can give her daughter just one of two things, *a* or *b*, for her birthday; there are no moral grounds for favouring one over the other (for if there were, each agent, being virtuous, would go for the one that the grounds favoured). And one does *x*, giving her daughter *a*, and the other does *y*, giving her *b*. So virtue ethics does not give me action guidance here—which is just what we want, if we want our normative ethics to embody the fact that there are such irresolvable pleasant dilemmas, in which there is nothing that counts as *the* morally right decision.

What of action assessment—what shall we say about $x$ and $y$? Well, according to the virtue ethics account, both agents do what is right, what gets a tick of approval, despite the fact that each fails to do what the other did.

Now if your linguistic ear is not offended by that claim (both agents do what is right, despite the fact that each fails to do what the other did), well and good. But if you think it sounds odd, the time has come to revisit the slogan that 'virtue ethics takes certain areteic concepts (*good* [*well*], *virtue*) as basic rather than deontic ones (*right, duty, obligation*)'.

As we have seen, this slogan should not be taken to mean that virtue ethics is concerned only with good or virtuous agents and not at all with right action; it can come up with an account of the latter. But it does this under pressure, only in order to maintain a fruitful dialogue with the overwhelming majority of modern moral philosophers for whom '*right* action' is the natural phrase. '*Right* action', with its suggestion of uniqueness, its implication of 'if not right then wrong', and its associations with 'required/obligatory', 'forbidden/prohibited', and 'permissible', is not a term it is happy with. It favours talking in terms of *good* action (*eupraxia*), of acting *well* (or badly), rather than in terms of *right* action. And if your linguistic ear is offended by the claim that both my two generous parents do what is right, despite the fact that each fails to do what the other did, perhaps you can see why.

Maybe it *is* odd to say that they both do what is right—neither action, after all, is required or obligatory—but certainly each acts *well*. Note here that saying only that each does what is permissible fails to capture that fact, and thereby fails to do justice to our two agents. What they do merits more in the way of assessment, for they do not do what is merely permissible, but act generously and hence well.

Now let us turn to distressing irresolvable dilemmas. The discussion of these has to be more extended and complicated.

Suppose (just for the sake of an example) that whether to ask the doctors to continue to prolong one's unconscious mother's life by extraordinary means for another year, or to discontinue treatment now, would be an irresolvable dilemma in some cases. Then virtue ethics embodies that fact by allowing for the possibility that two virtuous agents, faced with the same decision in the same circumstances, may act differently; one opts for asking the doctors to continue treatment, the other for asking them to discontinue it. So, as before, no action guidance is forthcoming, which is just what we want.

We cannot, however, proceed straight to the question of action assessment because just *what* possibility is being envisaged here is nothing like as clear as it was in the rather footling example of the choice between birthday presents. It is important to bear in mind that the possibility is supposed to embody the fact that the dilemma is genuinely irresolvable, that there *are* no moral grounds that favour doing the one thing rather than the other—and hence that anyone who thinks she has found something which favours doing one rather than the other is in error. It is not the rather different sort of possibility imagined by Pincoffs.

Pincoffs stresses the point that reference to *my* standards, *my* ideals, and hence *my* conception of what is and is not worthy of me, is 'an essential, not an accidental feature of my moral deliberation' and that two people can be equally virtuous without having exactly the same standards and ideals.[7] So suppose we have two such people. One might be a doctor herself, someone who had always striven to think of the human body as a living, and hence mortal, thing, not as a machine to be tinkered with; she knows that, if her mother were her patient, she would advise the discontinuation of treatment. The other might be someone who worked with apparently hopeless cases of mental disability, someone who said of herself, 'I never give up hope; I couldn't do the job if I let myself.' Faced with some such decision as the one just outlined, it seems that each might act differently, each believing, correctly, that she had a moral ground, or reason, for favouring the action she elected to take. The doctor says, perhaps, 'I must accept that the body is mortal'; the other, 'I mustn't give up hope.'

That may well be possible, but it is not the possibility envisaged, of an irresolvable dilemma. For here the dilemma *is* resolvable—for each agent, in the light of her own ideals and standards. Neither (*ex hypothesi*) is in error when she thinks she has found something which favours doing one thing rather than the other. Exactly what was meant by saying that the two virtuous agents were faced by 'the same decision, in the same circumstances' was not hitherto clear. But now it can be said that it is intended to rule out the Pincoffs's cases. What is envisaged is that the virtuous agents themselves rec-

[7] E. Pincoffs, 'Quandary Ethics', 564.

ognize the dilemma as irresolvable, as one in which, even given their particular standards or ideals or whatever, there is no moral ground for favouring one action rather than the other. That is why I described them, deliberately, as 'opting for' different courses of action, rather than exercising choice.

*How* do they decide then? This is a question we will come to presently; for the moment let us return to action assessment. One has opted to ask for treatment to be continued, the other for it to be discontinued. How shall we assess those two different actions?

As in the case of the pleasant dilemma—perhaps more so here— there is some awkwardness in saying that each did what was right: can it really be *right* both to guarantee that one's mother should die immediately *and* to make efforts to preserve her life? But now it may seem more plausible to rest content with saying that what each agent did was permissible. However, once again, we fail to do our agents justice. They both faced up to the decision, after all, in a way that less courageous and responsible people standardly fail to do in such cases. They both thought about it carefully, conscientiously, and wisely, arriving, after much agonized thought, at the conclusion that neither decision here was *the* correct one. This is all built in to the example, by my saying that the agents are *virtuous*. So surely we should say that they acted *well*—courageously, responsibly, thoughtfully, conscientiously, honestly, wisely—and not describe them merely as having done what was permissible, which any cowardly, irresponsible, thoughtless, heedless, self-deceiving fool could just as well have done in the circumstances.

So suppose we can, and should, say here that the two virtuous agents acted *well*. Irresolvable dilemmas of this sort, though distressing to confront and come through, are not as bad as some others may be. What of irresolvable dilemmas where the forced alternatives are even more terrible? These we may call, *pro tem*, tragic dilemmas—those from which, as the familiar phrase goes, 'it is impossible to emerge with clean hands'. What can virtue ethics find to say about them?

## TRAGIC DILEMMAS

The familiar phrase about the clean hands does not quite capture what is needed, for 'there are situations from which it is impossible to emerge with clean hands' is not equivalent to 'there are situations such that whatever you do you necessarily emerge with dirty hands'. There are, undoubtedly, some things a virtuous agent must die rather than do. This is recognized in common morality, which condemns at least some cases of saving one's own life by betraying or killing others. In such cases it is indeed impossible to 'emerge' with clean hands, but we know what virtuous agents would do, and actually have done, all right—they allow themselves to die or be killed; perhaps even commit suicide. The dilemma is resolvable, though its resolution is exceptionally demanding, and the agent does not 'emerge' from it at all.

So let us insist that we are talking about irresolvable dilemmas in which one's own death is not an option, being either impossible to achieve, or itself a cowardly abnegation of responsibility. What can virtue ethics say about them? Well, in so far as they are irresolvable, it begins by saying what was said before—that two virtuous agents, in the same situation, may act differently. But here it seems to be quite inappropriate to say that each acts well, mirroring the fact (I take it to be a fact) that it is quite inappropriate to say, with respect to tragic irresolvable dilemmas, that both agents do what is right. If anything, the temptation is to say that both do what is *wrong*. So it looks as though I am going to be forced to say that both agents act *badly*.

Here, it may seem, we find a version of the 'conflict problem' which lands virtue ethics in real trouble. The difficulty is not that virtue ethics cannot provide action guidance for such situations—for, *ex hypothesi*, the dilemma is irresolvable, and so no adequate normative ethics should provide action guidance. The trouble is that virtue ethics, employing the notion of the virtuous agent, seems to be trapped in a contradiction, as follows:

> Our supposedly virtuous agent is faced with a tragic dilemma. She acts, for act she must, and whatever she does is *wrong*, impermissible; she can only emerge from the situation with dirty hands. But then, how can we call her virtuous without contradiction? There was, perhaps, always a slight suspicion that the very idea of a virtuous agent was an idealization; now we see that it is an impossibility. If there are tragic dilemmas, there cannot be such a thing as a virtuous agent.

This may seem an obvious conclusion. But it seems obvious only because we have lapsed back into thinking of the concept of the virtuous agent as captured in a truism which relies on a prior identification of right and wrong action. The truism here is 'The virtuous agent never does what is wrong', presupposing a prior identification of wrong action. But the concept of the virtuous agent does not figure, in virtue ethics, riding on the back of a prior concept of right, or wrong, action. A virtuous agent is one who has the character traits of, for example, charity, honesty, justice . . . So the conclusion amounts to the claim that, if there are tragic dilemmas, then no one can have the character traits of charity, honesty, justice . . . And that does not seem so obvious.[8]

Can the apparent contradiction be reconstructed? Suppose this were said:

> Tragic dilemmas, situations from which, perforce, the agent emerges with dirty hands, are situations in which the supposedly charitable, honest, just . . . agent is forced to act callously, dishonestly, unjustly . . . But if someone acts callously or dishonestly . . ., she cannot be charitable or honest . . .; that would be a contradiction. So, if there are tragic dilemmas then no one can really be charitable or honest or . . .; no one can really have those character traits. There cannot be such a thing as a virtuous agent.

But there are no such situations; the claim embodies a conceptual confusion created by a misinterpretation of the adverbial qualifications 'callously', 'dishonestly', 'unjustly', etc. The charitable, honest, just agent, even when faced with a tragic dilemma, does not act callously, dishonestly, unjustly, that is '*as* (in the manner) the callous, dishonest, unjust agent does'. She acts with immense regret and pain instead of indifferently or gladly, as the callous or

---

[8] It can only be some such lapse which leads people to say that the doctrine of the 'unity of the virtues' (the claim that, if you have one virtue, then you must have them all) rules out tragic dilemmas. They must be thinking that a (putative) virtuous agent emerging from a tragic dilemma would necessarily display, and thereby possess, some particular vice or other. If she has some vice then, if the doctrine of the unity of the virtues holds, she has no virtues at all. So either there are no virtuous agents or, given the unity of the virtues, there are no tragic dilemmas. But who would ascribe to someone the whole character trait of a particular vice simply because she was faced with a tragic dilemma and acted? Doing what is, say, dishonest solely in the context of a tragic dilemma does not entail being dishonest, possessing that vice; it does not even provide any evidence for it.

dishonest or unjust one does. So we are not forced to say that the virtuous agents faced with tragic dilemmas act badly. They don't; it is the vicious who act badly.

However, if a genuinely tragic dilemma is what a virtuous agent emerges from, it will be the case that she emerges having done a terrible thing, the very sort of thing that the callous, dishonest, unjust, or in general vicious agent would characteristically do—killed someone, or let them die,[9] betrayed a trust, violated someone's serious rights. And hence it will not be possible to say that she has acted *well*. What follows from this is not the impossibility of virtue but the possibility of some situations from which even a virtuous agent cannot emerge with her life unmarred.

'How can this be?' someone might ask. 'Mustn't actions be good, bad, or morally neutral even on the virtue ethics account?'

The possibility arises because, within virtue ethics, 'good action' is *not* merely a surrogate for 'right action', *nor* is it simply determined by 'action of the virtuous agent'. Virtue ethics does not hold that actions are good, bad, or indifferent, as some people hold that actions are right, wrong, or permissible; nor does it call what the virtuous agent does (for the most part) 'good action' for want of any other phrase. 'Good action' is so called advisedly, and although it is conceptually linked to morally correct (right) decision and to 'action of the virtuous agent', it is *also* conceptually linked to 'good life' and *eudaimonia*.[10]

The actions a virtuous agent is forced to in tragic dilemmas fail to be good actions because the doing of them, no matter how unwillingly or involuntarily, mars or ruins a good life. So to say that there are some dilemmas from which even a virtuous agent cannot emerge having acted well is just to say that there are some from which even a virtuous agent cannot emerge with her life unmarred—not in virtue of wrongdoing (for *ex hypothesi*, in making a forced choice, the agent is blameless), and not in virtue of having done what is right or justifiable or permissible (which would

---

[9] I should stress, in relation to these examples, something that is widely overlooked, namely that killing can be as contrary to charity as it is usually taken to be to justice, and that letting die, if not also taken to be contrary to justice, should certainly often be taken to be contrary to charity. See Foot, 'Euthanasia'.

[10] As I noted in Chapter 1 (n. 5), I am keeping all discussion of 'good life' and *eudaimonia* for the theoretical chapters in the last part of the book. But I do need to just mention the concepts here.

sound very odd), but simply in virtue of the fact that her life pre-sented her with *this* choice, and was thereby marred, or perhaps even ruined.[11]

Some people think of Williams's Jim and Pedro case[12] as pre-senting an irresolvable dilemma, and what they want to say about it is that whether they killed the one, or refused, and allowed the twenty to be killed, what they would then have to do is kill them-selves when the opportunity came—i.e. that is what the virtuous agent would do, because no one decent could live with themselves after they had emerged from such a situation. Some other people say no, that would be cowardly, so the virtuous agent cannot do that. So she must live out the rest of her life haunted by sorrow.

The 'must' here is not action-guiding but conceptual:'One who is truly compassionate and just cannot ever rest content with the knowledge that she did not save the twenty (or did kill the one); one who is truly courageous cannot kill herself to escape the knowledge. It follows that a compassionate, just, courageous agent who has done what she has done will never rest content again: her life will be forever marred.'

A situation from which even a virtuous agent cannot emerge with her life unmarred sounds to me one which deserves to be called 'tragic'. If that is right, it suggests that it is a mistake to think of 'tragic dilemmas' as *ipso facto* irresolvable. I mentioned earlier that, within the literature discussing irresolvable dilemmas, there were some writers who wanted to insist that even some resolvable dilem-mas are not resolvable 'without remainder' or 'moral residue', and we are now in a position to say more about the form such remain-der or residue might take.

Some cases are straightforward, and there is little dispute about them, namely those in which, having correctly chosen to do *x* rather than *y*, the agent thereby creates a fairly obvious new obligation for herself. For example, she owes an explanation to the person to whom she made the promise she has just broken. Dispute breaks

---

[11] Cf. Aristotle's discussion of the misfortunes that befell Priam, *Nicomachean Ethics* 1101a5–14. Aristotle, I take it, would allow that the virtuous person's life can be marred, but not, I think, ruined. If truly virtuous, he cannot become wretched (*athlios*), for this involves 'doing what is hateful and mean', and he would surely want to say the same about the only way in which one's life can be ruined.

[12] B. Williams, *Utilitarianism: For and Against* (with J. J. C. Smart) (1973).

out when the remainder or residue is said to be guilt, or remorse, or regret.

Suppose someone is faced with a dilemma, through no fault of her own. Not only is it, *ex hypothesi*, resolvable, but she can see quite clearly that this is so, that in this case there is nothing for it but to do *x*, terrible as it is. So she does *x*. Should she feel guilt or remorse about having done so? Some say 'of course', but others say 'not so'. For *guilt* and *remorse* are, going strictly by their dictionary definitions, directed to a *wrong* or *sin* committed and what wrong or sin has she committed? That she did *x*? But she has a cast-iron justification for having done *x*: *ex hypothesi*, she had to do *x* because doing *y* would have been so much worse. She is quite blameless (given that she is faced with the dilemma through no fault of her own), and how could guilt or remorse be appropriate if she is blameless?

What about regret—should she feel that? The difficulty here is to find a suitable sense of 'feeling regret' which is sufficiently powerful to be a suitable reaction to having done *x*, this terrible thing. Guilt and remorse are powerful enough—they can haunt one, fill one with despair, mar and even ruin one's life. But can regret? We might say the agent should feel regret in that she should wish, passionately, that she had not done what she has done. But then we seem to be suggesting that she should wish that she had done *y* instead; that she regrets not having done so, and, if the situation is as described, how can we say such a thing? For, *ex hypothesi*, she should *not* have done *y*, that would have been a terrible mistake.

Hence we seem driven to saying that, when the dilemma is resolvable (and the agent is in it through no fault of her own), the only feasible emotional remainder is that the agent deeply regrets the circumstances that made doing *x* necessary. This certainly takes the remainder well away from guilt and remorse, but at the price of severing its connection with the agent. After all, a virtuous third party, agreeing that the agent had to do *x*, would doubtless deeply regret the circumstances that made it necessary. To get the connection back again, we have to say that the agent deeply regrets the circumstances that made *her* doing *x* necessary.

However, even this may sound insufficiently powerful. Can regret over the circumstances that made my doing *x* necessary, however deep, and with however much emphasis on the 'my', fill me with despair, mar and even ruin my life? If not, then anyone who insists that such regret is the only feasible emotional remainder in the cases under discussion seems to be painting too rosy a picture of life. For those who insisted on the appropriateness of guilt and remorse in these cases were surely right to insist that the mere fact that one had intentionally done *x should* haunt the rest of one's life if *x* were very terrible, even granted that one was blameless.

The thing to do here is to give up trying to describe the form 'remainder' should take in terms of guilt or remorse (suitably powerful, but inappropriate when the agent is blameless) *or* regret (inappropriate or insufficiently powerful), and go straight for the point that a virtuous agent's life will be marred or even ruined, haunted by sorrow that she had done *x*. Here again, we arrive at a situation that deserves to be called 'tragic'—not because the dilemma was irresolvable, but because, resolving it correctly, a virtuous agent cannot emerge with her life unmarred.

Now we might look back at the other sort of resolvable dilemma in which a virtuous agent might find herself—that in which the correct resolution is to allow oneself to be killed or even to commit suicide. That too, deserves to be called tragic, and for the same reason with a different twist. A virtuous agent cannot emerge from it with her life unmarred, because she cannot emerge from it with her life; she has to give it up.

## RIGHT ACTION AGAIN

We have come a long way from action guidance and action assessment. Let us go back to them. Our point of departure was the discussion of a dilemma which, though, supposedly irresolvable and undoubtedly distressing, did not merit being called 'tragic'. The reason why it did not merit this description was that both agents could be described as acting *well*, and our picture of tragic dilemmas is that they are situations from which an agent, somehow, cannot emerge having acted well, but only, in some way, damned. We have now worked out an account of this which neither paints a rosy picture of life in which there are no tragic dilemmas, irresolvable or resolvable, nor, in admitting their existence, commits us to saying that there are no virtuous agents. Yes, there are tragic dilemmas, namely situations from which a virtuous agent cannot emerge having acted well. These are not situations from which she emerges having acted *badly*, but those from which she does not emerge at all, or emerges with her life marred—she is damned, or condemned, to death or sorrow. And there seems to be no reason to suppose that these are always irresolvable dilemmas.

Now when a dilemma is tragic, my original specification of right action will not do.[13] I said, 'An action is right iff it is what a virtuous agent, would, characteristically, do in the circumstances.' When the dilemma is resolvable, this provides the appropriate action guidance (the morally right decision is to do what a virtuous agent would, characteristically, do in the circumstances); but if we take it as also providing the action assessment, it says the wrong thing (except in the case of self-sacrifice), giving this terrible deed, the doing of which mars the virtuous agent's life, a tick of approval, as a good deed. When the dilemma is irresolvable, it appropriately provides no action guidance, but still says the wrong thing if we take it as providing action assessment.

One might try to wriggle out of this problem by putting a loaded interpretation on 'characteristically'. Suppose that the right decision *is* to kill someone, or let them die, to betray a trust, to break a terribly serious promise. That is what the virtuous agent does—in the circumstances. But, given that they are charitable, true to their word, just, do they not act 'uncharacteristically', out of character, when they do these terrible things?

But this is too *ad hoc*. The straightforward interpretation of 'characteristically' in the specification just is as an adverb included to rule out the everyday ways in which virtuous people act 'out of character'—when they are exhausted, dazed with grief, ill, drunk (through no serious fault of their own, we must suppose), shell-shocked, and so on. These are the sorts of conditions in which we are not surprised if people are 'not themselves'. But it would not be correct to describe a virtuous agent who resolved a tragic dilemma rightly as thereby 'not herself'. If anything, she might have to have been quite especially herself, calling on all her virtue and moral wisdom in order to resolve the dilemma rightly in the first place. And recognizing a tragic dilemma as irresolvable might well make the same demands.

---

[13] I was led to see this, and thereby the importance of tragic dilemmas, in a conversation with Michael Slote and Christine Swanton.

I would rather qualify the original specification quite explicitly and say the following:

An action is right iff it is what a virtuous agent would, characteristically, do in the circumstances, except for tragic dilemmas, in which a decision is right iff it is what such an agent would decide, but the action decided upon may be too terrible to be called 'right' or 'good'. (And a tragic dilemma is one from which a virtuous agent cannot emerge with her life unmarred.)

That the original account needs to be qualified in relation to tragic dilemmas is hardly surprising. Precisely what utilitarianism or deontology might say about them, I leave to their proponents to determine, but surely everyone will want to recognize that at least resolvable ones present us with cases in which, apart from self-sacrifice, action guidance and action assessment come apart. So some amendment will be needed of any account which, as is standard, provides both. And any account which insists that in irresolvable dilemmas both actions are just plain wrong, forbidden, prohibited, will have to give up their truism, 'The virtuous agent never does (characteristically) what is wrong (but only what is right).' So I do not regard the necessity of the qualification as casting any doubt on the basic idea behind the original account.

However, we might now raise a question about what that 'basic idea' is, or was, supposed to be. Is it the idea that character has 'primacy' over action, a claim that is usually supposed to be 'central to any form of virtue ethics'?[14] This question cannot be given a straightforward answer, because the claim 'character has primacy over action' can mean so many different things. In just what respects the version of virtue ethics I am exploring can be described as endorsing the 'primacy of character' will not emerge fully until the final chapters of the book. At this point, I want to disown some points that may be taken to fall under it.

Let us consider, firstly, a passage from Stephen Hudson. Having quoted Aristotle as saying 'Actions then are called just and temperate when they are such as the just or temperate man would do', he continues,

---

[14] Oakley, 'Varieties of Virtue Ethics', 129.

The very notion of a courageous act—taking courage to be our paradigm for moral virtues, for the moment—is secondary to and dependent upon the notion of a courageous person. The former acquires its sense from the latter. How so? An act gets rightly called courageous when and only when it is such that the courageous person would perform it in those circumstances. The courageous man is thought of as an ideal type, who is the exemplar of courage; it is by reference to that type that we select which acts are typical of courage. Once we have, so to speak, got our hands on such an exemplar, we can, by reference to what he would do, decide whether what we and others do is in fact courageous. That task, of appraising the courageousness of acts, relies essentially on our understanding of the trait of courage, a characteristic of a type of person.[15]

The suggestion here that we cannot understand 'courageous act' ('honest act', 'loyal act', 'temperate act', 'charitable act', etc.) until we have (so to speak) got our hands on the exemplar, the agent with the virtuous character, is an assertion of the 'primacy of character' with a vengeance. I would certainly want to disown the idea that we cannot understand the v-rules 'Do what is courageous, do what is honest, do what is loyal, etc.' until we have understood what it is to be a courageous, honest, loyal, etc. person. Quite small children can understand those rules to at least some extent, and when you look up those adjectives in a good dictionary, the dictionary does not simply say 'of acts, typical of someone with the virtue of . . .' and refer you to the corresponding noun. (Contrast an adjective such as 'Pickwickian'. Now this has come to have a broader application than to words misused or misunderstood to avoid offence, all a dictionary can say is 'of or like Pickwick'.)[16]

I initially described the v-rules as 'generated' by the terms for the virtues and vices, and thereby I am happy to say that the notion of 'v-acts' is, in some way, 'secondary to and dependent upon the notion of ' a virtuous person. But I construe 'secondary to and dependent upon' as something more complicated than 'only to be defined or understood at all in terms of'. The v-adjectives applied to actions have a certain amount of independence—especially, I think, the vice adjectives—which is encapsulated in dictionary entries and mother's-knee rules. The notion of the virtuous per-

[15] Hudson, *Human Character and Morality*, 42–3.
[16] This, again, is Anscombe's point that the answer to 'Is it unjust? Is in untruthful?', etc. 'would sometimes be clear at once' ('Modern Moral Philosophy', 33).

son—the courageous, or honest, or loyal one—is 'primary' in the
sense that it is needed to go beyond those and provide the fine tuning. ('Face danger or endure pain when and only when a courageous
person would,' 'Eschew being economical with the truth when and
only when the honest agent would.')

It seems that the fine tuning we get from our understanding of
what a virtuous agent would do works on the vice terms as well as
the virtue terms. We do not need an 'exemplar' of cowardice or dishonesty; on the contrary, we fine tune 'cowardly' and 'dishonest'
applied to actions as we come to understand that, on occasions, discretion may be the better part of valour and even the courageous
flee for their lives, in which cases their fleeing is not cowardly, and
that, on occasions, the scrupulously honest may be economical with
the truth and deceive others, in which cases their deception is not
dishonest.

But the possibility of tragic dilemmas shows us that the fine tuning does not work across every case. In a tragic dilemma, a virtuous agent does something terrible or horrible and although the fact
that she does it may suffice to tune out 'cruel', 'appallingly cal-
lous/irresponsible', 'horribly unjust', 'utterly disloyal' as correct
descriptions (people's intuitions about this differ), it certainly does
not tune out 'terrible' or 'horrible'. Indeed, it is just because she
regards herself, rightly, as having done something terrible and horrible—something that cannot possibly be described as 'acting
well'—that her life is marred. And if the claim that 'character has
primacy over action' is supposed to commit one to a reductive definition of terrible or horrible acts in terms of the virtuous (or perhaps the vicious?) agent, then I want to disown that too.

Of course, I do not disown a conceptual connection. Terrible acts
will in general indeed be, as I said above, the very sort of thing that
the most callous, dishonest, unjust . . . i.e. *wicked* characteristically
do, and the very sort of thing that 'for the most part' would never
even cross a virtuous agent's mind as a possible course of action.
But the reason why it would normally never cross her mind is that
through it a very great evil would be brought about (or perhaps a
very great good lost?). No virtue ethics inspired by Aristotle is committed to a reductive definition of the concepts of *good* and *evil* in
terms of that of the *virtuous agent*, only to maintaining a close connection between them. To anticipate the discussion in the later
chapters very briefly, let me just point out that, as Foot says, the

virtue of charity is 'the virtue that gives attachment to the good of
others, and because life is normally a good, charity normally
demands that it should be saved or prolonged'.[17] What constitutes
the (true) good of others, and when life is and is not a good, are
amongst the things that the virtuous person knows and can recognize, but they are so not because she recognizes them but because
of facts about human nature.

Once again, we see the danger of slogans. It is surprisingly common to find virtue ethics, given its committal to the 'primacy of
character', treated as though it maintained that the concepts of the
virtuous and vicious agent were the only pieces of conceptual appa-
ratus relevant to moral philosophy, as though it promised to be able
to give a reductive analysis of all our other moral concepts in terms
of them. (As I have noted elsewhere,[18] Foot is criticized for 'helping
herself ' to the concepts of a *good* and a *benefit* in the paper on
euthanasia just referred to, the implication being that if she is going
to apply a virtue ethics approach to euthanasia, discussing it in
terms of justice and charity, this is illegitimate; she is not allowed to
employ those concepts until they have been given their reductive
analysis in terms of the virtuous agent.)

But although, given its specification of right action, virtue ethics
may be committed to some sort of reductionism of the concept of
the Right, it is far from committed to a wholesale reduction of other
moral concepts. On the contrary, it relies on a lot of them. Not only
does it rely on the concept(s) of the *good* of human beings and what
(truly) *benefits* them, by means of which we define charity, but also
on those of, for example, the *worthwhile*, the *advantageous*, and
the *pleasant* which are inseparably related to them. If I have the
wrong conception of what is worthwhile, advantageous, or pleasant, then I shall have the wrong conception of what is good for, and
harmful to, myself and others and, with the best will in the world,
will lack the virtue of charity, which involves getting all of this right.
And the concept of what is a very great evil in human life would be
a further example.

So where do I stand on the 'primacy of character'? For a start, I
need a phrase which explicitly disavows any foundational or reduc-

[17] Foot, 'Euthanasia', 54.
[18] 'Applying Virtue Ethics' (1995).

tivist role for it,[19] so I shall say I subscribe to the thesis that the concept of the virtuous agent is the focal concept of ethics.[20] Then, summing up the preceding discussion, I shall say that by this I mean, at least, that we need it to understand both action guidance and action assessment, to understand why it is sometimes so difficult to see what should be done and why we accept advice, to understand irresolvable and tragic dilemmas and the unity of the virtues, and to fine-tune, and thereby fully understand, our virtue and vice concepts. (In later chapters I shall argue that we also need it to understand so-called 'moral motivation'.)

## Absolutism Again

The preceding discussion of tragic dilemmas, especially its recognition that the correct resolution of a dilemma may be to allow oneself to be killed, should serve as a corrective to another misunderstanding of virtue ethics: the idea that it denies that there are any absolute prohibitions, some particular actions that one is categorically required not to do. It is sometimes criticized for this but, disconcertingly—and dangerously—it is sometimes praised for taking a 'flexible' or 'situation-oriented' approach to problems, considering each case on its own merits and hence avoiding the inflexible pronouncements of deontology, or indeed, utilitarianism. This tends to come about when virtue ethics is seen as, desirably, avoiding the problems with which textbooks frequently confront the other two. The thought goes something likes this:

> Utilitarianism says there is nothing intrinsically wrong with lying; so, presented with the case in which a bare-faced lie to a patient who trusts one would have good consequences, keeping everyone happy, it recommends the lie. Such examples drive us to deontology and the importance of abiding

[19] Cf. Julia Annas on ancient virtue theories. 'In them, the notions of the agent's final end, of happiness and of the virtues are what may be called *primary*, as opposed to basic. These are the notions that we start from; they set up the framework of the theory, and we introduce and understand the other notions in terms of them. They are thus primary for understanding . . . However they are not basic in the modern sense: other concepts are not derived from them, still less reduced to them.' *The Morality of Happiness* (1993), 9.

[20] See Michael Slote, 'Virtue Ethics' (1997), for the differences between agent-based and agent-focused versions of virtue ethics.

by the rule or principle that one must not lie, regardless of the consequences. But then we are confronted with the famous cases such as protecting the Jews hidden in one's cellar from the Nazis at one's door, where the consequences of telling the truth are so frightful that we are driven back to utilitarianism. In steps virtue ethics, which, rejecting all appeal to general rules or principles, rejects both the monistic 'maximize happiness' and the exceptionless 'Do not lie', and bids us consider each case on its own merits. The wise eye of the virtuous agent discerns that it is the fact that one would be lying to one's trusting friend which is morally relevant or 'salient' in the first case, not the consequences, whereas it is the consequences, not the lie, which are relevant in the second; it is this capacity for moral perception, not following rules, that enables her to act well—how refreshingly sensible!

Now although that paragraph is not, I think, entirely wrong, it embodies a number of mistakes. For one thing, it takes us straight back to the old idea that 'virtue ethics does not come up with any rules or principles', forgetting the existence of the v-rules. For another, in its ready, albeit implicit, acceptance of lying to the Nazis, it suggests that virtue ethics inevitably rejects 'absolutism'—that is, that it is always ready to adapt its 'rules' to circumstances. And the combination of the two can lead to a dangerously tempting third mistake—the thought that virtue ethics is somehow soft and conciliating, that it will let us off a number of uncomfortable hooks that deontology, in particular, hangs us up on. Hence the surprise when it is said that there may be situations in which the virtuous agent will be condemned to death or sorrow, or called upon to let herself be killed.

Suppose that two of virtue ethics' rules are 'Do what is honest' and 'Do not do what is dishonest'. Why might one think that these were rules that could be adapted to circumstances in such a way that virtue ethics spared us the uncomfortable demands of deontology?

Someone inclined to the picture of virtue ethics as soft and conciliating might begin by thinking that the virtue of honesty was consistent with telling white lies:

> When I hear someone I had always thought of as very honest
> tell a small social lie I do not infer that my previous assess-

ment of their character was mistaken; I recognize their good manners. Someone who makes a point of never telling such lies, I might say, is not thereby more honest than someone who, always scrupulous in telling the truth about important things, allows herself the occasional white lie when etiquette demands it. She is, on the contrary, someone who has made the mistake of thinking that there is something sacrosanct about the rule 'Do not lie', or perhaps the mistake of thinking that 'one lie leads to another' is an inescapable law of human psychology or the human condition.

This conciliatory line of thought might continue thus:

I would not condemn someone as dishonest if they lied to the Nazis about the Jews in their cellar either. *If* I think that the only way out of this situation is to lie, and my putatively honest agent lies, I do not say that this is any reflection on her honesty (that what she did was dishonest), though I do not say it was an exercise of it either. I say, 'Well, the considerations of honesty do not arise here, you see, because . . .' So possession of honesty is consistent with telling barefaced lies too. It seems that we tailor our virtue (and vice) concepts to fit the world as we find it; and we find it to be a world in which genuinely virtuous people sometimes break the deontologist's rules.

One question that has been begged here is just what we find the world to be like, for instance the question of whether or not we find it to be a world of God's making. It is often assumed that deontology is the only possible normative ethics for a theist, but this squares ill with the fact that Aquinas, Anscombe, and Geach are all virtue ethicists rather than deontologists. They all regard 'Do not lie' as an absolute prohibition, and, accordingly, would deny much of the above. For a start they would, I take it, deny that the virtue of honesty was consistent with telling white lies; someone who is scrupulous about telling the truth in other contexts is not dishonest the way someone who will lie whenever it suits her is, but is still failing in honesty. The rule 'Do not lie' *is* sacrosanct, and it is *not* a mistake to think that one lie leads to another; getting into the habit of telling small social lies 'corrupts our practical wisdom'.[21]

---

[21] Geach, *The Virtues*, 113.

Geach says that 'if you can *see* no way out but a lie, the lie may
be the least wicked of the alternatives you can discern; [but] it is still
wicked, and you should blame yourself that you lacked the wisdom
of St. Joan or St. Athanasius, to extricate yourself without lying'.[22]
He is discussing the absolute prohibition against lying in the context of the claim that God does not require of any his faithful servants the choice between sin and sin; hence, if you are in the
situation through no fault of your own, and lying is a sin, and is the
only alternative *you can see*, you are thereby lacking in virtue, perhaps in that practical wisdom which is an essential aspect of each
of the moral virtues. Yes, we tailor our virtue (and vice) concepts to
fit the world as we find it, but we do not find it to be a world in
which *genuinely* virtuous people break the rule against lying; we
know it is not.

Many may well not agree with Geach concerning the absolute
prohibition against lying and God's guarantee that the genuinely
virtuous can avoid lying without doing something even worse such
as betraying the Jews to the Nazis. But disagreeing with Geach's
case is a far cry from thinking quite generally that 'we find the world
to be such that genuinely virtuous people quite often break the
deontologist's rules', let alone thinking that, because of virtue
ethics' original specification of right action, when they do, they 'do
what is right'.

What he is certainly correct about is that the situations in which
we find it very difficult to decide what to do do not come to us conveniently labelled as distressing or tragic *dilemmas*, and that it will
be the mark of someone lacking in virtue that they too readily see
a situation as one in which they are forced to choose between great
evils, rather than as one in which there is a third way out. Hence it
is a mistake to allow oneself to think that someone genuinely honest is likely to tell a bare-faced lie as soon as she recognizes something else 'relevant' or 'salient' in the situation; that someone
genuinely charitable and just is likely to kill someone off if this will
prevent great suffering. For the thought that we find the world to
be such that one is not infrequently forced to lie or kill is the thought
of someone not virtuous but seriously lacking in virtue. (Compare
Anscombe: 'if someone really thinks, *in advance*, that it is open to
question whether such an action as procuring the judicial execution

---

[22] Ibid. 121.

of the innocent should be quite excluded from consideration . . . he shows a corrupt mind.')[23]

And he may well be right about there being some absolute prohibitions too. I am quite willing to stick my neck out and say that we find the world to be such that no genuinely virtuous person would ever sexually abuse children for pleasure—that, in Aristotle's terms, the description of the act 'connotes depravity'.

[23] Anscombe, 'Modern Moral Philosophy', p. 40. I was horrified to find some of my Open University students inventing an example of a woman killing her husband to stop him sexually abusing their children and saying that 'This is what a virtuous agent would do'. What they meant by saying that was, 'I wouldn't blame her, wouldn't say she was lacking in virtue, would regard her as justified, because she was protecting her children in *the only way* she could.' But there's the corruption of thought. Who says it was 'the only way'? The people who thought of the example are also imagining the woman saying, 'There wasn't any other way to protect them; I couldn't do anything else,' and themselves instantly *accepting* this. But they shouldn't accept it. A too great *readiness* to think 'I can't do anything but this terrible thing, nothing else is open to me' is a mark of vice, a flawed character. I argue that what one is 'compelled' by ('I couldn't do anything else') is a mark of one's character, for well or ill, in 'Acting and Feeling in Character: *Nicomachean Ethics* 3. 1' (1988).

PART II

# EMOTION AND MOTIVATION

# 4

# Aristotle and Kant

In the last chapter we referred to some of the emotions a virtuous agent would feel on certain occasions, in particular, regret and even extreme grief as reactions to what had to be done. Virtue ethics is often praised, especially at the expense of Kant's deontology, for giving a better account of the moral significance of the emotions than the other ethical approaches, and, in particular, for giving a more attractive account than Kant of 'moral motivation'. But just what this account is, and whether and if so how Kant in particular, and deontologists and utilitarians in general, are cut off from it, has not been made clear. As I said above (Chapter 2, p. 48), it does not seem to me that either approach is cut off from recognizing the significance of regret simply in virtue of being 'act-centred' rather than agent-centred and it may be that neither is intrinsically debarred from incorporating a quite general and plausible account of the moral significance of the emotions. I have always thought that virtue ethics does give a better account than the other two approaches—that was, indeed, one of the things that attracted me to it in the first place—but I am no longer sure, as I used to be, that this is much more than a historical accident.

The central issue people seem to have in mind when they think of virtue ethics as giving the superior account of the moral significance of the emotions is, I think, the issue of the feelings of agents who act charitably. The debate concerns a famous passage in the first section of Kant's *Groundwork*, and an apparent conflict between what this passage says and a central thesis of Aristotelian ethics. If I am right in thinking that this is the central issue people have in mind, we should pause to note a few oddities about it. First, it can hardly aspire to showing that virtue ethics is superior to both deontology *and* utilitarianism on the emotions since the latter, in its simplest forms, is uncommitted on what agents should feel when they act. Second, it fails to engage with non-Kantian deontology—and surely a deontologist might still be recognizably Kantian while still repudiating some of Kant. Third, it does not look as though it will suffice to ground a general claim about the moral significance of *the* emotions. Even if it shows that sympathy, compassion, and love are morally significant, what about fear, anger, joy, sorrow, hope, pride, shame, despair, admiration, gratitude, embarrassment, and so on? Nevertheless this issue is worth considering in some detail, to deepen the understanding of neo-Aristotelian virtue ethics and to explore the extent to which it is at loggerheads with Kant in the *Groundwork*.

At the end of Book 1 of the *Nicomachean Ethics*, Aristotle introduces a distinction between the 'continent' or 'self-controlled' type of human being, (who has *enkrateia*) and the one who has full virtue (*arete*). Simply, the continent character is the one who, typically, knowing what she should do, does it, *contrary* to her desires,[1] and the fully virtuous character is the one who, typically, knowing what she should do, does it, desiring to do it. Her desires are in 'complete harmony' with her reason; hence, when she does what she should, she does what she desires to do, and reaps the reward of satisfied desire. Hence, 'virtuous conduct gives pleasure to the lover of virtue' (1099a12); the fully virtuous do what they (characteristically) do, gladly.

[1] I follow modern convention in giving this general description of continence, despite the fact that, when Aristotle comes to discuss continence and 'incontinence' (akrasia, weakness of will) in Book 7, he says explicitly that 'we must regard as continence and incontinence only those states that are concerned with the same pleasures as temperance and licentiousness'. He does allow that the word 'incontinence' may, by analogy, be used in relation to states concerned with other things, such as temper, honour, gain, and one's family (interestingly, he does not include fear), but he is markedly less interested in these cases of 'incontinence only by analogy' than the others. It seems, oddly enough, that he has overlooked the possibility that those who 'care too much' for such things might *act* in a way they knew was wrong; the passage (1148a20–b15) suggests that they feel too much (and know it) but that this is not a thing that is condemned because 'there is no actual wickedness involved', unlike incontinence proper. But we have thought of hosts of examples in which agents do what is wicked because, contrary to reason, but driven by passion, they exact undeserved revenge or do what is unjust or dishonest for the sake of honour, gain, or their family. If he has, indeed, overlooked these possibilities and is thinking only of people who, feeling as they should not, nevertheless always manage to act as they should, then his 'incontinent by analogy' cases would be included under our modern conception of continence, to which we add further cases such as helping others without any delight in their well-being.

So Aristotle draws a distinction between two sorts of people—the continent or self-controlled, and the fully virtuous—and he weights that distinction, as the phrases show, a particular way; the fully virtuous agent is morally superior to the merely self-controlled one.

In the *Groundwork* passage, Kant says,

To help others where one can is a duty, and besides this there are many spirits of so sympathetic a temper that, without any further motive of vanity or self-interest, they find an inner pleasure in spreading happiness around them and can take delight in the contentment of others as their own work. Yet I maintain that in such a case an action of this kind, however right and however amiable it may be, has still no genuinely moral worth. It stands on the same footing as other inclinations—for example, the inclination for honour, which if fortunate enough to hit on something beneficial and right and consequently honourable, deserves praise and encouragement, but not esteem; for its maxim lacks moral content, namely the performance of such actions, not from inclination, but *from duty*. Suppose then that the mind of this friend of man were overclouded by sorrows of his own which extinguished all sympathy with the fate of others, but that he still had power to help those in distress, though no longer stirred by the need of others because sufficiently occupied with his own; and suppose that, when no longer moved by any inclination, he tears himself out of this deadly insensibility and does the action without any inclination for the sake of duty alone; then for the first time his action has its genuine moral worth. Still further: if nature had implanted little sympathy in this or that man's heart; if (being in other respects an honest fellow) he were cold in temperament and indifferent to the sufferings of others—perhaps because, being endowed with the special gift of patience and robust endurance in his own sufferings, he assumed the like in others or even demanded it; if such a man (who would in truth not be the worst product of nature) were not exactly fashioned by her to be a philanthropist, would he not still find in himself a source from which he might draw a worth far higher than any that a good-natured temperament can have? Assuredly he would. It is precisely in this that the worth of character begins to show—a moral worth and beyond all comparison the highest—namely that he does good, not from inclination, but from duty.[2]

On the standard reading of this passage, Kant draws the same distinction as Aristotle, but weights it the contrary way—the self-controlled agent is claimed to be morally superior to the agent who

---

[2] I. Kant, *Groundwork of the Metaphysics of Morals*, trans H. J. Paton (1964), 66.

would, in Aristotle's terms, have full virtue, because she desires to
do what she does. He describes the benevolent actions of people 'of
so sympathetic a temper that . . . they find an inner pleasure in
spreading happiness around them and can take delight in the contentment of others as their own work' as having 'no genuinely
moral worth', and contrasts them unfavourably with the benevolent actions of two other people, who, unmoved by any feelings of
sympathy, act 'without any inclination for the sake of duty alone';
their actions have 'genuine moral worth'. And this looks like bad
news for Kant, for it seems to be (and has been claimed to be) tantamount to the wildly implausible claim that the person who visits
her friend in hospital 'because she *is* her friend' is morally inferior
to the one who visits her 'out of a sense of duty'.[3] I used to read the
*Groundwork* passage in this way, but have now come to believe
that Aristotle and Kant are much closer than is usually supposed.[4]


### PHILIPPA FOOT IN 'VIRTUES AND VICES'


I was initially led to change my mind by Foot's penetrating discussion of Kant's passage in 'Virtues and Vices'.[5] Foot introduces her
discussion by pointing to an apparent contradiction in our everyday thoughts about morality.

[W]e both are and are not inclined to think that the harder a man finds it
to act virtuously the more virtue he shows if he does act well. For on the
one hand great virtue is needed where it is particularly hard to act virtuously; yet on the other it could be argued that difficulty in acting virtuously
shows that the agent is imperfect in virtue: according to Aristotle, to take
pleasure in virtuous action is the mark of true virtue, with the self-mastery
of the one who finds virtue difficult only a second best. How then is this
conflict to be decided?

[3] The example is now standardly used in this abbreviated form. In its original
form, it was much richer in details which, importantly, made the characters of the
agents clear. See Michael Stocker, 'The Schizophrenia of Modern Ethical Theories'
(1976).
[4] Robert Louden in 'Kant's Virtue Ethics' and Christine Korsgaard in 'From Duty
and for the Sake of the Noble' also find more agreement between them than is
allowed on the standard reading.
[5] 'Virtues and Vices' (1978), 10.

One rather weak response to the difficulty, which she does not consider, might be to say that common-sense morality just *does* contain contradictions, that different approaches (Kantian, Aristotelian) pick up on different sides, and that the only thing for moral philosophers to do is go for one approach rather than the other and give up, or remake, common-sense morality. So, one might say, it is just a brute fact that the Kantian approach captures the common-sense view on courageous actions, whereby the one who shows most courage is 'the one who wants to run away but does not', and the Aristotelian one captures the common-sense view on benevolent or charitable actions, whereby the one who shows most benevolence or charity is the one 'who finds it easy to make the good of others his object'.[6] Enlightened by the correct moral theory, we must revise our pre-theoretic ideas about courage or charity, comforting ourselves with the thought that we have, at least, managed to remove contradiction.

But Foot finds a better response; she finds some points in Kant with which Aristotelians may, and indeed should, agree. Her discussion forces us to note that the continent/fully virtuous distinction needs to be applied with some discretion and that the claim 'virtuous conduct gives pleasure to the lover of virtue' needs careful qualification. Moreover, as I shall go on to argue, there are points of agreement beyond those that she mentions.

So, how are we to resolve the conflict between the thoughts 'the harder it is for a man to act virtuously, the more virtue he shows if he acts well' and 'the harder it is, the less virtue he shows'? Foot's answer is that each may be true with respect to different cases, depending on what it is that 'makes it hard' to act well. Some things that 'make it hard' for someone to act well 'show that virtue (in him) is incomplete',[7] less than full virtue, for what 'makes it hard' pertains to his character. These are the cases of which it is true that 'the harder it is for him, the less virtue he shows', and the ones that the continent/fully virtuous distinction—which is a distinction between different *characters*—applies to. But other things that 'make it hard' for someone to act well do not pertain to their character; rather, they are circumstances in which the virtuous character is 'severely tested' and comes through. These are the cases of which it is true that 'the harder it is for him, the more virtue he

---

[6] Ibid.      [7] Ibid. 11.

shows', and here the continent/fully virtuous distinction does not apply.

Consider courage. This has always looked like a somewhat awkward virtue for the continent/fully virtuous distinction, and it is significant that Aristotle himself regards it as necessary to qualify his claim that the exercise of every virtue is pleasurable with respect to it (1117b10). Although his remarks in this passage are open to different interpretations,[8] what seems beyond dispute is that someone who wants to risk and endure frightful pain or death, and enjoys doing so, is not thereby courageous but a masochist, or a daredevil maniac. Even when the courageous are not acting contrary to an inclination to run away or preserve themselves, they are not, in any ordinary sense, 'doing what they want to do' and thereby reaping the pleasure of satisfied desire.

Nevertheless, there still seem to be neo-Aristotelian cases (off the battlefield) where the distinction applies. Parents who find it hard to go to the rescue of their children because they have to conquer their fear of danger to themselves do not compare favourably with those parents who fly to the rescue with no thought of their own safety; Hume's friends marvelled at the way in which he conducted himself towards the end of his life, in such a way that 'Death for the time did not seem dismal', as Boswell reported, let alone fearful. Those who find it harder to put their impending death out of their minds for the sake of their friends are less admirable. In such cases, fearlessness, rather than the conquering of fear, merits the highest esteem, since it reflects the agent's values and, thereby, character. But if the fear that has to be conquered does not connect with one's values, but is, as we say, pathological, the judgement goes the other way. As Foot points out, 'if someone suffers from claustrophobia or a dread of heights he may require courage to do that which would not be a courageous action in others'.[9] Being subject to some pho-

---

[8] John McDowell, for example, maintains that the virtuous understand the notions of 'benefit, advantage, harm, loss and so forth' in such a way that no sacrifice necessitated by virtue counts as a loss: 'The Role of *Eudaimonia* in Aristotle's Ethics' (1980). I shall be discussing this view in Chap. 8.

[9] Foot, 'Virtues and Vices', 12. Louden, 'Kant's Virtue Ethics', fudges Foot's distinction, committing her to the blanket claim 'that the agent who does not even want to run away shows more courage than the one who wants to run away but does not'.

bia is being in circumstances that *call* on one's courage; if one comes through, one merits esteem.[10]

Consider honesty. If it is 'hard for me' to restore the full purse I saw someone drop because I am strongly tempted to keep it and have to conquer the temptation, I am less than thoroughly honest and morally inferior to the person who hastens to restore it with no thought of keeping what is not hers. But there are two different examples of the agent who thus hastens to restore the purse. There is the one who has a nicely full purse of her own, and the one who is poor. The former *may* be as thoroughly honest as the latter but, if she is, her honesty has not been, on this occasion, severely tested, because it is easy for her to restore it—what is a full purse to her? For the poor agent, 'it is hard' to restore it, hard in so far as she is hardily circumstanced, and the poorer she is—the harder it is for her to restore the purse—the more honesty she shows in unhesitatingly and readily restoring it. Here again, we should note qualifications that must be put on 'virtuous activity gives pleasure to the lover of virtue'. If the purse that the poor agent restores goes to someone who is manifestly a 'profligate debauchee', then Hume has a point when he says that there cannot be any 'natural motive' involved, only the motive of restoring to someone that which is theirs. As I shall stress later, no Aristotelian should take on Hume's vocabulary here, but I see no reason why we should deny to the fully honest the thought that it is a damned shame that this had to be done. The 'pleasure' the fully honest agent derives from this particular act is of an attenuated, not a characteristic, sort.

Consider now the (non-Aristotelian) virtue of charity or benevolence which Foot discusses. It might seem that the successful exercise of this could not fail to give straightforward pleasure to one who genuinely possesses the virtue, for should not a genuine attachment to the good of others guarantee joy in their joy, pleasure in their pleasure? Must it not quite generally be the case that anyone who 'finds it hard' to help another possesses only the inferior, 'continent' form of this virtue? No, for here we come to one of Kant's

---

[10] This is a 'neo-Aristotelian' point. Had Aristotle recognized claustrophobia, it seems likely that he would have regarded it as a defect that made the virtue of courage unobtainable, since the concept of pathological fears is a distinctly modern one. Nor does it seem likely that he would recognize, as we can, the admirable courage, fortitude, and hope of people who struggle with and triumph over addiction.

philanthropists, the one whose mind is 'overclouded by sorrows of his own'. To say of him, when he does what is charitable, with difficulty and without pleasure, that he thereby acts less well, or shows himself to be less perfect in the virtue of charity, than someone else who does the same gladly, would be a mistake, for what 'makes it hard' for him to act well here does not show that his virtue is incomplete.

There is no reason why an Aristotelian should not agree with Kant that there is something particularly estimable about the action of the sorrowing philanthropist. For here, the 'difficulty that stands in the way' of his virtuous action is of the sort that 'provides an occasion' for much virtue.[11] It is his sorrow which makes noticing and attending to the needs of others particularly difficult; and as Foot rightly remarks, if he still manages to act with charity this 'most shows virtue', because 'this is the kind of circumstance that increases the virtue that is needed if a man is to act well'.[12] The fact is that it is difficult to do anything much when one's mind is overclouded by sorrow, and impossible to take pleasure in anything; the difficulty and lack of pleasure in acting which this man finds, spring from the nature of sorrow, not from his character,[13] and it is only difficulties that spring from one's own character that show the virtue to be incomplete. So if the answer to 'Why does this person find it hard to make the good of others her object?' is 'Her mind is overclouded by sorrow', then the fact that she finds it hard may be no reflection on her virtue; she may still count as being fully virtuous rather than merely 'continent'.

So, following Foot, we may conclude that Kant's estimation of the sorrowing philanthropist should not be read as a straightforward denial of Aristotle's weighting of the continent/fully virtuous distinction. Instead, that distinction, and the concomitant Aristotelian claim that 'virtuous conduct gives pleasure to the lover of virtue', should be given qualified and particularized interpretations in a way that does justice to Kant's example.

---

[11] Foot, 'Virtues and Vices', 11.     [12] Ibid. 14.
[13] Or so, at least, we charitably suppose when reading Kant's passage. It would have a very different ring if we imagined him 'no longer stirred by the need of others' because, appallingly conceited, he has been cast into despair by his failure to receive some trivial public recognition. Then the sorrow itself would manifest a defect in character, and the difficulty in attending to the needs of others would spring from it.

But what about his other examples? Surely we can discern the denial in what he says about the happy philanthropists who 'find an inner pleasure in spreading happiness around them', acting from inclination, not from duty? Foot does indeed imply that, in denying that their charitable actions have 'genuine moral worth', Kant has simply made a mistake about the virtue of charity. 'For charity is,' she says, 'a virtue of attachment as well as action, and the sympathy that makes it easier to act with charity is part of the virtue.'[14] She is right that he has made a mistake about the virtue of charity, but I suspect too that Kant may have a picture of the happy philanthropists in mind which would justify his dismissal of their actions as 'lacking moral worth'. This is the point at which I leave Foot's discussion and seek to show that there is even more agreement between Kant and the Aristotelian approach than she identifies.

## ACTING 'FROM INCLINATION'

What does Kant take the happy philanthropists at the beginning of the passage to be like? What *is* it to be the sort of agent who acts 'from inclination not from duty'? Later, I shall suggest that the answer to the latter question is not the same as the answer to the first. But, for the moment, let us construct a picture as follows.

Suppose we began by thinking of certain emotions, say sympathy, compassion, and love, as good or nice ones. Without committing ourselves to tendentious details about what an emotion is, or what it is to feel one, we can say safely that each characteristically involves such desires as the desire to help others, to comfort them in their affliction, to give them what they want and need; in other words, that they motivate one to do such things, and also that they characteristically involve emotional *reactions*—felt pain or sorrow at another's pain or grief, felt pleasure or joy at another's pleasure or joy.

Now we note an important difference between people: some are very prone to feel these emotions, others very little or not at all. (Some are in between, but let us leave them out of it.) This seems to be a difference in their characters; the former are charitable (or, as

---

[14] Foot, 'Virtues and Vices', 14.

people tend to say nowadays, benevolent); the latter callous and selfish. So we might regard possessing the virtue of charity (or benevolence) as being very prone to feeling these emotions on suitable occasions. Can we note a further difference between people—that some are very prone to feeling these emotions without being prompted to many actions by them, whereas others are thus prompted? Given that we said that the emotions in question characteristically involve desires to act, this seems unlikely, but, just in case, we could make it explicit and say: possessing the virtue of charity is being very prone not only to feeling but to acting from the emotions of sympathy, compassion, and love, prompted by the desires associated with them.

Is this an adequate conception of the virtue of charity or benevolence? Well, it passes two tests. It certainly grounds the continent/fully virtuous distinction; someone who tends to help others and to spread happiness around, but feels no joy over their joy or sorrow when she cannot help, lacks the virtue in question, though clearly coming closer to it than someone who does not tend to do such things. It also makes the virtue of charity out to be, as Foot requires, 'a virtue of attachment' which corrects 'a deficiency of motivation' common to human nature. And it is not, I think, an uncommon conception.[15] If not Hume's [16] it is at least recognizably Humean, and it is plausible to suppose that Kant's target in this passage is Hume.

It is Hume who has said that 'If any man from a cold insensibility, or narrow selfishness of temper, is unaffected with the images of human happiness or misery, he must be equally indifferent to the images of vice and virtue'[17]—which is to say that he will never do

---

[15] It is, I think, Lawrence Blum's. Near the end of *Friendship, Altruism and Morality* (1980) he says: 'it is possible to cast much of the arguments of this book in the language of character and of virtues. For I have regarded compassion, sympathy and concern (or concernedness) as virtuous traits of character, associated with the emotions denoted by the same terms.' He assumes that I have the virtue of compassion if I have a compassionate character, and that I have a compassionate character if, simply, I am prone to feel and act out of the emotion of compassion on suitably moving occasions. It is also, I suspect, the conception that leads Frankena to coin the phrase 'principles without traits [virtues] are impotent and traits without principles are blind', *Ethics*, 65.

[16] I do not claim that it is Hume's. Oddly enough, Hume never says explicitly what he thinks possession of a virtue consists in, and how Humean passions might figure in a virtue when rendered suitably 'calm' is a large topic.

[17] D. Hume, *Enquiry Concerning the Principles of Morals* (1902), § 183.

what is benevolent or refrain from doing what is callous or cruel, because inclination, or 'passion', will never move him to do so. To which Kant, we may suppose, replies, echoing his words, that suppose a man were 'cold in temperament and indifferent to the sufferings of others', assuredly he *would* still find in himself a source that would enable him to do what is benevolent; he will do it, not from inclination, but from duty. So perhaps Kant's happy philanthropists have this sort of Humean benevolence.

It will indeed be true of them that, as described, they are 'of so sympathetic a temper that, without any further motive of vanity or self-interest, they find an inner pleasure in spreading happiness around them and can take delight in the contentment of others as their own work', in Kant's words. That is just what makes them, at first sight, so attractive—just the sort of character, one might think, that one wants to visit one in hospital. And when, in action, they hit on 'what is beneficial and right', their actions deserve praise and encouragement, as he says. But there is the rub, for, as described, they are liable to go wrong in a number of ways. How come?

In Kantian terms, they are liable to go wrong because the emotions are unreliable as sources of acting well. But this is not something with which any Aristotelian need disagree. In Aristotelian terms, we reach the same conclusion at greater length and on different grounds.

We may say that sympathy, compassion, and love attach one to 'the good' of others, involving desires to benefit and not harm them. But, more cautiously, we should say that they attach one to 'the apparent good' of others (and, correspondingly to 'apparent benefit' and 'apparent harm')—their 'good' as conceived by the one who feels the emotions. And a misconception of what is 'good' for others and of what benefits and harms them may result in someone's being prompted to act wrongly by the emotions in question. (For example, compassion misguided by a misconception of 'good' may prompt someone to lie rather than tell the hurtful truth that the other needs to know.) Moreover, even when guided by a correct conception, the emotions may prompt one to actions that other considerations should tell against; perhaps this person does not merit sympathy and charitable action but others, unnoticed, do; perhaps, not having paused to think, one will wind up doing more harm than good; perhaps others would make a much better job of it (there is sometimes a sort of greediness and vanity in wanting to be the one who helps); perhaps one *can't* help, not because it is physically impossible, but because it is morally impossible in that it involves breaking a certain promise, or violating the other's, or another's, rights. And finally, one may fail to feel the emotions (and hence to be prompted to action by them) when other emotions get in the way—hatred or embarrassment or self-pity, or, indeed, personal sorrow—and thereby fail to act as one should.

In short, the emotions of sympathy, compassion, and love, viewed simply as psychological phenomena, are no guarantee of right action, or acting well. There is nothing about them, *qua* natural inclinations, which guarantees that they occur 'in complete harmony with reason', that is, that they occur when, and only when, they should, towards the people whose circumstances should occasion them, consistently, on reasonable grounds and to an appropriate degree, as Aristotelian virtue requires. Moreover, even when they are 'fortunate enough to hit on something [in some sense] beneficial and right', they still need to be regulated by *phronesis* or practical wisdom. They may prompt one to a good end, but the agent still has to be good at deliberation to be (reasonably) sure of attaining it, and the good of others, though a good end, is not the only good to be pursued in acting well.

So if Kant's happy philanthropists, who act from inclination, not from duty, are as described, they cannot be regarded as having an Aristotelian version of the non-Aristotelian virtue of charity or benevolence. Kantians and Aristotelians agree on the fact that this sort of agent cannot be relied upon to act well. And now for the further question: can Aristotelians agree with Kant that, when even their actions do hit on 'something beneficial and right', those actions lack genuine moral worth, *because* they are done from inclination not from duty? Well, not in those terms, of course, since 'duty' and 'moral worth' are terms of art in Kant, and nothing straightforwardly corresponding to them can be found in Aristotle nor even reconstructed in neo-Aristotelianism. But, in other terms, there is a significant measure of agreement to be found.

We should not forget that Kant and Aristotle significantly share a strongly anti-Humean premise about the principles or springs of movement (or 'action' in the broad sense of the term). According to Hume, there is only one principle of action, the one we share with animals, namely passion or desire; according to both Aristotle and Kant there are two, one which we share with the other animals, and one which we have in virtue of being rational. Of course we all know that the ideal Kantian agent acts from a sense of duty, not from inclination, but if 'inclination' is that-principle-of-movement-we-share-with-the-other-animals, then the virtuous Aristotelian agent doesn't act from inclination either, but from reason (*logos*) in the form of 'choice' *(prohairesis)*.

In the *Eudemian Ethics* Aristotle says, 'with the other animals the action on compulsion is simple (just as in the inanimate), for they have not inclination and reason (*logos*) opposing one another, but live by inclination; but man has both, that is at a certain age, to which we attribute also the power of action; for we do not say that a child acts, or a brute either, but only a man who does things from reasoning'.[18] So, in Aristotelian terms, we could say that the happy philanthropists, supposing them to have 'Humean' benevolence as described, do not *act* in the strict sense of the term at all. They live *kata pathos*, by inclination, like an animal or a child; their 'doings' issue from passion or emotion (*pathe*) not 'choice' *(prohairesis)*. And here is the sense an Aristotelian may attach to the Kantian claim that their 'actions' (in the broad sense) lack genuine moral worth because they act from inclination not from duty. It is *actions* proper, which issue from reason, that are to be assessed as virtuous (or vicious), but their 'doings' are not actions, and thereby cannot be said to be, and to be esteemed as, virtuous ones.

So, in contrast to the standard reading of this passage, I maintain that neither the esteem Kant gives to the sorrowing philanthropist nor his (relative) denigration of the happy philanthropists should be regarded as drawing Aristotle's continent/fully virtuous distinction and, implausibly, reversing the weighting he gives to it. The esteemed sorrowing philanthropist need not be regarded as having mere continence (because of Foot's points), and the denigrated happy ones should not be regarded as having full virtue (because they do not act 'from reason').

However, those who have detected something deeply wrong about Kant in this passage, wanted to sum it up by saying 'Kant cannot give a proper account of the moral significance of the emotions', and thought that, somehow, virtue ethics gives a better account, have not been quite astray. The key example in this passage is the third philanthropist, the one who is 'cold in temperament and

---

[18] *Eudemian Ethics* 1224a25–30.

indifferent [!] to the sufferings of others' but who nevertheless manages to do good, whose character Kant describes as having 'a moral
worth and *beyond all comparison the highest*' (my italics). But, in
the terms of the Aristotelian distinction, the third philanthropist
clearly has, at best, continence rather than full virtue, and in reserv-
ing for his character the highest moral worth, Kant displays in this
passage, not a reversal of Aristotle's weighting of the continence/full
virtue distinction but a total lack of recognition of its existence.
Moreover, the explanation of this failure of recognition is Kant's
picture of the emotions; he does not have the understanding of them
that generates that distinction. The issue is not so much over 'moral
motivation', nor Kantian problems with impartiality versus friendship or love, but over the nature of full virtue and the role emotion
plays in it.

The fact is that the agent with, in neo-Aristotelian terms, the full
virtue of charity, does not appear in this passage. I pretended he did
when following Foot on the sorrowing philanthropist, in order to
make clear that Aristotelians can accommodate the point that it is
sometimes hard for the agent with full virtue to act well. But, sticking to the text, the sorrowing philanthropist is someone with
Humean benevolence, liable to go wrong in a variety of ways, who
hitherto has acted only from inclination and now 'for the first time'
acts 'for the sake of duty alone'; not a new sort of philanthropist
who has been introduced in contrast to the happy ones. And, in
Aristotelian terms, this is hardly a coherent picture.

Let us ask again, what is it to be the *sort* of agent who acts 'only
from inclination', not from 'a sense of duty', or reason, or whatever,
that is, someone who acts 'only from inclination' not just on a particular occasion but as a way of going on? (I said above that this
question did not have the same answer as the question 'What does
Kant take his happy philanthropists to be like?') In Aristotelian
terms, as we just said, it is to be the sort of agent who lives *kata
pathos*, like an animal or child—that is the way children and animals go on. But what fairly ordinary adult lives like an animal or
child?

It might be thought that, for Aristotelians, the answer to that
question is 'the adult with natural virtue', but Aristotle's tantaliz-
ingly brief remarks on natural virtue near the end of Book 6 of the
*Nicomachean Ethics* do not clearly bear this out. He says that the
natural dispositions (towards, say, temperance or courage) are

found in (some) children and animals, notes that without 'intelligence' (*nous*)[19] they are apt to be harmful, and says that if the subject with the natural disposition(s) acquires 'intelligence', his disposition, while still resembling the natural one, will now *be* virtue in the full sense. But he does not say explicitly that natural virtue can be found in adults[20] and, when we look at what he says about prodigality in Book 4, we may see the omission as deliberate. The prodigal man is said to be open-handed and eager to give, much closer to having the virtue of liberality than the illiberal or mean one; if he could be trained or otherwise changed (to give and receive 'in the right degree or manner') he would have the virtue. But there is no suggestion that he has the natural virtue of liberality; on the contrary, prodigality is said to be a vice.

Now a child who was 'open-handed and eager to give' would surely have the natural virtue of liberality; since she has not yet reached 'the age of reason', her mistakes in giving and receiving do not manifest culpable ignorance. But once one is an adult, such mistakes *do* betray culpable ignorance and one is blameworthy. An adult can't just say to herself, 'I am preserving my childish innocence, acting only from inclination with no thought of whether I am thereby acting well', and make that true by saying it. On the contrary, this would count as, culpably, being inconsiderate, feckless, and self-indulgent, as acting that way *not* 'from inclination' but from choice (*prohairesis*), having decided (for some reason) that acting in accordance with one's inclinations *was*, in general, acting well.[21] Although those who have reached 'the age of reason' do,

[19] It is not clear whether Aristotle is using *nous* here in the casual popular sense—as we use it—or in the technical sense he has been discussing earlier. But either way, it is not something the children and animals have.

[20] I do not deny that one can interpret Aristotle here as implying that adults can have natural virtue. I do deny that this is the most plausible interpretation.

[21] Gary Pendlebury has pointed out to me that this is the point Hegel is making in his ringing phrase, 'When man wills the natural, it is no longer natural.' Christine Korsgaard, in 'From Duty and for the Sake of the Noble', recognizes the plausibility of the point in relation to Kant, but is so determined to identify the philanthropists who act 'from inclination' as, in Aristotelian terms, adults with natural virtue, that she does not allow Aristotle the same insight. According to Korsgaard, 'Kant's view seems to be that the capacity for reflective choice, whether exercised or not, makes a difference to every action: adult human actions take place in the light, so to speak, of reflective thought, and can no longer be exactly like the actions of children and animals' (234, n. 21). In contrast, 'Aristotle's view suggests that a merely voluntary [but not chosen] action performed "on the spur of the moment" is not a

occasionally, act 'from inclination', they do not then act from the same state as small children, for their state includes their knowledge that such action is up for assessment as innocent or deplorable, unjustifiable or justifiable in the circumstances. Once one has acquired reason, the only thing that would clearly count as being the *sort* of agent who acts 'only from inclination' and not from reason is being the sort of agent who is akratic or 'weak-willed' in character.

I take Marcia Baron's description of a certain sort of agent in her first (so-called) 'variety of ethics of virtue'[22] to be an instructive failure to attach sense to there being a sort of fairly ordinary agent who acts 'only from inclination'. This agent, she says, 'desires to help others' and so on, but has 'no moral concepts in the abstract: *no concept* of . . . goodness' (my italics.) But what sort of fairly ordinary adult, one who has learnt to use language and engages in the practice of explaining and justifying their actions in response to questions, could conceivably desire to help others but have 'no concept of goodness'? When small children act from their inclination or desire to help others, and get it wrong, saying, for example, 'She wanted the bandage taken off', we do not ascribe a mistaken conception of goodness to them. They are too young to have a concept of goodness, and we start teaching it to them when we say such things as, 'Yes, I know you wanted to do her good, but it's not good for babies to have their wounds unbandaged; she needs it to be left on.' But an adult who has acted similarly can't excuse themselves by saying, 'I was trying to help, but have no views about whether what I did benefited or harmed her, no concept of what is good or bad for human beings.'

So full virtue, which can be possessed only by adults, cannot be

proper subject of moral judgement, since the agent is just following nature, and it is choice, not the merely voluntary that reveals character' (ibid.). I would say that, on the contrary, there is nothing in Aristotle to suggest that actions of adults which are voluntary but not chosen are not proper subjects of moral judgement, and everything against it, for the primary examples of such actions are those of the akratic or weak-willed which he certainly takes to be blameworthy.

22 'Varieties of Ethics of Virtue' (1985). Baron thinks that Lawrence Blum would be drawn to this picture of the virtuous agent. I am not sure she is right to suppose that Blum's compassionate agents have *no* concept of goodness, but she is certainly right that he seems quite blind to the fact that there can be right or wrong conceptions, and thereby a difference between compassion as a virtue and compassion as a tendency to be moved to action by the emotion of compassion.

a child's natural virtue with reason, in the form of practical wisdom simply added on. It is only with respect to the doings of children, brutes, and the weak-willed (and perhaps occasional, uncharacteristic, impulsive doings of virtuous adults) that it makes sense to say that they act (in the broad sense) 'from inclination'.

What, now, is to be said about the simple contrast between the two agents who visit a friend, one 'because she *is* her friend', the other 'out of a sense of duty'? With hindsight, it is revealed to be far less simple as a criticism of Kant on 'moral motivation'. If we take it as the contrast between a child moved by inclination, by the emotion of love (or friendship or sympathy—it doesn't matter which) and an adult moved by reason (either with full virtue or continence), then it is far from implausible to say the first is morally inferior to the second. But if we try to take it as embodying the Aristotelian contrast between continence and full virtue, it has been set up in the wrong way. In so far as it makes sense to talk of Aristotle's view on 'motivation', the continent and the fully virtuous have the same 'motivation'—they each act from reason in the form of 'choice' (*prohairesis*). The difference between them lies not in their 'motivation' or reasons for action, but in their condition; the fully virtuous are better disposed in relation to their emotions than the self-controlled.

We shall be looking directly at the question of 'moral motivation' in Chapters 6 and 7. Before that, I want to describe the role emotions do play in full virtue, to make good the claim that virtue ethics gives an account of the moral significance of *the* emotions, not merely a few, such as, on the one hand, regret and grief, and on the other, compassion and love.

# 5

# Virtue and the Emotions

Now let us turn to the role emotions play in full virtue. I begin by stating, without argument, what I think an Aristotelian ought to mean, minimally, by 'the emotions are morally significant'. This is basically made up of three claims.

(1) The virtues (and vices) are morally significant.

(2) The virtues (and vices) are all dispositions not only to act, but to feel emotions, as *re*actions as well as impulses to action. (Aristotle says again and again that the virtues are concerned with actions *and* feelings.)

(3) In the person with the virtues, these emotions will be felt on the *right* occasions, towards the *right* people or objects, for the *right* reasons, where 'right' means 'correct', as in 'The right answer to "What is the capital of New Zealand?" is "Wellington".'

We should note immediately that the second claim really does give something like a logically proper ground for the *general* claim '*the emotions are morally significant*'. It thereby stands in marked contrast to some rather weak literature which seeks to support that general claim by a piecemeal approach which at best justifies no more than 'a few emotions (love and sympathy, or regret and pride) are morally significant'.

We should note too that the claims in combination give some cash value to the view that the feeling of certain emotions on certain occasions has intrinsic *moral* value, rather than merely instrumental value or some other sort of intrinsic value. Feeling this emotion then could be said to have 'intrinsic moral value' simply in so far as it is the manifestation of virtue. It is here, I think, that the (initially, apparently rather minor) issue about regret should figure as significant. Cases of emerging, with regret, from distressing or tragic dilemmas are, in the context of 'the moral significance of the emotions', to be thought of as but some amongst a great range of situations in which we want to say 'The way to feel here/what one should feel about this/what anyone decent would feel about this/is . . .'. Another way to describe the very same fact would be that it has intrinsic moral value in so far as the emotional response had the right, i.e. correct, rational content.

Finally and most importantly, we should note that the third claim introduces the crucial notion of feeling emotions rightly or correctly, where that is a cognitive notion. When we recall that the agent with Humean benevolence, and children with natural virtue, notably fail to feel emotions correctly on every occasion, we are in a position to see that virtue is not merely a matter of being disposed to act well with a few dispositions to feel 'nice', sympathetic (or perhaps empathetic) reactions thrown in to make up the full weight. Just as Augustine's famous instruction 'Love, and do what you will' turns out not to be a license to follow one's heart, but to embody extremely stern directions concerning what really counts as love, so the claim that full virtue involves feeling emotions correctly makes it clear that this would not be possible (in general) without the influence of reason.

What account of the emotions allows this claim to be true? One account that will *not* allow for it is one that makes the emotions no part of our rational nature. And there is indeed much in Kant to suggest that, although he shares with Aristotle the view that we have not just one, but two principles of movement, in other respects his philosophical psychology is Humean. He seems committed to the view that our emotions or inclinations are no part of our rationality. They come from the non-rational, animal side of our nature; if they happen to prompt us to act in accordance with the judgements of reason about what ought to be done we are lucky; if they incline us against them we find life difficult, but their prompting us in the right direction is no mark or indication of their rationality. The emotions are not rational in any way.

A different account, with a tradition that dates back to the Stoics, has it that the emotions are indeed part of our rational nature, for they are, or are partially constituted by, judgements, at least some of which are evaluative. On the face of it, this account marries well with the claim that emotions may be had rightly or correctly;

roughly, an emotion is had correctly when the judgement (or set of judgements) which (partially) constitutes it is true (or, perhaps, reasonable given the evidence available). As an enormous literature on this topic has made clear, this 'cognitive account' faces numerous difficulties; for my present purposes, it suffices to mention just two. One is the difficulty in finding a suitable judgement (or set of judgements) to ascribe to someone who is only too aware of the fact that her emotion is irrational in some way, but is in the grip of it notwithstanding. I know perfectly well that the insect is harmless but am still terrified of it, that the tin-opener is not defying me and did not cut my thumb on purpose but am still furious with it, that my partner is a worthless skunk but I still love him, heaven help me. The second is that, even if we allow that toddlers and the higher animals can have some beliefs, there really is something very odd about maintaining that they make judgements, especially evaluative judgements; but unless they do, then, on the cognitive account, they do not have emotions either. These two objections might be summed up as one more general one; that on the cognitive account, the emotions are *too* rational, too akin to the judgements of theoretical reason.

What seems needed is an account which avoids these two extremes—of animal/non-rational and utterly rational. On Hume's, and Kant's, picture of human nature, there is no logical space between the two. But Aristotle's division of the parts of the soul into rational and non-rational is not so hard and fast. We may classify the desiderative part of the soul with the nutritive part, as non-rational, he says—but then we must divide the non-rational part of the soul in two, distinguishing the desiderative part by saying that it participates in reason as the nutritive soul does not. Alternatively, we may classify the desiderative with the reasoning part of the soul as rational—but then we must divide the rational part of the soul in two, and say that the desiderative listens to, or obeys, the reasoning part.[1]

So the Aristotelian picture of human nature creates a space for the emotions—in what is called the desiderative part of the soul— which allows them to be, shall we say, Janus-faced; animal and/or non-rational one face; rational the other. And this allows us to be struck—as surely we should be—not only by the fact that human

---

[1]  *Nicomachean Ethics* 1102b10–1103a1.

beings are subject to some emotions which non-rational animals are also subject to, and not only by the fact that human beings are subject to some emotions that non-rational animals notably lack (for instance, pride, shame, and regret), but, much more significantly, by the way in which reason can radically transform an emotion that human beings certainly share with animals, such as fear. How very unlike the other animals human beings are when they endure agony, and risk their lives, for justice and truth, or are terrified by the prospect of university examinations; when they are ready to die for glory, but tremble at the prospect of humiliation. The emotion that in the other animals is essentially connected to physical self-preservation or preservation of the species can be transformed in human beings into an emotion connected with the preservation of what is *best*, most worth preserving, in us and our species. And the correctness (or incorrectness) of our view of that is an aspect of our rationality.

What then is an appropriate account of the emotions? The details need not concern us here; what will suffice, I believe, is the broad claim that the emotions involve ideas or images (or thoughts or perceptions) of good and evil, taking 'good' and 'evil' in their most general, generic sense, as the formal objects of pursuit and avoidance. (Readers who find 'good' and 'evil' odd in this context may substitute 'value' and 'disvalue'.)

Many philosophers have noticed the fact that our emotions involve ideas, or thoughts, of good and evil. Some use the phrase 'of pleasure and pain' as (supposedly) interchangeable with 'of good and evil'; others distinguish the phrases. Some emphasize the fact that (most) emotions are in part constituted by, or at least generate, a desire to do something, construing these desires as themselves involving ideas or thoughts, of good and evil (pleasure and pain). Hence it may be said that fear is in part, or generates, the desire to run away from something, this desire itself involving the idea of staying put as evil or painful; that love is in part, or generates, the desire to be with the loved one, this desire itself involving the idea of being with the loved one as good or pleasant. Some emphasize the way the causes, or objects, of the emotions are, or must be, thought of, or perceived, or construed: something we fear or hate must be thought of, perceived as, evil (painful) in some way; something we hope for or love, as good (pleasant). Some, noting that the desires characteristic of (some of) the emotions actually involve the objects (or causes), introduce further complexity: hence hatred may be said to involve the idea that evil's coming to someone thought of as evil is (or would be) itself good; anger to involve the idea that evil's coming to someone who has caused evil is (or would be) itself good . . . and so on.

In short, there is much variety and disagreement, but a discernible common ground, namely the vague remark 'our emotions involve ideas, or thoughts, or perceptions, of good and evil', taking 'good' and 'evil' in their most general, generic, sense.[2]

In his otherwise admirable paper 'Morality and the Emotions', Bernard Willliams appears to overlook this point.[3] Seeking, in 1965, to explain why 'recent' moral philosophy in Britain had neglected the emotions, Williams found part of the answer to lie in the preceding and prevailing preoccupation with 'the most general features of moral language, or . . . evaluative language' and the consequent concentration on 'such very general terms as "good", "right" and "ought"'. This concentration, he said, 'has helped to push the emotions out of the picture', for '[i]f you aim to state the most general characteristics, and connexions of moral language, you will not find much to say about the emotions; because there are few, if any, *highly general* connexions between the emotions and moral language'.

But Williams was too kind to his predecessors and contemporaries; the highly general connection between the emotions and the very general terms 'good' and 'bad/evil' was sitting there, right under their noses, *manifest* in the accounts of, at least, Plato, Aristotle, the Stoics, Aquinas, Descartes, Locke, and Hume. They left the emotions out of the picture not for lack of any general connection between them and the terms they were obsessed with, but because they fed on a very one-sided diet of examples.

Now note that the vague remark stating the general connection falls far short of the much more explicit claim that the emotions involve, or are, evaluative *judgements*. The burnt child fears the fire and is distressed by its mother's anger long before it is of an age

---

[2] For the kind of discriminating detail which makes the vague remark into a plausible and illuminating thesis, the best source is still Aquinas, not just in *Summa Theologiae* Ia2ae (QQ. 22–30) on 'The Emotions', but all through IIa2ae (QQ. 1–189) on hope, fear, despair, charity (*caritas*), joy, hatred, *accidie*, envy, anger, curiosity, etc. Descartes, in *The Passions of the Soul*, gives a rather watered-down but still instructive version.

[3] Reprinted in his *Problems of the Self* (1973).

where we can talk of its making judgements, evaluative or otherwise. Indeed, even the claim 'the emotions involve thoughts of good and evil', when applied to small children, has to be construed with some care. It signifies the appropriateness of our talking to them in terms of generic good and evil when responding to their manifested emotions, rather than the appropriateness of the ascription of views to them.

However, the vague remark is obviously related to the more explicit one, and, vague as it is, it is sufficient to ground the claim that no emotion *in us* is just the same as it is in the other animals. For, in virtue of our reason, we, unlike the other animals, draw the distinction between what appears to us to be so, and what is really so in language. Unlike the other animals we can express our ideas or thoughts or perceptions about generic good and evil in sentences which figure, in our languages, as expressions of how things appear to us to be—as beliefs which are up for assessment as true or false, correct or erroneous, reasonable or unreasonable.

## THE EDUCATION OF THE EMOTIONS

Another fault of Williams's predecessors and (1965) contemporaries was that, though concentrating on 'the most general features of . . . evaluative language', they failed to think about the fact that such language has to be taught, and thereby failed to think about moral education and upbringing. We are taught to use sentences which contain the words (equivalent to) 'good' and 'evil' and their cognates and species from a very early age, at the same time as we are taught how to conduct ourselves. And a central aspect of this teaching is the training of the emotions.

The immense complexity of the ways in which the emotions are trained, and values thereby inculcated, can be called to mind by considering a paradigm case of *bad* training, namely, the inculcation of racism.[4]

---

[4] It is a tricky question whether 'racism' connotes rejection of another race or, more particularly, rejection in the context of oppression. My first two sets of remarks about the ways in which a racist upbringing affects our emotions are, I think, fairly uncommitted on this; blacks and whites, Gentiles and Jews may be affected in the same way. But the third set tends toward the concept of racism that necessarily involves oppression. It is the oppressing race, the one that imposes the myths and metaphors, whose charity and justice are liable to be perverted by that imposition.

Recall, firstly, how extreme racism expresses itself in emotion, the way it generates not only hatred and contempt, but fear, anger, reserve, suspicion, grief that one's offspring is going to marry a member of the rejected race, joy when evil befalls them, pity for members of one's own race who are bettered by them, pride when one succeeds in doing them down, amusement at their humiliation, surprise that one of them has shown signs of advanced humanity, horror or self-contempt at the discovery that one has felt fellow-feeling for one—it is hard to think of a single emotion that is immune to its corruption.[5] It can even extend its influence to the appetites, since the rejected race's food and drink can be found disgusting, and sexual relations with its members perversely attractive.

Recall, secondly, that no one relatively free of racism thinks that *any* of these emotional responses is in any sense natural; they all have to be inculcated, and from a very early age. Children have to be taught to fear, particularly, adults of a different race; to hate and suspect and despise its younger members; to be amused or otherwise pleased when they are hurt; to be angry or suspicious when they are friendly; to join in rejoicing when it is heard they have been done down; to admire those who have brought about their downfall; to resent, or dismiss, their doing well or being happy.

And recall, thirdly, what we are beginning to understand about how racism is inculcated and how hard it is to eliminate. The last thirty years or so have seen a growing awareness of the ways in which we are influenced by the representations of racial stereotypes, of the racism implicit in many of our myths and metaphors, our images and archetypes, and a corresponding awareness that the most dedicated and sincere concern for charity and even justice is liable to be perverted and misdirected until we have both recognized, and rooted out, the racism that expresses itself in *emotional responses* we still defend as innocent, or justified, or reasonable—or beyond our control.

When we bear this real example, of the inculcation of racism, in mind, it becomes vividly clear that 'the' way in which the training of the emotions shapes one's thoughts of generic good and evil cannot be divided neatly into the rational and the non-rational. On the

---

[5] In discussion, someone optimistically suggested love. But although there are heartening examples of love's triumph over racial prejudice, there are also examples of its failure to survive the discovery that the loved one has 'tainted' blood.

one hand, it is rational, in so far as children being inculcated in it are being taught applications of the generic terms 'good' and 'evil' (such people are *dangerous, ignorant, perverted*; he tried to get you to go to his place!/to eat his food? what *cheek*, how *disgusting*; she wouldn't have anything to do with him/she pushed him over?, quite *right* too, how *brave*, how *sensible*—these are all terms whose application we pick up from those who bring us up). And it is rational, further, in so far as some explanatory or justifying putative facts will be interwoven with the training—such people are dangerous *because* they can't control their passions, *because* they hate us, *because* they are cunning and devious, are not being brave *because* they don't feel pain the way we do, do not deserve pity *because* they always make a fuss—and putative evidence given for such claims. In these two ways it is a training peculiarly appropriate to rational animals.

On the other hand, it is non-rational in so far as it proceeds, one might say, by unconscious imitation, Humean sympathy, and conditioning; the children just come to respond emotionally in the same way as those who are bringing them up, in a way that is at least akin to the way in which the young of some other species acquire their emotional responses.

Finally, it is, of course, non-rational, or irrational, in the sense that the whole system of the application of the terms, their putative explanations and justifications, is a tissue of falsehoods and inconsistencies. But, as we know to our cost, the recognition of this fact does not suffice to undo the training. Coming to realize that some of one's emotional reactions have been not only entirely stupid but wicked is no guarantee that one won't go on having them.

Is it possible to extirpate them, to undo a childhood training in racism and re-train emotional reactions, in this area, into 'complete harmony' with reason—given the presence of a dedicated concern for charity and justice? The answer to this, I think it must be said, is that we still do not know.

We do know that reason can, directly, achieve a certain amount; one can catch oneself having the emotional reactions, drag the relevant stupid thoughts about good and evil to the surface of consciousness and hammer them with rational beliefs—I have *nothing* to fear from this person; she did *not* insult or patronize me, but asked a reasonable question; I have every possible reason to trust this person, and none not to; it is not at all surprising that she should be a mathematician. And we know that familiarity, in the sense of habitual acquaintance and intimacy (once again, given the dedicated concern), far from breeding contempt, breeds fellow-feeling, and can achieve much by way of casting out fear, hatred, suspicion, and misplaced surprise.

But total re-training may nevertheless be impossible. Aristotle, acknowledging his debt to Plato, emphasizes 'the importance of having been trained in some way *from infancy* to feel joy or grief at the right things';[6] given the emotions' non-rational face, it may be that reason cannot entirely unseat bad training in childhood, and that relationships of love and trust formed in adulthood cannot entirely undo a kind of unconscious expectancy of evil which still manifests itself in racist emotional reactions.

If, sadly, that is so, what follows? It certainly does not follow that anyone subject to such reactions can shrug them off and say, 'Oh well; they are beyond my control; I just can't help reacting that way.' For since we know that some re-training is possible, and do not know when, if ever, it ceases to be effective, anyone decent must be anxiously seeking ways to control them, refusing to give up hope. But what does seem to be entailed is that those of us who had racism inculcated in us early are unlucky; through no fault of our own, and despite our greatest efforts, we may remain morally inferior (though not thereby necessarily blameworthy) to those who, in virtue of good training in childhood and rational principle, achieve complete harmony between their emotions and reason and thereby full virtue.

What would be involved in denying this entailment? We would have to insist that we can be as perfect in charity and justice as any human being can be, despite being subject to racist emotional reactions, as long as we keep them from manifesting themselves in action or omission (and, perhaps, as long as we continue to try to extirpate them). Well, someone might insist on saying that, but it sounds astonishingly arrogant, and one doubts that members of the rejected race will agree.[7] And perhaps it is examples such as racism

---

[6] *Nicomachean Ethics* 1104b11–12; my italics.

[7] I here disassociate myself strongly from Blum's lamentable claim that a 'formerly racist man who now believes in equality', who has striven, with some success, to extirpate his racist emotional reactions, but who still has 'occasional feelings of dislike and distrust towards blacks . . . can no longer be identified with them. He is not to be criticised for having them. They are thus external to his moral self',

that are needed to unseat the distaste that many people feel for what Williams has christened 'constitutive moral luck'.[8]

If we try to think of Kant's third philanthropist as 'indifferent to the sufferings' of a particular oppressed race, because of his racist upbringing (which is a great deal easier than trying to imagine someone who is genuinely indifferent to the sufferings (*any* sufferings?) of other human beings (*any* other human beings?)), we would surely not think of him as a moral exemplar just because he acts to benefit a member of the oppressed race 'out of duty', notwithstanding the indubitable fact that he had no control over his upbringing. If he has not devoted any effort to trying to undo the effects of his upbringing but is resting content with the claim that it was not his fault and his emotions are beyond his control, then he is corrupt. If he has tried but not succeeded at all then he has not tried hard enough (for we know that some re-training is possible) and is at least suspect. What if he is still fairly young, has only recently started trying, and hence has not succeeded much? Then, naturally, he will find it harder to do what is charitable and just than someone who, with the same bad upbringing, has been trying to undo it for longer, but his finding it harder does not make him morally superior to the one who now finds it easier than it used to be—quite the contrary.[9]

Why do those of us who had racism inculcated in us think that we must strive, and continue to strive, to undo the effects of that upbringing? Not because we think it will make it easier for us to do what is charitable and just (though it will), but because we think it will make us better people, more charitable and just than we are at present. Why do we try to bring up our children differently? Not in the hope that it will make their moral lives less a matter of striving than ours have been (though, with respect to racism, it should), but in the hope that they will turn out better than we have, more

*Friendship Altruism and Morality*, 181. It seems worth recording that, when I read out this passage to a graduate class in Stanford in 1996, its members gasped with horror.

[8] Williams, 'Moral Luck' (1976).

[9] It is often said, even by virtue ethicists, that justice does not involve the emotions, but the example of racism seems to me to show that this is a mistake. A white person who was not horrified and grieved by Martin Luther King's assassination and overjoyed by the eventual emergence and triumph of Nelson Mandela is far from perfect in justice, no matter how impeccable their every action.

charitable and just. How could we think that we ought to give our children a good upbringing, that we owed it to them, if we thought that it had no effect on whether they turned out better or worse? But whether or not we ourselves had a good upbringing is just a matter of luck.

It should be noted, in this context, where we are all (I assume) vividly aware of the fact, that the whole idea that a human agent *could* do what she should, in every particular instance, while her emotions are way out of line, is a complete fantasy. Our understanding of what will hurt, offend, damage, undermine, distress or reassure, help, succour, support, or please our fellow human beings is at least as much emotional as it is theoretical. Dedicated adherence to rules or principles of charity and justice achieves a great deal, but it is only someone arrogant and self-righteous who supposes, given a conventional upbringing in which racism is embedded, that they can apply such rules and principles with the *right* imagination and sensitivity to other groups.

And even if, *per impossibile*, such correctly imaginative and sensitive application of the rules could be written into them, the grasp of, and adherence to, the rules would *still* not take us all the way to 'what we should do'. For sometimes 'what we should do' is just, as we say, 'be there' for other people. They tell us what they have suffered, and the tears come to our eyes; they tell us what they have endured and our faces flush with indignation or anger. It is all in the past, there is nothing we can do to undo it, no comfort or assuagement we can offer in the form of action. Such comfort and assuagement as we can offer, as we should, springs solely from our emotional reactions. If we can't come up with the right ones, we fail them, and it is a moral failure.

The same remarks apply, *mutatis mutandis*, to the question of whether one can fail in full virtue because of 'natural temperament'.[10] No one who is thoroughly cold-hearted as an adult is so through no fault of his own unless he is a psychopath. One preserves a cold heart and indifference to the sufferings of others in oneself as an adult by wilfully abnegating responsibility, blaming it all, childishly, on nature or one's upbringing. Or, worse, one pre-

---

[10] For a detailed defence of this view see Gregory Trianosky, 'Natural Affections and Responsibility for Character: A Critique of Kantian Views of the Virtues' (1990), an article from which I have greatly benefited.

serves and positively fosters it by allowing oneself to think such thoughts as that one is 'endowed with the special gift of patience and robust endurance [in one's own] suffering' and assumes 'or even demand[s]' it of others, as Kant (rather revealingly) allows.[11] It is hard to imagine a more uncharitable and unjust thought in relation to the sufferings of the innocent, the helpless, and the oppressed, but one way in which we keep ourselves uncharitable and unjust while, quite sincerely, espousing charity and justice as virtues is precisely by *not* thinking such thoughts in relation to such cases. We think about the suffering of the feckless, dishonest, and self-indulgent, classify them as 'the underclass' and, conveniently forgetting about the sufferings of the feckful, honest, and hard-working who have been unlucky, the people who would need exceptional virtue (which we should recognize we lack) to rise above their social environment, and the *children*, we harden our hearts. And when we do so, it is all our own fault.

## CONCLUSION

It is, I think, true, that where Aristotle, and thereby the Aristotelians, have an edge over Kant (and, indeed, Hume) with respect to the moral significance of the emotions is in the account Aristotle gives us of human rationality, an account that allows the emotions to participate in reason and thereby play their proper role in the specification of full virtue. Much modern moral philosophy, deontological and utilitarian, has followed Kant, or Hume, rather than Aristotle, on human rationality, and thereby still suffers from the fault to which Anscombe drew attention back in 1958—it lacks 'an adequate philosophy of psychology'.[12] But although this may give the Aristotelians an edge over Kant, I do not see, offhand, any deep reason why it should give them an intrinsic edge over Kantian deontologists. The Kantians can repudiate Kant's unattractive claims about the cold-hearted, as Aristotelians discard Aristotle's unattractive claims about women and natural slaves, without dismembering the philosophy. As the recent revived interest in *The Doctrine of*

---

[11] See the passage quoted at p. 93 above.
[12] Anscombe, 'Modern Moral Philosophy', 26.

*Virtue* reveals, there are, in fact, hints in Kant's later writings[13] that he did acknowledge some rational emotions; but even if there were not, deontological moral philosophers might still, it seems to me, be recognizably Kantian (in so far as they start with the Categorical Imperative) and add on an Aristotelian account of the emotions, just as virtue ethicists are still recognizably Aristotelian (in so far as they start with the Aristotelian account of the virtues) when they add on non-Aristotelian virtues such as charity and repudiate Aristotle's sexism. Nor do I see any immediate inconsistency in utilitarians' adding on the Aristotelian account of the emotions. Once they have noticed how optimific it would be if everyone were brought up, or trained themselves, to have the right emotions, on the right occasions, to the right extent, towards the right people or objects, should they not welcome the idea?

It might turn out that thoroughly worked-out attempts to add on the Aristotelian account of the emotions changed the deontology and utilitarianism into virtue ethics in all but name; then indeed we might claim that virtue ethics is intrinsically superior in this regard. But until we see what such attempts look like, that should remain an open question; perhaps its current pre-eminence in this area will turn out to have been an historical accident.

[13] See Louden, 'Kant's Virtue Ethics'. Note, further, 'Sympathetic Feeling is Generally a Duty' (in *The Doctrine of Virtue*, § 34), where Kant commends 'the capacity and the will to share in others' feelings' as an appropriate feeling, for 'a human being [is] regarded [here] not merely as a rational being but also as an animal endowed with reason' (204).

# 6

# The Virtuous Agent's Reasons for Action

It is standardly assumed that virtue ethics cannot give an account of 'moral motivation'—that is, of acting from (a sense of) duty, on or from (moral) principle, because you think you (morally) ought to, or are (morally) required to, or because you think it's (morally) right—taking all these different phrases to be equivalent for present purposes. Even its own supporters tend to assume this, and, making a virtue out of necessity, resort to arguing that 'moral motivation' is, in various ways, a rotten notion.

I, however, think it is rather a good notion, an important feature of our ethical thought, and in this chapter and the next, I aim to give virtue ethics' account of it.

Why is it standardly assumed that virtue ethics is incapable of providing such an account? Largely, I take it, for reasons that should have been dispelled by the last two chapters. Contrary to the common view, virtue ethics is not, as we have seen, starkly opposed to Kant and his followers on the issue of 'moral motivation'. Virtue ethicists who rely on Aristotle's philosophy of action rather than Hume's need not, and should not, say that the virtuous agent acts 'from desire' as opposed to reason, for, as we saw, Aristotle and Kant share the non-Humean premise that we have two principles of movement, not just one. The virtuous Aristotelian agent does not characteristically act from that principle-of-movement-we-share-with-the-animals, as a child does, but from reason (*logos*) in the form of 'choice' (*prohairesis*).

Once this point is recognized, the question of whether, according to virtue ethics, the virtuous agent, when she acts virtuously, acts 'from (a sense of) duty', 'on or from principle', 'because she thinks it's right' (regarding all those phrases as, for present purposes, equivalent), is a question to be explored, not one whose answer is determined by saying she does not act from reason.

Why have moral philosophers disinclined to follow Kant regarded 'moral motivation' as a rotten notion? In part for reasons which, once again, should have been dispelled by the preceding chapters. Recognizing something amiss in the *Groundwork* passage quoted at p. 93 above, they have misidentified it as an issue about motivation instead of an issue about the nature of full virtue and the quasi-rational role the emotions play in it.

But there is more to the rejection of the notion of 'moral motivation' than that. The very phrase, and all but one of its glosses, explicitly rely on the word 'moral', and even the exception ('from (a sense of) duty') does so implicitly. Since there are particular duties that go with particular jobs, 'from (a sense of) duty' must be understood in this context as 'from (a sense of) moral duty', if rubbish collectors (and concentration camp officers) are not to count as 'morally motivated' when they do what their job requires. But ever since Anscombe's 'Modern Moral Philosophy', philosophers sympathetic to its claims have heeded her demand that 'the concepts of obligation and duty—*moral* obligation and *moral* duty, that is to say—and of what is *morally* right and wrong, and of the *moral* sense of "ought", ought to be jettisoned' (26).

Amongst their reasons has certainly been Anscombe's point that 'the term "moral" . . . just doesn't seem to fit, in its modern sense, into an account of Aristotelian ethics'. Bernard Williams claims that ancient Greek thought 'basically lacks the concept of *morality* altogether, in the sense of a class of reasons or demands which are vitally different from other kinds of reason or demand'.[1] Moreover, without adverting to the Greeks, Philippa Foot has fought a long-running battle against attempts to give the adjective 'moral' distinctive, magic, reason-giving force. And, altogether, this makes it look as though virtue ethics should have no truck with the notion of 'moral motivation'. Doesn't it depend on a special, and dubious, notion of obligation? Hasn't it just been foisted on us by Kant? If it's not in Aristotle, isn't that enough to show that we do not need it?

But although the term 'moral motivation' and its various glosses are particularly associated with Kant and his followers, it is far

[1] B. Williams, 'Philosophy' (1981), 251.

from clear that the notion is not to be found in Aristotle, nor indeed ancient Greek philosophy more generally.[2] True, 'the' notion has, by now, acquired so many accretions that it may not be quite accurate to say that it is the very same one, but I think it is certainly sufficiently analogous to deserve the same phrase and the same glosses.

What is unfortunate and dangerous about the phrase and its glosses is, I think, not so much the presence of 'moral' but the way in which they do indeed suggest that what is at issue is acting for a special kind of reason. On the account that I shall give, being 'morally motivated' is not solely a matter of acting, on a particular occasion, for a special kind of reason, let alone one that is 'vitally different from other kinds of reason', as Williams puts it, but, primarily, of acting *from virtue*—from a settled state of good character. The central idea of this chapter, and the next, is that 'because she thought it was right' ('from (a sense of) duty', etc.) is an ascription that goes far beyond the moment of action. It is not merely, as grammatically it may appear to be, a claim about how things are with the agent and her reasons at that moment. It is also a substantial claim about the future (with respect to reliability) and, most importantly, a claim about what sort of person the agent is—a claim that goes 'all the way down'. A consequence of this idea is not only that occurrent thoughts somehow equivalent to 'This is right, virtuous, noble, my duty' are not necessary for 'moral motivation'; they are not sufficient, either. This idea does not seem to me to be obviously inconsistent with Kant's claims about the 'morally motivated' agent who acts *from* a good will; indeed I think that much he says entails it. But whether Kantians will, or should, agree, and whether they will agree with what I claim follows from it, I leave to them to decide.

## ACTING VIRTUOUSLY

What is it to act virtuously, or well, on a particular occasion?

(1) For a start, it is to do a certain sort of action. What sort? 'A virtuous, good, action', we might say—and truly, but this is hardly an illuminating way to begin laying down

---

[2] See Julia Annas's response to the quoted remark from Williams in *The Morality of Happiness*, 121–4.

what it is to act virtuously, or well. So we'll give examples—it is to do something such as helping someone, facing danger, telling the truth, repaying a debt, denying oneself some physical pleasure, etc.

This is clearly insufficient, for suppose someone does such an action by accident, unintentionally—helping when she meant to harm, in great danger without knowing it, telling the truth when she thought she was saying what was false, etc. Or suppose the agent acts, as a small child might, in uncomprehending obedience to someone's instruction. Hence we add:

(2) The agent must know what she is doing—that she is helping, facing danger, telling the truth, etc.

It is standard to add a further condition, namely: The agent acts for a reason. I do not want to get bogged down in the many disputes about what, in detail, is involved in acting 'for a reason' so, following Williams,[3] I shall gloss this, I hope neutrally enough, by saying that if we ask them why they helped or told the truth or whatever, they would, if articulate, be able to give us an honest answer which enables us to understand what it is about the situation and the action that made this action in this situation something that would seem to them an appropriate thing to do.

What is this condition doing? It is, in fact, doing a lot of work. Part of what it is doing is ruling out someone's doing such an action knowingly but 'for no particular reason'—on impulse, or a whim, or just because she feels like it at the time, or akratically; acting 'for a reason' contrasts with 'acting from inclination'. It is also ruling out acting in comprehending, but blind, knee-jerk obedience to an order. As Anscombe rightly remarks, 'Because he told me to' can give one's reason for doing something, when the agent is thinking of obeying him as something that is good about what she has done. But it can also give no more than a 'mental cause'.[4]

It is also a condition that needs further elaboration. Stated in full it is something like:

(3) The agent acts for a reason and, moreover, for 'the right reason(s)'.

[3] B. Williams, 'Acting as the Virtuous Person Acts' (1995).
[4] G. E. M. Anscombe, *Intention* (1963), 23.

This rules out helping, or facing danger, or telling the truth, or whatever, for ulterior reasons or under compulsion. (It is common, but a little misleading, to describe such cases as 'doing the right thing for the wrong reason(s)'. What is misleading about this phrase is that it obscures the fact that, in one way, the agent is not 'doing the right thing'. What she is doing is, say, trying to impress the onlookers, or hurting someone's feelings, or avoiding punishment.[5]

Is any further condition necessary? One might maintain, plausibly, that we have got enough, in outline, for 'acting morally'. But here we should note an interesting difference between 'acting morally' on the one hand and 'acting well' on the other. The former is not hospitable to such qualifications as 'quite', 'fairly', 'very', or 'perfectly'; the latter is. Hence we can, comprehensibly, ask 'Have we all the conditions for acting very well, perfectly ("excellently"), or only for acting fairly well?' And this leads us to think of a fourth condition.

Suppose an agent fulfils the first three conditions, but helps someone or repays the debt with difficulty, reluctantly, and another agent does the same easily and gladly; suppose one agent fulfils the first three but tells the hurtful truth with zest and enjoyment while another does the same, regretting the necessity, and so on. True, there will be occasions where the inappropriateness of the feelings of the first agent in each pair is such as to cast doubt on whether the agent really is acting for the right reason(s). But take the cases where this is not so. Then we may have to admit that the agent with the inappropriate feelings 'acts morally' and acts (fairly) well, but we can insist that the agent with the appropriate feelings acts better. And, according to virtue ethics, the agent with the inappropriate feelings does not act virtuously, in the very way or manner that the virtuous agent acts. To capture acting (really) well, excellently, or virtuously, we need the further condition:

(4) The agent has the appropriate feeling(s) or attitude(s) when she acts.

The first three conditions are related to, though not identical to, the first two conditions Aristotle gives, in *Nicomachean Ethics*, Book 2, ch. 4, for a virtuous act's being done 'in the way' a virtuous

---

[5] This was the complication in relation to 'right action' that I put to one side in Chapters 1–3.

man does it. Suppose a just or temperate act to be done (cf. Condition 1 above), then, Aristotle says, the agent acts 'in the way' someone with the virtues of justice and temperance acts only if (i) he knows what he is doing (cf. Condition 2), and (ii) he chooses it (cf. acts for a reason) and chooses it 'for its own sake' or 'because of itself' (cf. Condition 3).

Aristotle's third condition is that the agent acts from a firm and unchanging state, i.e. (in this context) from (a) virtue. Given the emotional aspect of the virtues, this certainly relates to the fourth condition above; whether it imports more, and if so what, will be considered later.


## CHOOSING THE ACTION 'FOR ITS OWN SAKE'

What is involved in Condition 3, the agent's acting 'for the right reason(s)'? In the context of Kantian ethics, we say that this means that the agent acts on or from (moral) duty or principle or because she thinks that what she is doing is (morally) right, or what she (morally) ought to do—taking all these phrases as equivalent. What can we say in the context of virtue ethics?

A helpful place to look for an answer is in the discussions of the related condition in Aristotle—the claim that the virtuous choose virtuous actions 'for their own sake' and that this is required for acting virtuously. What is puzzling about this claim is that, in one way, we can all see what it means in context, but when we try to state what it means in other terms that seem, at first sight, obviously equivalent, we wind up saying things that threaten to be far too philosophically sophisticated to be plausible. There are some fairly standard lines on what Aristotle means—or should have meant— by the virtuous choosing virtuous actions 'for their own sake'. The virtuous agent chooses the virtuous act as or *qua* just or courageous, or more generally, *qua* virtuous, or as an instance of doing well (*eupraxia*), or for the sake of the noble (*to kalon*). But all of these interpretations, unless further developed, run up against the same difficulty. What are we insisting must be the case if the agent chooses her action for this reason (whichever it is claimed to be)?

Of course we are not insisting that the agent must, consciously, act under that very description—that precisely those English (or Greek) words must occur to her; that is obviously false. Are we insisting that the thought, involving the relevant concepts 'This is just (or 'virtuous' or 'doing well' or '*kalon*', etc.), must occur to her? Perhaps, but, unless Quine has written in vain, we know that moving from specific sentences in a specific language, to Fregean thoughts, concepts, and propositions, is fraught with difficulties. Does a modern English speaker who has not read the ancient Greeks have the concept of *to kalon*? Is someone who chooses to tell the truth because—they say sincerely—they think that truth-telling is commanded by God, or the gods, or is a duty, choosing it as honest (or virtuous or doing well or *kalon*)? Always? Never? And if sometimes but not always, when? If we are going to ascribe grasp of the concepts of the ancient Greeks, or virtue ethics, to every virtuous person, we must say something more about what grounds such ascription.

Let us think for a moment about the sorts of reasons we expect the virtuous to give for their particular virtuous actions, bearing vividly in mind the obvious fact that we do not want to limit acting virtuously to those who have done moral philosophy, let alone Aristotelian moral philosophy. Virtue must surely be compatible with a fair amount of inarticulacy about one's reasons for action, and we cannot expect everyone virtuous to give the sorts of reasons offered above. We expect variety, not the same reason every time ('This is doing well, or virtuous'). And we do not automatically expect the variety to be expressed in the full vocabulary of the virtues and vices ('This is honest, courageous'); many people nowadays use very few such words, and some indeed are embarrassed by the suggestion that what they have done is courageous or generous and explicitly disavow it.[6]

We may then turn away from the above very general descriptions of what is involved in choosing an action 'for its own sake' and try to provide a more detailed specification, along the following lines:

'The virtuous agent chooses virtuous actions "for their own sake"' means 'the virtuous agent chooses virtuous actions for at least one of a certain type or range of reasons, X',

---

[6] A striking example of this is provided by some of the recorded statements of the admirable non-Jewish people who risked their lives to help the Jews during the Holocaust. One Dutch woman said, 'I don't think it such a courageous thing to do. For certain people it is a self-evident thing to do.'

where 'the type or range X' is typical of, and differs according to, whichever virtue is in question.

What are reasons 'typical of' a virtue? They will be the sorts of reasons for which someone with a particular virtue, V, will do a V act. So, thinking of the sorts of reasons a courageous agent might have for performing a courageous act, we can come up with such things as 'I could probably save him if I climbed up there', 'Someone had to volunteer', 'One can't give in to tyrants', 'It's worth the risk'. Thinking of the range of reasons a temperate agent might have for a temperate act, we can come up with 'This is an adequate sufficiency', 'I'm driving', 'I'd like you to have some', 'You need it more than I do', 'She said "No"'. With respect to the liberal or generous, 'He needed help', 'He asked me for it', 'It was his twenty-first birthday', 'She'll be so pleased'. With respect to the agent with the virtue of being a good friend, 'He's my friend', 'He's expecting me to', 'I can't let him down'. For honesty we get such things as 'It was the truth', 'He asked me', 'It's best to get such things out into the open straight away'. And for justice we get such things as 'It's his', 'I owe it to her', 'She has the right to decide', 'I promised'. And so on and so forth.

Reasons that more manifestly involve reference to the virtue in question, or a corresponding vice, such as 'This is the honest thing to do', or 'It would be cowardly not to', or 'That would be mean, greedy', certainly count as belonging to such ranges. And the general ones, such as 'It would be dishonourable (or 'a bit low') not to' or 'This is what the virtuous (or 'any decent person') would do' or 'What else could I do?' can count as belonging to every range. But neither of these two sorts is given any privileged position.[7]

---

[7] Sarah Broadie, in *Ethics with Aristotle* (1991), gives (what I take to be) an abstract version of the detailed specification. She says (p. 87), 'the description "A" under which it is deemed the sort of thing that a just or temperate person would do is the primary description for the agent. In other words, the agent is virtuous only if the action which observers describe as "A" is done by him as A or because it is A. That is what is meant by "doing it because of itself". If someone eats no more than is good for him now in preparation for enjoying a binge tomorrow, then *what* he is now doing is preparing for tomorrow's binge, and this is not the description of a temperate act.' My version of the detailed specification, simply in terms of a sort of reasons associated with a particular V is given in Williams's 'Acting as the Virtuous Person Acts'. I hit upon the same idea when writing on the *Ethics* for the Open University (*Aristotle: Ethics* (1979)), in the context of trying to work out what reasons children who were being well-trained in the virtues might give for their V actions.

A virtuous agent's reason, I said, enables us to understand what made the action in question seem, to a virtuous agent, an appropriate thing to do in the circumstances. And when we imagine the above reasons sincerely given, in the situation in question, in appropriate tones of voice, with appropriate further answers to further questions about why alternative courses of action are ruled out and so on—as, of course, we must—they are all such as to reveal this to us. They all show, or indicate, what the agent took as relevant or salient, advantageous or disadvantageous, good or evil, decisive or compelling, about the action or the situation or both.

The virtuous agent, *ex hypothesi*, gets these things right, and this is what provides the contrast between acting virtuously, in the way the virtuous agent acts, and doing what she does but for the wrong reasons. In showing or indicating what the virtuous agent took as relevant (salient, good or evil, compelling, etc.), the reasons given distinguish the way she is acting from the way the cowardly or licentious or greedy or self-seeking or merely docile agent happens to do the same sort of action. The latter see the world differently and pursue different ends, so they will be taking quite different things as relevant (salient, etc.)—that one's commanding officer will shoot one if one does not go forward into battle, that one's pleasure will be heightened if one delays gratification now, that one's error is bound to be found out—doing what is courageous or temperate or liberal or honest or just for the wrong reasons (in the particular case).

Williams says, I think rightly, that we can take 'The V agent did the V act for an X reason' (where X is one of the range appropriate to the V in question) as the proper way to understand 'The V agent chose the V act *qua* V (courageous, generous)'.

We say that the agent did the generous (e.g.) thing because it was the generous thing to do, and we understand what this means because we understand what it is about the situation and the action that makes this action in this situation something that would seem to a generous person the appropriate thing to do.[8]

What seemed right about saying that the virtuous agent chooses her V acts *qua* courageous, generous, etc. (rather than, say, 'virtuous' or '*to kalon*'), as a gloss on 'chooses her V acts for their own sake', was that it rightly implied that the virtuous agent did not act

---

[8] Williams, 'Acting as the Virtuous Person Acts', 17.

for the same reason every time. What seemed wrong about it was
that we naturally understood it to imply, implausibly, that the agent
had a mastery of the virtue terms and moreover would not disavow
that their action was correctly described by one. Following
Williams, we can now keep the first good point but understand
'choosing a V act *qua* V' in such a way as to free ourselves of the
implausible implication.

Williams goes on to make an important point. He continues

> It will follow from this that the philosophical understanding of the various
> virtues will require some, at least, of the understanding that comes from
> having the virtues: which is of course what Aristotle holds.[9]

Naturally, the reasons the virtuous agent gives will not make her
actions fully comprehensible to the cowardly, intemperate, untrust-
worthy and dishonest. She thinks saving Mozart's original
manuscript from the fire is worth the risk—how can she? She would
like someone else to have some of what's available—why, when she
could take it herself? Why is she making such a point of keeping her
promise or telling the truth in this case when all it's going to do is
cause her trouble?—It's pointless. To the vicious, the virtuous will
seem reckless, foolishly self-denying, unrealistically obsessive about
promise-keeping and truth.

But this is just what we should expect. One's detailed grasp of
what is involved in acting virtuously, in acting for the *right* reasons,
is not separable from one's grasp of what each of the virtues
involves, and one's grasp of that is not separable from possession of
the virtues themselves, at least to some degree. As Aristotle rightly
remarks, 'the coward calls the brave man rash, the rash man calls
him a coward and similarly in all other cases'.[10]

A further advantage of this account is that, in exposing the variety of reasons a virtuous agent may have for acting, but grouping
them into those typical of one virtue rather than another, we make
it clear how it might be that a less than ideal agent can be exem-
plary with respect to some virtues but not all. One way in which
people just do vary is that they are more sensitive to the sorts of considerations cited in the X reasons of one virtue than they are to

---

[9] Ibid.
[10] *Nicomachean Ethics* 1108b25–6.

those cited in another.[11] But the virtues do not thereby become completely discrete, isolable character traits, for not only do the ranges overlap but the same sorts of judgements about goods and evils, benefits and harms, what is worthwhile and what is unimportant crop up all over the place.

This is an attractive account of the V agent choosing a V act 'for its own sake', but it leaves unsettled the question of what truth, if any, there is in the other accounts of 'choosing a V action for its own sake'. If the virtuous, in choosing a V action for an X reason, is choosing it *qua* V (courageous, generous, etc.), is she *also* choosing it *qua* virtuous, and (or?) as an instance of doing well, and (or?) for the sake of *to kalon*? I shall discuss this later (p. 136).

## ACTING 'BECAUSE ONE THINKS IT'S RIGHT'

Now let us return to the question of what is involved in acting 'for the right reason(s)'. Does choosing to do a V action for its own sake, as characterized above, and bearing all the examples of the X reasons in mind, give a satisfactory equivalent in virtue ethics of acting on principle, or because one thinks the action is right, or one's duty, or what one 'morally' ought to do? Has something in Kant's thoughts been missed out? And, if it has, is it something that we think is important in ethics?

True, the specific words 'principle', 'right', 'duty', 'morally ought' do not occur in any of the X reasons given, and it might be thought that thereby something important has been missed out. But we do not want to tie acting for the right reason too tightly to specific words, or concepts corresponding to them, that figure in the agent's reasons, any more than we want to tie choosing an action for its own sake and thereby acting virtuously too tightly. The ancient Greeks, as is well known, do not have words that can be readily translated as 'principle', 'right', 'duty', or 'morally ought' (in the senses they are used here), but we do not want to say that none of them ever acted for the right reasons.

Moreover, as critics of some oversimplified interpretations of Kant have pointed out, there seem to be cases in which the fact that

---

[11] I have heard Williams make this point in lectures, but I do not know of anywhere he has said it in print.

something is required by principle, or is right, or your duty, is not, in a sense, 'the right reason' for doing what is V at all. On the contrary, someone who does whatever it is—visits a friend, jumps into the river to save her child, contradicts a lie, for the consciously formulated reason 'This is required by principle A', or 'This would be the right thing to do', or 'This is my duty', is repellently self-righteous or self-conscious. The right reason is, say, 'She's lonely', 'She's my child', 'That's a lie'; that should be sufficient to prompt the action in the circumstances.

The standard Kantian response to such examples is that one can act 'on principle', or 'because one thinks it is right', or 'from (a sense of) duty' on a particular occasion without actually thinking in terms of principle, or what is right or one's duty. And, at least with respect to how the first two phrases are ordinarily used outside the context of academic moral philosophy, this is surely true. Indeed, they are the very phrases we might naturally use to describe the way in which the agent who acts for X reasons acts. In response to a query about whether someone did a V act for some ulterior reason or under compulsion, we might say 'No, she did it because . . .' and cite the X reason, or we might say 'No, she did it on principle', or 'because she thought it was right'. (Perhaps in earlier centuries we might just as naturally have said 'She did it from (a sense of) duty'; the unattractive connotations of the phrase seem to have developed in the nineteenth century.)

So could we say that, if an agent does a V act for an X reason, she has, in effect, acted 'because she thought it was right' or 'on principle' or even ' from (a sense of) duty'? She hasn't acted merely from desire or inclination; she hasn't acted under compulsion, she has acted for a virtuous reason, not an improper or ulterior one—what more could one ask for in the way of 'moral motivation'?

When we think of obvious examples of agents doing V acts for X reasons, it may well seem that nothing else is required. But some less obvious examples may give us pause.

Consider, for a start, small children. Do they, sometimes, do V acts for X reasons or not? Sometimes they do V acts just because they are told to, and sometimes just because they want to do them. But sometimes they act because they promised, because someone is their friend, to help or please someone else, giving X reasons for what they do. Have they acted 'because they thought it was right'?

Consider, by a natural extension, the mentally handicapped. They too sometimes act because they promised, because someone is their friend, to help or please someone else, giving X reasons for what they do. Do they act 'because they think it is right'?

Now consider a different sort of case, an adult agent who does a V act for an appropriate X reason but thereby acts uncharacteristically. Someone whose other intentional actions, reactions, and talk license the descriptions 'selfish', 'unjust', and 'timorous' (or, more weakly, 'hardly generous', 'not particularly concerned with justice', 'not courageous') suddenly surprises us. She gives with an open hand, spurns the offer of an unfair advantage, she speaks out boldly in defence of an unpopular colleague—and gives the appropriate X reasons. It turns out that she is in love, or on top of the world because of a recent success; love or success has momentarily transformed her. And shortly afterwards, she lapses back into behaving as she did before. When she did what was V for the X reasons, was she acting 'because she thought it was right'?

Consider again those who tell the truth or help others for X reasons and also because—they say sincerely—they think that truth-telling or helping others is commanded by God and that if they act thus they will go to heaven (and to hell if they do not). Or suppose that they are blindly following an inculcated code, contrary to (we will suppose) their deeply repressed desires and views about what is important in life, what it is worth pursuing and having. Do they do what they do 'because they think it is right'? If you are inclined to say 'Yes', would you say the same if I added to the example the further proviso that, if they were to lose their faith in God, or their belief in the necessity of the code, they would never (given their hitherto repressed desires and views) do a V action for an X reason again?

Some people may still want to say 'Yes', and may want to say 'Yes' to at least some of the other examples as well. But I want to say 'No', all the way through (with a later qualification on those who take themselves to be obeying God's commands), because I believe that when we talk of agents acting 'because they thought it was right', 'from duty', etc. we are ascribing something to the agent that is clearly absent from all of the above cases. It is not being a moral agent, or being morally responsible, because though that is lacking in the cases of the small children and the mentally handicapped, it is not lacking in the other cases. And it is not 'acting morally', for, in my view at least, whatever that means is too obscure to be clearly absent in all the above cases. So what is it?

Intuitively, we might think it has something to do with reliability or predictability, in some loose sense. An agent of whom it can be truly said that she did what was V 'because she thought it was right', etc., on a particular occasion is, thereby, an agent who, by and large, will act in similar ways on similar occasions, an agent who can, by and large, be brought to act in certain ways by giving her certain reasons, and one who will make, and agree to, certain judgements about the actions of others.

I here invoke, though perhaps in an unfamiliar setting, familiar thoughts about the 'universalizability' and 'overridingness' of 'moral reasons' or 'moral principles'. There is much that is confused and plain mistaken in the accounts that have been given of these familiar thoughts, not least their reliance on some magic that is supposed to be done by the word 'moral', but the examples that got the accounts going always seemed very plausible. If we think someone did something 'because he thought it was right' and then find him failing to do the very same sort of thing the next day, for no better reason than (he says) that he doesn't feel like it, we say he couldn't have done the first thing 'because he thought it was right'. If we think someone did something 'because he thought it was right' but find him condemning someone else for doing the very same sort of thing for no better reason than that he, uncomfortably, is on the receiving end, we say he couldn't have done the first thing for that reason.

So we might say that 'the more' we ask for in the way of 'moral motivation', beyond doing what is V for an X reason, is something to do with reliability or predictability. But this does not seem to capture what is amiss with the agents who do what is V for appropriate X reasons and also say, sincerely, that they act thus because it is commanded by God, or that they will go to hell if they do not. Are they not reliable and predictable? 'Well,' someone might say, 'maybe they are, actually, reliable. But they are not so counterfactually, for if (as you said) they were to lose their faith in God, they would never do a V action for an X reason again.' But to be plausible, this prediction needs something like the same proviso as I added in the case of those who were blindly following a code. *If* they were previously acting 'contrary to their deeply repressed desires and views about what is worth pursuing and having', then we might suppose that, if they were to lose their faith, they would cease to act well. But some people who used to say 'I do this because it is commanded by God', and have now lost their faith, continue to do what is V for X reasons, as they did before.

So the stress on 'contrary to the agent's deeply repressed desires and views about what it is worth pursuing and having' in these two cases is significant. What is it doing? We could say that it picks out, in just these cases of failing to be 'morally motivated', a lack of something that is generally needed, namely the agent's being 'really committed' to the value of her V acts. Thereby, we would try to capture the fact that in all the cases considered above, in which I, at least, do not want to say that the agent acted 'because she thought it was right', despite her having done what was V for an X reason, there seems to be something rather amiss about the agent's valuing of the V act. Small children and the severely mentally handicapped are not, by and large, capable of having their own values; in so far as they recognize the value of doing what is V they recognize what they have been taught to do, not what they value on their own behalf. Their values are those they have been given, not, yet, their own. The agent who surprises us by her virtuous actions when momentarily transformed by love or success seems to recognize the value of the V actions only when it is, as it were, lit up for her by her love or success. Those who do what is V for X reasons and also because they think the actions are commanded by God or required by a code seem to divide into two sorts. There are those who recognize the value of the V acts as such, and also believe that God, or the code, requires them because of their value. But (we suspect) there are also those who would not do what is V for X reasons if they lost their faith in God or their belief in the necessity of the code, those who recognize the value of the V acts only under the further descriptions 'something God or the code requires me to do' but not 'as such'.

But what is it for an agent to be 'really committed to the value of her V acts'? That is hardly a perspicuous phrase. It is for her to be such that the valuing of them goes 'deep down', we may say; that it governs and informs her whole life and conduct. That is better, but still not very perspicuous. In Kant, I take it, it is for her to possess a good will, a will which acts steadily from the motive of respect for the moral law. And in Aristotelian ethics it is for her to possess the virtue in question. What it is that makes the agent who does what is V for X reasons on a particular occasion both actually and counterfactually reliable and predictable, if she is—what it is for her to be 'really committed to the value of her V act'—is that she acts 'from a fixed and permanent state', namely the virtue in question.[12]

So here is virtue ethics' version of the Kantian claim that the ideal agent acts 'on (or from) principle', 'out of (a sense of) duty', 'because she thinks it's right'. The neo-Aristotelian ideal agent chooses a V act for X reasons, from a fixed and permanent state— from a virtue. Like the ideal Kantian agent, she may be truly described as doing what is V 'because she thinks it is right/her duty/on principle' without those explicit thoughts occurring to her; that she does what is V for X reasons and acts from virtue is sufficient for 'moral motivation'.

Here too, I think, is how we answer the question I raised above ('If the virtuous, in choosing a V action for an X reason, is choosing it *qua* V (courageous, generous, etc.), is she *also* choosing it *qua* virtuous, and (or?) as an instance of acting well, and (or?) for the sake of *to kalon*?'). The answer, in an Aristotelian context, is that yes, the *virtuous*, in choosing a V action for an X reason, *is* choosing it *qua* virtuous and as an instance of doing well and for the sake of *to kalon*, because *she* is acting from virtue. In ascribing full virtue to her, complete with practical wisdom, we are, speaking in Aristotelian terms, ascribing to her a love of the noble and a correct conception of *eudaimonia* and thereby of doing well as acting in accordance with the virtues.

## AVOIDING THE PLATONIC FANTASY

Are we thereby ascribing to her what Sarah Broadie describes as 'an explicit, comprehensive, substantial vision of the good'?[13] Broadie

---

[12] Given, as usual, that we are in the area where 'things are true for the most part', the claim that virtue is a *permanent* state allows for a few exceptions. As I noted in the introduction (p. 12) the virtues (and the vices) are the sorts of character traits that are strongly entrenched, such that a sudden change in them calls for special explanation. But such explanations are sometimes forthcoming, and in some cases loss of religious faith might be such an explanation. Counterfactual reliability is not a strict necessary condition of virtue; given the way in which, in the devout, their faith and values are interwoven, the past virtuous actions of someone who falls apart and goes to ruin when he loses his faith need not necessarily be reassessed, with hindsight, as not having come from virtue after all.

[13] Broadie, *Ethics with Aristotle*, 198.

dubs this 'the Grand End theory', dismissing it as over intellectual, and in one way that is obviously right. When philosophers start implying that it is a necessary condition of virtue that the virtuous have reflected long and hard about what *eudaimonia* consists in and worked out a picture of what is involved in acting well so comprehensive and substantial that it can be applied and its application justified in every suitable case, we may be sure that they are falling victim to what could be called 'the Platonic fantasy'. This is the fantasy that it is only through the study of philosophy that one can become virtuous (or really virtuous), and, as soon as it is stated explicitly, it is revealed to be a fantasy that must be most strenuously resisted. Of *course* people can be virtuous, really virtuous, without having spent clockable hours thinking about *eudaimonia*, coming to the conclusion that it is a life lived in accordance with the virtues and working out an account of acting well, just as they can possess a really good will without having spent clockable hours working out whether various maxims can be willed as universal laws.

But notwithstanding the obviousness of that fact and the absurdity of the fantasy, it is very hard for those of us who follow Aristotle, or indeed Kant, to avoid falling into some version of it when we are talking about 'moral motivation'. Another version, as Broadie notes, is to ascribe ludicrous philosophical sophistication to people who have never studied the subject through the device of making the philosophical knowledge 'implicit'. However hard we try not to (and, it must be said, many moral philosophers have not noticed that we need to try), we always, at best, tremble on the verge of implying that our ideal agents have beliefs or capacities or ideas (albeit, perhaps, 'unconscious') that are far too *fancy*.[14]

The way to avoid the mistake, at least for virtue ethicists, is to insist that it is the ascription of virtue that (in this context at least) is basic. Loving the noble, having a correct conception of *eudaimonia* and a grasp of the universal *acting well*, are not tests for virtue,

---

[14] Christine Korsgaard, who really does try to avoid the fantasy, cites an amusing example of it in Kant himself: 'Everyone does, in fact, decide by this rule whether actions are morally good or bad. Thus *people* ask: If one belonged to such an order of things that anyone would allow himself to deceive when he thought it to his advantage . . . would he assent of his own will to being a member of such an order of things?' (my italics). *The Critique of Practical Reason* (C2 69), quoted in Korsgaard, 'From Duty and for the Sake of the Noble'.

or the grounds on which we ascribe virtue, nor are they the specification of an ideal of virtue to which everyone should aspire. They are what philosophers ascribe to ordinary virtuous people in the belief that they are thereby saying something illuminating and important, that if we philosophers were to think of ordinary virtuous people as possessing these 'fancy' things, *we* would have a better philosophical understanding of various topics that interest us—moral motivation, moral reasoning, practical wisdom, a correct conception of *eudaimonia*, virtue itself. And thereby, of course, we disagree about what is to be ascribed, and indeed how to construe what is ascribed, according to whether we think, for example, that moral reasoning is to be best understood as the application of general principles to particular cases, or whether the ascription of a grasp of the universal *acting well* is to be construed as making that claim.

Just how hard it is to get clear about what is at issue here is well illustrated by two different reactions to Broadie's dismissal of 'the Grand End theory'. Terence Irwin worries that she has not ascribed enough to the virtuous agent. How, he wonders, is Broadie's virtuous agent, who does not employ any general principles, 'to answer the charge of inconsistency' given that on one occasion, he 'prefers the interests of his friends over those of strangers . . . [and] on another occasion . . . prefers the interests of strangers over those of his friends.'?

Is it not reasonable to ask him where the difference (between the two situations) lies? If it is, then it also seems reasonable for him to answer (for instance): 'In the first case, I was giving a party for my friends rather than for strangers, *since there is no general requirement to do all I can to benefit others*. In the second case, I refused to lie about my friends' collusion in insurance fraud, since friendship does not require complicity in fraud.' This sort of answer introduces general principles.[15]

Given the bit I have italicized, it would clearly be ludicrous to expect any non-philosopher, however virtuous, to give such an answer; indeed any non-philosopher would be hard put to see any 'inconsistency' between giving a party for one's friends and refusing to lie about their collusion in fraud. We have to take Irwin's remarks as amounting to (something like) the claim that we

---

[15]  T. Irwin, review of S. Broadie, *Ethics with Aristotle* (1993), 329 (my italics).

philosophers will best understand moral or practical reasoning if we think of the virtuous agent as deducing the permissibility of giving a party for his friends rather than strangers from the general principle that there is no general requirement to do all one can to benefit others. But Broadie would disagree. She not only thinks that this is an incorrect interpretation of Aristotle; she also thinks it is a misguided or plain wrong way to think about moral reasoning.

On both these points McDowell agrees, but he thinks that we can attribute 'choosing the action as an instance of acting well' without endorsing any such deductivist model of practical reasoning and without implying that anyone, let alone a virtuous non-philosopher, could produce the general principles that took one, step by step, from 'a blueprint, in universal terms, for doing well' to the instance at hand.[16] He thinks, as has been clear since his 'Virtue and Reason', that we will best understand moral or practical reasoning in terms of the 'reading' of particular situations, and that the illuminating philosophical account of the way in which right readings hang together is that 'actions that result from them are all indeed instances of a universal, doing well'. 'We might gloss "reading situations correctly",' he says, 'as: seeing them in the light of the correct conception of doing well';[17] and I take that 'we' to be 'we philosophers'. If *we* think of the virtuous agent this way, we will come to a better understanding of what is involved in that reasoning which issues in right conduct—and stop trying to construct deductivist models.

When some philosophers ascribe to the virtuous a correct conception of *eudaimonia*, and thereby a grasp of acting well as acting in accordance with the virtues, they probably have fallen for the Platonic fantasy and ascribed to them, ludicrously, 'an explicit, comprehensive, substantial vision of the good'. However, if one is sufficiently cautious, it is (just) possible to follow Aristotle in ascribing such things without making that mistake. Whether we are right to do so depends on whether such ascription gives us a better understanding of whatever topic is in question, and, in the present case, these Aristotelian ideas do not, I think throw much further light on 'moral motivation', so I shall not continue to mention them.

---

[16] McDowell, 'Deliberation and Moral Development', 25.
[17] Ibid. 26.

## CONCLUSION

There is growing enthusiasm for the idea that the ideal Kantian agent, the person with a good will, who acts 'from a sense of duty', and the ideal neo-Aristotelian agent, who acts from virtue—from a settled state of character—are not as different as they were once supposed to be.[18] As I have stressed, this goes hand in hand with recognizing that whatever disagreements we may have about which fancy things it is illuminating to ascribe to our ideal agent when we ascribe 'moral motivation' to her, we are not insisting that she have explicit thoughts about right action, duty or principle (nor indeed about virtue, good action, or *to kalon*). Such explicit thoughts are not a necessary condition for being morally motivated.

But the examples given above (pp. 132–3) of agents doing what is V for X reasons without thereby acting 'because they thought it was right', 'from duty', 'on principle', suggest a further, more unexpected thesis; namely that, speaking loosely, such explicit thoughts are not sufficient either. Speaking more precisely, the thesis is that neither an agent's sincere avowals of 'this is right/my duty/required by principle' (or their translations in other languages), nor those sentences (or their translations), complete with assertion sign, occurring in their mind at the time, is sufficient to license the ascription to them of the *belief* that what they are doing is right, their duty, or required by principle. And since they must have that belief in order to be morally motivated, in order to act because they think (i.e. believe) that what they are doing is right, their duty, etc., neither the avowals nor the occurrent sentences are sufficient for moral motivation.

This thesis will be explored in the next chapter.

---

[18] The idea has been developed by Stephen Hudson in 'What is Morality all About?', by Barbara Herman and Christine Korsgaard (see references in the Bibliography), and particularly by Marcia Baron, in the series of papers that has culminated in *Kantian Ethics Almost Without Apology* (1995). See also Robert Audi, 'Acting from Virtue' (1995).

# 7

# Moral Motivation

In the previous chapter we considered the question of whether, according to virtue ethics, the virtuous agent, when she acts virtuously, acts 'from (a sense of) duty', 'on or from principle', 'because she thinks it's right'—is 'morally motivated', in short—and I concluded that, in a sense, she does and is. That is, acting virtuously, in the very way the virtuous agent acts, namely from virtue, is sufficient for being 'morally motivated' or acting 'from (a sense of) duty'. In this chapter I want to defend a bolder thesis, namely that, ideally, it is necessary too. By this I mean that the perfectly virtuous agent, when she acts virtuously, from virtue, sets the standard for 'moral motivation', for acting 'because one thinks it's right', 'from duty', etc., a standard against which we assess the extent to which the less than perfectly virtuous do the same. The more an agent's character resembles that of the perfectly virtuous, the more he may be credited with 'moral motivation' when he does what is V for X reasons.

## MORAL MOTIVATION AS A MATTER OF DEGREE: BELIEF ASCRIPTION

An immediate consequence of this thesis, intimated in the phrase 'the extent to which the less than perfectly virtuous do the same', is that 'being morally motivated' turns out to be a matter of degree; and I know that this is something that many people find counterintuitive. 'Moral motivation', they think, acting 'on principle' or 'because you think it's right', must be an all-or-nothing matter. This conviction is no doubt often rooted in what I consider to be a false philosophy of mind,[1] a picture of the beliefs that explain virtuous

---
[1] Cf. Introduction, pp. 15–16.

actions as atomistic, as the kinds of thing that can occur independently of any other beliefs and behaviour. But I suspect that even those who in general subscribe to a different picture, recognizing, in some form or another, that belief ascriptions carry entailments about actual or counterfactual sayings and doings, tend to lose sight of this point when they think about such beliefs as 'This is right/my duty/required by principle'. There is a great temptation (in no way, I hasten to add, peculiar to, or even typical of, Kantians) to imagine the agent's mind as filled with glorious occurrent ideas about the rightness of what she is doing, the sacred claims of duty, the glory of the Noble, ' 'tis a far, far better thing that I do than I have ever done', and so on, and to think that, in imagining this, one has got hold of the agent's occurrently believing that what she is doing is right, or acting 'from duty', as an all-or-nothing matter.

One corrective to this is to remember, again, about children. I claimed in the preceding chapter that even quite small children sometimes do what is V and give X reasons for doing so, and I claimed further that, nevertheless, they do not act 'on principle', 'from duty', 'because they think it's right'. There is something absurd about attributing such deep, value-embodying reasons to children (or indeed to some mentally handicapped people) who, if they can be said to have values at all, do not have values which are yet their own.

But this absurdity does not diminish one whit when we suppose that instead of (or as well as) giving X reasons, the small children say 'It was the right thing to do' or 'It was my duty' or 'It's a matter of principle' or something similar. Indeed, if the adults around them regularly speak in certain ways or they have imbibed certain sorts of stories, they may come out with much more grandiose phrases concerning nobility or honour or the moral law.[2] Having

---

[2] In the modern, English-speaking world, it is easy to forget that many children used to be brought up on stories in which the heroes (and sometimes heroines) constantly spoke of what was noble, or what duty or honour required, and learnt to use such vocabulary themselves very young. It is also easy to overlook the extent to which other languages may be different from contemporary English. I am reliably informed that, in Iceland, the language of honour and dishonour, used throughout the famous Icelandic sagas, is still perfectly colloquial today—so colloquial indeed that many locutions employing it cannot be literally translated into English because they sound quaint. But, admirable as the Icelandic nation is, I do not suppose that their children, colloquially speaking in terms that (literally) translate as 'My honour demands that I do . . .', are morally more advanced than ours. (I am indebted to

been taught to use such phrases alongside being taught the X resasons, they may have lots of occurrent ideas involving them when they act. But we still do not suppose that they are acting because they think (i.e. believe) that what they are doing is right, or their duty, or required by principle or . . . They are simply too young to have those beliefs. They do not, and counterfactually would not, say and do a whole range of the other things required for the ascription of such beliefs.

I would claim further that, even in relation to (most) young adolescents, we do not want to say that they act 'on principle', 'because they think it is right', 'from (a sense of) duty', in just the same way as adults do. By and large, their moral beliefs, or their values, are still not entirely their own, but those of their mentors or their peer group. But we do not think that there is a determinate point at which small children start acting 'because they think it's right', 'from duty', in just the same way adolescents do, nor a later determinate point at which adolescents start doing it in just the same way adults do, because at that determinate point their values have become entirely their own. We know that human and moral development is gradual and forms a continuum. So 'moral motivation', acting because you believe that the action is right, can be a matter of degree.

True, it is important to remember again that we are in the area where things are true 'for the most part'. Some children do develop, as we say, a 'wisdom beyond their years' and become fully fledged moral agents, acting 'because they think it's right' remarkably young. I would not be surprised if the youthful Dalai Lamas, given their unique education, did. And it may happen for no apparent reason at all. I recently read a newspaper obituary of an astonishing Pakistani boy called Iqbal Masih, sold to a carpet manufacturer at four, who, by the tender age of twelve, when he was shot, had already been campaigning for two years (he addressed meetings) with extraordinary determination and courage for the rights of children in Pakistan. (He managed to escape from his bondage and somehow wind up at a school in Pakistan that looks after such children.) The obituary did not tell one much more than that, but even

Thorsteinn Gylfason for this point. See his fascinating introductory essay to *Njal's Saga*, Wordsworth classics (1998), for a learned and spirited defence of the view that 'the fundamental moral conceptions of *Njala* (*Nyal's Saga*) are shared by us'.)

that much certainly suggests that he had a range of mental capacities far beyond that of most adolescents. It is not absurd to ascribe to him some quite profound beliefs about what his life, and indeed human life, should be like, and what sort of person he should be, nor absurd to suppose that these were his own and arrived at by, in some sense, reflection. He can hardly have acquired them from his parents, or the other unfortunate children, or the adults who ran the carpet factory; and the obituary did not suggest that the school he escaped to encouraged the children in its care to risk their lives by becoming campaigners. It seems he thought of that for himself.

Well, perhaps he did not; perhaps indeed the story is not true. But surely it might be. Astonishing? Yes. Incredible? No—and not ruled out by the claim that 'for the most part' eleven- and twelve-year-olds do not act 'because they think it's right' or 'on principle'. Indeed, this claim is supported by the fact that Iqbal's story is so astonishing. Characteristically, there is nothing like enough in what eleven- and twelve-year-olds say and do to license our ascribing the profound beliefs to them that it seems reasonable to ascribe to him.

So if you are inclined to think that 'moral motivation', acting because you think it's right, must be an all-or-nothing matter, its presence determined by what is going on in the agent's mind at the moment of acting, do, please, remember children. For any ideas or thoughts that you ascribe to your 'morally motivated' agent as sufficient will be ones that children—ordinary children, not ones like Iqbal—can have if, as part of their day-to-day moral education, they have been taught a sufficiently fancy vocabulary. (And remember too that children brought up by philosophically sophisticated parents may be taught to give disconcertingly sophisticated answers to questions such as 'Why is it right to help people or tell the truth?' No doubt few children can give good answers to such a question. But children can be taught to answer 'Because the moral law requires it' or 'That's what we need to live together', just as a child I heard of was taught to answer 'Why is April the cruellest month?' by saying 'It breeds memory out of desire'. It may well be that teaching children a good general answer to the question 'Why is it right to do so-and-so?' speeds up their moral development, but that is not to say that teaching them to produce the good answer gives them moral understanding on the spot.)

I took it as a premise that it was (for the most part) absurd to ascribe 'moral motivation' to children, and, recognizing that some readers will not agree, I acknowledge that some may remain convinced that 'moral motivation' is always an all-or-nothing matter. I hope that those who do accept the premise will now accept that it can be a matter of degree, and hence may be brought to recognize some other ways, beyond the fact of the continuum of moral development, in which that may be so.

## CHARACTER ASCRIPTION

The thesis I aspire to defend in this chapter is that the perfectly virtuous agent, when she acts virtuously, sets the standard for 'moral motivation', for acting 'because one thinks it's right', etc.—a standard against which we assess the extent to which the less than perfectly virtuous do the same. This can certainly be taken to embrace the preceding remarks. The virtuous agent, when she acts virtuously, acts from virtue, from the relevant character trait which includes practical wisdom. Children, even young adolescents, however well brought up and nice, do not, 'for the most part', even get into the running for being morally motivated, because, except for cases such as Iqbal, they are not candidates for the possession of virtue. They may have personalities, they may have natural virtues, but they do not yet have character traits; their characters are forming but not yet formed and settled.

However, it might be said that we do not really puzzle over whether or not to ascribe the belief that what one is doing is right, or one's duty, to children; and the bolder, more embracing thesis I am after is that various puzzles we have about the ascription of that belief , or 'moral motivation' to adults—cases where we feel driven to say, 'Well, he believes it in one way but not in another'—are best understood by considering how we would describe their characters. And this introduces another dimension to the claim that 'Moral motivation is a matter of degree' beyond 'The capacity for it develops gradually as children grow up'.

As I noted in the introduction, whether or not an adult definitely has a particular virtue is often a matter of degree. For a start, the virtue words accept so many qualifiers that explicitly register degrees of virtue—'perfectly V, exceptionally V, thoroughly V, as V as you could reasonably expect any ordinary human being to be, fairly V, quite V . . .'. These, perhaps, do not do much more than

register degrees of reliability in doing what is V for X reasons
(though they may also register degrees of appropriate feeling). But
as Gary Watson rightly remarks, the reliability in question is not
just a statistical notion.[3] We shall see shortly that some failures in
reliability matter a great deal less than others, for the virtue words
also accept qualifiers such as 'basically/fundamentally V but . . .'
and 'as V as you could expect anyone to be given his upbringing or
his society'. Moreover, they can combine; people can be 'fairly V
but . . .' and 'exceptionally V, given their upbringing or society'.

Here is one puzzle about 'moral motivation'. Consider those
who, like the Nazis, or other extreme racists, or people committed
to the teachings of a wicked religion or cult (for example, one that
calls for the torture and murder of unwilling victims), have
embraced wicked moral beliefs. Many of them may well be hypocritical, entirely lacking in integrity, cowardly, dishonest, licentious,
self-indulgent, and utterly selfish as well as cruel and unjust. But a
few of them, although they pursue bad ends and characteristically
do terrible things without a qualm, and even with enjoyment, may
nevertheless be capable of actions that (at least apparently) are quite
splendid, ones that, we may be inclined to say, really call for
courage or honesty or generosity.

So imagine that one of them does something spectacularly self-
sacrificial or unusually demanding. He gives, sincerely, suitable X
reasons—one mustn't give in to tyrants who try to force one to do
immoral things, this sort of issue calls for the whole truth (even if
one's life hangs on revealing it), it's a deserving institution and needs
every penny it can get (whereas I don't need my inheritance). And
his action is not, in a way, uncharacteristic—none of the people who
knows him is particularly surprised. Let us even embroider the
example by supposing that he also says sincerely that all he did was
what was right, what duty required, that someone of principle
could have done no less in the circumstances. Was he 'morally motivated'? Did he do what he did 'because he thought it was right',
'from duty', 'on principle'?

The temptation to say 'Yes' conflicts with our recognition of the
fact that this man is wicked—how can we ascribe something as
noble or high-minded as 'moral motivation' or a sense of duty to
someone so vile? The way out of the puzzle is not, I think, to try to

---

[3] G. Watson, 'Virtues in Excess' (1984), 72, n. 18.

discredit his X reasons but to stick with our assessment of his character as thoroughly bad.

Thereby, far from resembling the character of the virtuous, it is at the opposite end of the spectrum. I am prepared, in such cases, to stick my neck out and roundly declare that such people have no virtues at all; that the Nazism or racism or religion (supposing them to be very bad) has poisoned their characters to such an extent that no character trait they have can count as one. And this means that I would go back to the apparently splendid act and, denying that it was done from virtue to any extent at all (since the agent has none), deny that the agent acted 'because she thought it was right' (or on principle, etc.). And this would allow me to say (what does not seem so far from the truth) that such people have no real idea of rightness or goodness in action, no moral principles, no real idea of moral duty, at all. They say that they have, they think that they have, and they are just wrong, hopelessly corrupted by the wicked doctrines they have embraced and made their own.

By the same token, when one of them does something vicious and claims, quite sincerely, to have done it because it was right, his duty, required by principle, etc., we need not puzzle over whether he merits at least some minimal amount of praise or respect because of his high-minded moral motive, his sense of duty. He doesn't, because he didn't act from a 'moral motive' or sense of duty at all.

Contrast these with another case. What are we to say about some of the people who lived in our countries in bygone years, in privileged echelons of societies in which various cases of unjust, callous, greedy, arrogant, cruel, thoughtless behaviour were not thought of as such because the victims of them belonged to underprivileged groups? We know, from diaries and letters, that some of them were distressed, even outraged, by the plight of the poor, or the slaves, or women; that some did a little and some a lot to try to change things—because, they said, the suffering or injustice must be ameliorated, it was wrong to let it continue, it was one's duty to do something, etc. But we know too that all of them continued to behave in some ways that nowadays we would condemn as unjust, callous, greedy . . .[4]

---

[4] Discussing 'a gloomy general feature of revolutions', Mary Midgley notes that '[i]nequalities above one's own level tend to be visible: those below it to be hidden', citing as examples Stokeley Carmichael's sexist remark that 'The only place for women in the SNCC is prone', the nineteenth-century women who, fighting for

Perhaps because we are so anxious to disassociate ourselves from the shameful actions of our forebears, there is some inclination to dismiss all their apparently virtuous endeavours as merely hypocritical, either to deny outright that they acted 'because they thought it was right' or 'on principle' or to insist that their principles, or what they (really) thought was right, were insufficiently universal or impartial to count as '*moral* motivation'.

But surely, in character, they resemble the ideal virtuous agent much more closely than did those of their contemporaries who were indifferent to the plight of any of the underprivileged groups, let alone those who enjoyed exploiting their position. Would any of us ever count as being 'morally motivated', as acting 'because we think it's right', if our descendants judge us with similar harshness instead of allowing that some of us were 'fairly virtuous, given the lamentable materialism, greed, and indifference to the Third World and non-human animals that characterized twentieth-century Western societies'?

It is extraordinarily difficult to determine when someone is to count as having embraced the wicked beliefs of a society, or religion, or cult, and when they can count as just, so to speak, having been landed with them. But difficult as it may be to do, and admitting that many cases are simply indeterminate, we can sometimes draw a distinction between views and attitudes prevalent in a society that any ordinarily decent person within it could reasonably be expected to see through, and those that only exceptional and extraordinary people might see through. One reason, I take it, that we judge the Nazis so severely is that, although it might well take a quite exceptional person to see through the anti-Semitism so well entrenched at the time (in the U.K. and U.S. as well as in Germany and Austria), there was nothing entrenched about the idea that it would be just policy to start drawing distinctions between the legal rights of your country's citizens on grounds of race, let alone the idea that it was consistent with compassion and justice to put them in concentration camps and slaughter them. Anyone reasonably

women's rights 'took for granted the cheap labour of uneducated female servants', and the American Declaration of Independence which proclaimed 'the proud belief that all men are created free and equal, while explicitly excluding women and implicitly (as far as some of the signatories went) non-European slaves as well'. *Animals and Why they Matter* (1984), 72.

decent in Europe at the time, however anti-Semitic their upbringing, was able to see that that was wrong.

Some blind spots we take as adequate grounds for denying any
virtue at all, notwithstanding the fact that some people with such
blind spots may do things that, coming from others, we should hail
as the mark of virtue. Other blind spots that we can assign to a person as the result of their socialization and think that only someone
exceptional might have seen past can be accommodated by suitably
qualified ascriptions of virtue; some people with such blind spots
can be fairly or even exceptionally V, given the society they live in.
But, thereby, not perfectly virtuous; hence, without ascribing
hypocrisy to them, we can still say that they are not morally motivated, do not act because they think it's right or from duty, to the
extent that the perfectly or even thoroughly virtuous do.

Blind spots are far from always being explicable in such terms.
Who does not number, amongst their family and friends, people
they will readily describe as pretty generous, considerate, just, compassionate, honest, but whose exercise of these virtues is patchy, in
some incomprehensible way? We are sure that they are, in general,
to be described as people who regularly and reliably act 'because
they think it is right'; as people of moderately high principle, as people who are morally motivated, perhaps, in general rather better
than ourselves—and yet, oh dear, they will do *this*. How can they?
I am not thinking of seriously vicious acts, but at least of ones that,
if you know the person well, and love them, you find distressing.
Someone may lie about their forebears, but nothing else; someone
may characteristically be unjust in minor ways to women they do
not know well; someone may lavish some money (not a big proportion of their income but a significant sum) on things you think
are decadent; someone may go in for sexual activity you think is
exploitative in a minor way. Or, more trivially, someone who is the
most lavishly generous and considerate of hosts is typically quite
horrid to you if you tip half a cup of cold coffee down the sink and
(they say angrily) '*waste* it!!'. Maybe you can often get them to
admit that they shouldn't have done what they did, (or said what
they said or reacted the way they did)—but on the next occasion,
there they are, cheerfully doing it or saying it or reacting the same
way again. Or maybe you can't get them to agree; you always make
the same objections, and they always make the same replies, and the
argument always trickles away.

Sometimes we might be ashamed to quiz them at all about their blind spots because, despite the fact that they have them and frequently do things that we find mildly repellent, or shocking, or flawed, we know them well enough to know that whenever anything serious is at issue, they always come up trumps, doing startlingly better than anyone else we know. Do they have principles (which they act on when they act well) or don't they? When they act well do they act 'because they think it's right' or don't they? On the one hand we want to say 'Yes' and on the other we want to say 'No'.

On the account of moral motivation given, there is no clear cut solution to these puzzles, and that seems to be a point in its favour rather than one that counts against it. According to the account given, all that we can say to ourselves, about these people we love and respect is, 'Well, they are, in general, quite honest, just, generous, temperate . . . but they do have this blind spot, namely, . . .', or, in the last case, 'Well, they are fundamentally virtuous, you can rely on them totally in a serious crisis, but oh dear, you have to be prepared to put up with them doing such-and-such.' And saying this should remind us that it is unlikely that many of the people nearest and dearest to us should have such blind spots while we had none.

A final example of ways in which people are not all of a piece is provided by the interesting phenomenon introduced as follows by Nomy Arpaly and Timothy Schroeder.

To act akratically is to believe one course of action to be, all things considered, the right one, yet to take some other course of action instead. The most commonly discussed examples of akrasia center around wrongdoing of one sort or another, in which desires override judgement . . . one is resolved to tell an awkward truth, but somehow the lie slips out. In the cases of interest to us, however, akrasia results in what, for lack of a better word, might be called rightdoing of one sort or another. That is, the akratic course of action is superior to the course of action recommended by the agent's best judgement. Because these cases reverse our usual expectations from akratic action, we shall call them cases of inverse akrasia.[5]

The authors begin with three examples of inverse akrasia: Huck Finn's 'failure' (by his own lights) to turn in the runaway slave Jim;

---

[5] N. Arpaly and T. Schroeder, 'Praise, Blame and the Whole Self' (1999), 162.

Neoptolemus's 'failure' to cheat Philoctetes; and Oskar Schindler's 'failure' to make as much profit as possible from the Jews working for him.[6] They claim, rightly, that not only the actions but also the motives of the three agents merit praise and argue that meriting praise (or blame) for actions and motives depends largely on the extent to which the action and its motives express the agent's 'Whole Self' or character.

I agree with almost everything they say, but my concern here is not exactly the same as theirs. They leave unquestioned, I think, the standard assumption that whatever praiseworthy motives Huck, Neoptolemus, and Schindler may have had for their praiseworthy actions, it is absolutely clear cut that they cannot have acted 'because they thought it was right' , 'from duty', or 'on principle'.[7] But it is precisely the grounds for that assumption that I sought to dispel in the last chapter. Once it is agreed that the ideal Aristotelian agent who does what is V for X reasons, and acts from virtue, may well be indistinguishable from the ideal Kantian agent as far as 'moral motivation' on a particular occasion is concerned, then the grounds for supposing that in order to be 'morally motivated' the agent must have explicit, occurrent thoughts about the rightness of what they are doing, or about its being required by duty or principle, have been given up. Agreed, Huck, Neoptolemus, and Schindler did not have those thoughts, but that fact, on its own, is not enough to rule out the possibility that they acted 'because they thought it was right', 'from duty', 'on principle'. So far, that is still an open question. So let's consider it.

We naturally imagine, whether the story fills this in or not, that the minds of our three inverse akratics are somewhat preoccupied around the time of acting with various occurrent thoughts about the *wrongness* of what they are doing—robbing Jim's poor old owner, dishonourably failing to obey Odysseus, not only feeling but giving in to slavish sentimentality unbecoming to a decent man—and one might think that that was surely enough to rule out, absolutely, the

---

[6] Neoptolemus is a character in Sophocles' play *Philoctetes,* and his praiseworthy refusal to obey Odysseus is mentioned by Aristotle (1146a19). The authors stress that the motivation of their Schindler is as portrayed in the film, not necessarily in either the book or real life.

[7] They speak throughout of their three inverse akratics as being motivated by desire.

idea that they are nevertheless acting 'because they think it's right'. But what are their characters like?

The stories do fill in enough to make it clear that, notwithstanding any occurrent thoughts they may have about the wrongness of what they are doing, the three do all act for X reasons. Huck does not report Jim because Jim is his friend; Neoptolemus tells Philoctetes why Odysseus sent him because it's the truth; Schindler protects the Jews because they are in desperate need of protection. Moreover, the stories fill in enough to make it clear that in thus doing what is V for X reasons they are not acting atypically. Neoptolemus is honest, Schindler is compassionate and courageous, and Huck, in his own youthful way, is loyal and a good friend; these aspects of their characters, or fledging characters, manifest themselves in all sorts of ways. The two adults are not thoroughly so (nor Huck thoroughly so for his age), for it must be the case that sometimes they would act and react as no thoroughly virtuous agent would. But, as we say, 'their hearts are in the right place'.

On the strength of the extent to which Neoptolemus's and Schindler's characters are like that of the perfectly honest or compassionate and courageous agent, I would say that, notwithstanding the fact that they categorize what they are doing as wrong, they are both 'morally motivated'; they both act 'because they think it's right', 'from (a sense of) duty', 'on (or from) principle'. True, they both believe that what they are doing is wrong, contrary to duty or some principle they hold *too*, in a way; that is the respect in which they are not as virtuous as the perfectly virtuous. So, although they are 'morally motivated', acting 'because they think it's right', 'from duty', they do not manage to do so to the full extent that the perfectly virtuous do.

Huck, given his youth and the fact that he is no Iqbal, does not make it. What we might optimistically say is that, given this flash of independence from the racism he has had inculcated in him, he is beginning to think for himself about justice and may, given his loyal and friendly impulses, be setting his feet on the path to virtue. Pessimistically we might note that, according to the story, he decides that he is a bad boy and that there is no point in his trying to be anything else. Unless those beliefs change and he acquires, poor child, some self-esteem and the courage of his present heartfelt convictions, he may well be setting his feet on the path to vice, due to wind up excusing all his selfish, unjust, and dishonest actions as things he couldn't help because he's just bad.


## THE UNITY OF THE VIRTUES

The preceding examples, in acknowledging a variety of ways in which people are not, ethically, all of a piece, might be taken as illustrating the falsity of the doctrine of the unity of the virtues: that to have any individual virtue one must have them all. However, if we interpret that doctrine in the way Aristotle does, this is not obviously so. Having discussed practical wisdom in Book 6, Aristotle concludes as follows:

One might on these lines meet the dialectical argument by which it would be contended that the virtues exist independently of each other, on the ground that the same man is not equally well endowed by nature in respect of them all, so that he will be the possessor of one, but not yet the possessor of another. As far as the natural virtues are concerned, this is possible; but it is not possible when the virtues are those that entitle a person to be called good *without qualification*; for the possession of the single virtue of practical wisdom will carry with it the possession of them all.[8]

The cases we have been discussing are all ones in which the agent is not entitled to be called 'good without qualification'. Assessed against the standard of the ideal virtuous agent, their individual virtues, or virtue in general, are to be qualified, by such phrases as 'not thoroughly but his heart's in the right place' or ' fairly/remarkably, given the society they lived in' or 'basically, but . . .'. And despite the fact that we do accept, as a fact, that people are rarely all of a piece as far as their virtue is concerned, we also recognize that the virtues do form some sort of a unity.

What sort? 'The' ( so-called) doctrine of the unity of the virtues can take a surprising variety of forms[9] and this is not the place to

---

[8] *Nicomachean Ethics* 1144b33–1145a2 (my italics).

[9] Timothy Chappell, in an unpublished paper (now, alas, lost), once argued that there were (something like) thirty (!) versions of the doctrine of the unity of the virtues. I cannot now remember how he did it, but I think the first eight came from '(i) The possession of any one virtue is necessary and sufficient for (or (ii) necessary for or (iii) sufficient for or (iv) conducive to) the instantaneous possession (or (v–viii) the eventual possession) of all the other virtues too' and the next eight from the same structure with 'The possession of some one virtue (e.g. *phronesis*)' as the opening clause.

go into it in much detail. But it is worth saying a little about it here.[10]

Consider again a view of the virtues that I denied on p. 131 above, that they are discrete, isolable ('independent') character traits. The Humean form of benevolence discussed in Chapter 5 was such a character trait, consisting simply of a tendency to feel concern for others and be prompted to action by that concern. Courage is quite commonly thought of in such a way, as consisting simply of fearlesness or the readiness to face danger in pursuit of one's ends. Similarly, temperance is thought of as self-restraint or moderation in the face of the prospect of immediate physical pleasure, honesty as the readiness to avoid deception, and so on. (It is not clear to me that one can think of justice in this way.) Thought of in such a way, they can readily co-exist with, and, at least in the cases of 'courage' and 'temperance', actually aggravate, various vices—and thereby, it may be thought, clearly disprove any substantial version of the doctrine of the unity of the virtues.

But, as I noted in the Introduction, to think of the 'virtues' in this way is not to think of the character traits in question as virtues at all. They are not excellences of character, not traits that, by their very nature, make their possessor good and issue in good conduct. They can be faults or flaws rather than excellences and they can lead their possessors to act badly. What this way of thinking about the virtues omits is the Aristotelian idea that each of the virtues involves practical wisdom, the ability to reason correctly about practical matters. And, as the earlier discussion of the V agent acting for X reasons revealed, this ability does not exist in discrete, independent packages, peculiar to each virtue, allowing again for the possibility that someone might be, for example, courageous but totally lacking in charity, or charitable but totally lacking in temperance. The same sorts of judgements about goods and evils, benefits and harms, what is worthwhile and what is relatively unimportant crop up across the ranges. (Someone who does not see the relief of others' suffering as a good worth pursuing, something it is worth facing danger to achieve, lacks the virtue of courage (though without, thereby, being cowardly). And someone who is prepared to do a

---

[10] What follows has been greatly influenced by two excellent articles on the doctrine of the unity of the virtues, Gary Watson's 'Virtues in Excess' and Neera K. Badhwar's 'The Limited Unity of Virtue' (1996).

great deal for others at great cost to himself but is happy to deceive his wife about his adulteries 'because what she doesn't know won't harm her' is lacking in charity.)

That we do not believe in the disunity of the virtues is, I think, shown by our reaction to certain sorts of stories we sometimes read in the newspapers. We read of people doing what seems splendid; the sort of action that seems to call for an exceptional level of, say, courage or generosity. And then we learn about them that they have also done something morally repellent and we are surprised and often puzzled. I do not only mean something repellent in the same area—cowardly or selfish, as the case may be, which might immediately lead us to say that we had obviously made a mistake in ascribing courage or generosity to them in the first place. I mean something in a different area; the agent who dashed into the burning building and saved a stranger turns out to be a rapist; the one who has given a huge proportion of his income to the homeless turns out to be someone whose lies are keeping an innocent person in gaol. And we are surprised and puzzled: how could they be so splendid in the one instance and so despicable in another, we wonder? Now isn't that an interesting fact—that we are surprised and puzzled?

If we thought of the virtues as discrete, isolable traits, such that someone could be, for example, truly courageous but also cruel and licentious in character, or truly charitable but also cowardly and dishonest, there would be no reason to be surprised or puzzled. We would expect one who acts from courage to be reliable and predictable as far as courageous acts were concerned, but have no expectations about their kindness or honesty. But we do. We believe the virtues form some sort of unity.

But again, what sort? The discussion in the last chapter, which stressed the ways in which the X reasons appropriate to one particular virtue were not independent of the X reasons appropriate to any other, also highlighted Williams's point that one way in which people vary is that they may be more sensitive to the sorts of considerations cited in the X reasons of one virtue than they are to those cited in another. Who does not know of people who, though admirable in many respects, are hardly exemplars of others? And the above discussion of blind spots suggests further that people may vary within particular ranges, either systematically across them (as some of our admirable (not our despicable) forebears had their blind spots about working-class women, or, indeed, women) or simply within them (as someone otherwise impeccably honest may lie about their forebears). So it seems that what we believe in is what Neera Badhwar calls 'the limited unity' of the virtues and Gary Watson 'the weak unity thesis'. This is a view that simultaneously recognizes the fact that practical wisdom cannot occur in discrete packages, limited in its area of competence to just this virtue or that, and also the fact that it is not an all-or-nothing matter. According to this thesis, anyone who possesses one virtue will have all the others to some degree, albeit, in some cases, a pretty limited one.

Now let us relate this back to the proposed account of 'moral motivation'. On this account, when we believe that we have correctly identified 'because she thought it was right', 'on principle', etc. as the agent's motivation on a particular occasion, we believe that we have thereby identified them as acting from virtue. And given even the weak unity thesis, this means that we believe that we have thereby identified them as being a certain sort of person all round—that we have seen, manifested in just this one action, what they are like, pretty much 'all the way through', 'deep down'. In ascribing to them a settled state of, say, charitableness or honesty, we have thereby ascribed to them at least some possession of all the other virtues as well. Hence our surprise and puzzlement when some other act of theirs inclines us to say—but they are cruel! They are dishonest through and through! We are surprised and puzzled because we thought we had them identified as someone who was at least fairly virtuous all round.

Now this is to locate the puzzlement, not to dissolve it. But, having located it, we know where to look for solutions—in the agent's character over all. Maybe we made a mistake about the morally repellent act; perhaps it was, unbeknownst to us uncharacteristic and a case of akrasia in the face of extreme temptation or under extreme circumstances. Maybe we made a mistake about the splendid act—perhaps it was, unbeknownst to us, not done for X reasons, but ulterior ones all too characteristic of the agent. Maybe it was utterly uncharacteristic. Or maybe it was not simply uncharacteristic but nevertheless did not actually spring from a character that resembled that of the virtuous at all, as in the examples of the Nazis or extreme racists. Once we are clear about the agent's character, and the extent to which it resembles that of the virtuous, we can see to what extent he may, or may not, be credited with 'moral motivation'.

## FIRST OCCASIONS OF ACTING VIRTUOUSLY

There is a residual stronghold of the idea that 'moral motivation', acting because you think it's right, can be correctly ascribed independently of any ascription of virtuous character, which is the attachment to a vision of there being a first occasion of a 22-carat 'morally right act', a right act which, for the first time in his undistinguished, or rather selfish, or perhaps even wicked life, the agent does 'because he thinks it's right'. I suspect that this vision has its roots in religious views about the possibility of redemption; no sinner is so far gone that he may not find in himself that divine spark, the source of all rightness in action, that would enable him to do what is right. But even people apparently uninfluenced by any thoughts about redemption still cling to the vision, citing various examples as cases of it. I shall claim that the vision is confused, the result of not filling in enough details in the examples.

One favoured sort of example concerns unexpected courage. Someone described as 'absolutely ordinary', 'not courageous at all', suddenly 'uncharacteristically' does something quite heroic. 'One often reads of such cases in the newspaper,' it is said. But do the newspapers describe the person in question thus, or say her action was uncharacteristic? And if so, on what grounds? She may indeed be a timorous driver and scared of mice; she may, hitherto, have led an ordinary life in which there have been few, if any, occasions in which the virtue of courage was called upon; but that's not enough to license saying that she lacks the virtue. If she thinks that people who risk their lives to withstand tyrants or save others are admirable, rather than unrealistic sentimental fools or reckless dolts, if she is trying to bring up her children to be courageous, if she is horrified by reports of parents who have run away and left their children to be mauled by Rottweilers, then her action is not uncharacteristic. Try to imagine her as the opposite in those respects and her action is uncharacteristic, all right—but also unintelligible as 'morally motivated'. If a newspaper report gave me the opposite of those sorts of details and also reported that she had done some heroic deed 'because she thought it was right', I would dismiss the report as incredible.

But might she not have been inspired? This brings us to the other favoured sort of example. I discussed a case in the previous chapter in which love or success had a momentarily transforming effect on someone's actions and outlook, leading them to act uncharacteristically. But although we know love can have this merely transitory effect, do we not also believe that it can have a more profound one and actually change people's characters? Fable ascribes this occasional effectiveness to the love of a good woman; religion to the workings of God. Without committing ourselves to either we might still think that sometimes—very rarely perhaps, but sometimes—people can be brought 'to see the light', to have their eyes opened to what is truly good and truly bad in human life, to become reformed characters, in the twinkling of an eye.

It is true that many born-again Christians die again almost immediately and that penitent hedonists lapse back into their old ways, but not all of them do. And surely we can ascribe 'moral motivation' to the first acts of their new lives. Is it to be said of the ones who do not lapse that their first V acts, the first occasions, after a life of selfish profligacy and self-indulgence, in which they do what is temperate, or just, or considerate, that they cannot be acting virtuously—because they think it's right—because they do not act from a settled state of virtuous character?

No, indeed, but that does not show that 'moral motivation', acting because you think it's right, can be correctly ascribed independently of any ascription of virtuous character. For it is an essential part of such stories that the agent is acting from a settled state of virtuous character, because she has been transformed. True, the state has only just settled, born, fully formed in a sudden conversion, and this is far from being the way in which settled states of character usually come to be. But we are in the area where things are true 'for the most part', and I did say that such cases are rare. And of course, as far as knowledge goes, I shall not be being unduly sceptical, given the usual rate of recidivism, if I say, concerning the first few temperate or considerate acts of someone who has hitherto been a profligate debaucher, that I do not know whether they are acting virtuously or not. But if you draw a picture of the first just or temperate act and label it as 'first just or temperate act of a reformed character' then I can consistently add the further label 'Paul acting virtuously, because he thinks it's right, i.e. from a virtuous character'. A virtuous character is what the vision on the road to Damascus has, according to the story, converted him to having.[11]

However, if you draw a picture of a just or temperate act and then draw a cartoon strip featuring the same agent cheerfully ignoring other opportunities for such acts, and doing downright unjust and licentious ones, labelling the beginning of the strip 'first and only V act of Saul' I will claim that it is incoherent to suppose that Saul could have done that V act 'because he thought it was right' or 'on principle' or 'from (a sense of) duty'. You can no more label the first picture 'Saul acting because he thinks it is right' than you can label it 'Saul's whole character changed for just five minutes of his life, after which it changed back again'. A change in character has to be profound, to go all the way down, and part of what is meant by saying that it is profound is that it is not transitory.

Furthermore, the re-formed character's first V act is not quite the '22-carat morally right act' that was initially imagined—unless by the grace of God. For even if we allow sudden transformation of character, nothing but supernatural intervention could transform someone hitherto quite lacking in virtue to anything better than, say, fairly virtuous. Not only do old habits of acting and reacting die hard, but our re-formed agent has a lot to learn about people and about life before he acquires the sensitivity, perception, and imagination necessary for being thoroughly virtuous. An adult who has hitherto thought only of himself will be poorly equipped to put his new-found love of his fellow human beings into good practice; one who has hitherto ruthlessly pursued money and power and now sees them as dross is not in the best position to deal with people of modest ambition as he should. So, as fairly, but far from perfectly, virtuous, he will, on that first occasion act 'because he thinks it's right', 'from duty', 'on principle' only to some, not to the full, extent.

## CONCLUSION

The thesis of these two chapters has been that what is both necessary and sufficient for a virtuous act to be 'morally motivated' is

[11] This is the obverse of the possibility I allowed for in the previous chapter, where sudden loss of faith transforms one's character for the worse.

that it is done from a state of character that adequately resembles the state of character from which the perfectly virtuous agent acts. The central idea, to repeat what I said at the outset, has been that ascribing 'moral motivation', 'because she thought it was right', is ascribing something that goes far beyond the moment of action. It makes a claim about what sort of person the agent is—a claim that goes all the way down. (Hence, in my view, the fact that it is an important feature of our ethical thought. We can give no higher praise to an agent with respect to her action than to ascribe it.) One consequence of this idea is not only that occurrent thoughts somehow equivalent to 'This is right, virtuous, noble, my duty', or what have you, are not necessary for moral motivation; they are not sufficient either.

A further consequence, worth noting in conclusion is that this, of course, remains true when the ascription is in the first person. Although I am, barring advanced self-deception or neurosis, usually pretty much an authority on what my reason for doing something is, I am not necessarily an authority on whether I am acting 'because I think this is right' or 'on principle' or 'from (a sense of) duty', any more than I am on whether I know or understand something. For what is required for 'did it because she thought it was right' to be true of me goes well beyond what I know about myself in the moment of acting, to the state of my character and whether it adequately resembles that of the perfectly virtuous, concerning which my self-knowledge is distinctly fallible—as Kant himself might well agree.[12]

---

[12] 'We are pleased to flatter ourselves with the false claim to a nobler motive, but in fact we can never, even by the most strenuous of self-examination, get to the bottom of our secret impulsions; for when moral value is in question, we are concerned, not with the actions which we see, but with their inner principles, which we cannot see.' *Groundwork*, 75.

# PART III

# RATIONALITY

# 8

# The Virtues Benefit
# their Possessor

## PREAMBLE

This final section of the book ventures into the extremely difficult and tendentious territory of 'the objectivity (or rationality) of morality' in relation to virtue ethics. No reasonable reader could suppose that, in these four remaining chapters, I am going to prove that 'morality is objective/rationally justifiable', and no charitable one that I would be foolish enough to attempt such a task. My aim is considerably more modest and also programmatic. I believe that the neo-Aristotelian virtue ethics approach has something distinctive and largely unrecognized to contribute to discussion of the issue and my aim is to say what that is. It is programmatic in so far as 'the proof of the pudding is in the eating'. As things are at the moment, academic philosophers and their research students are beavering away at the problem of the objectivity of morality and very few are trying to crack it by pursuing anything like the line I am about to describe in these chapters.[1] For all I know they are, if not on the right track, still on a good one, but I think the virtue ethics track I propose looks just as promising, if not more so, and I put it forward as something that merits serious attention. We'll just have to wait and see what happens if and when a whole lot of philosophers try following it through.

But what version of 'the' problem am I concerned with (for it can take many different forms)?

In the first chapter, comparing the different ways in which act

[1] From my point of view, the two notable exceptions are Foot and McDowell. But although it seems to me that I have derived most of what I say in these chapters from them, I know that Foot disagrees with much of it and strongly suspect that McDowell would disagree with even more.

utilitarianism, simple deontology, and virtue ethics specify right action, I noted that the latter two had a particularly acute epistemological problem. The deontologists, in their second premise, have to come up with a completion of

P2.  A correct moral rule or principle is one that . . .

and the virtue ethicists have to come up with a completion of

P2.  A virtue is a character trait that . . .

and, I said, we both thereby lay ourselves open to the threat of moral cultural relativism or, even worse, moral scepticism. If we complete our second premises simply by saying 'is on the following list' and then give one ('Promises must be kept', 'Do not lie', 'Do not kill persons/human beings/the innocent . . .' or 'temperance, courage, charity, honesty . . . ') we are inviting the question '*Is* that the right list? How do you know?' But can we complete our second premises adequately in any other way? The threat is that maybe we cannot. Maybe, I said, we can do no more than list the rules, or character traits, accepted by our own culture or society, and thereby admit that our action assessments are culturally circumscribed, true 'for us' but not for others. Or, even worse, maybe we have to accept that there isn't anything that counts as knowing that a particular action is right; all there is is feeling convinced that it is because it is in accordance with a rule one personally wants to adhere to, or because it is what would characteristically be done by the sort of person one wants to be.

The question of whether, and how, deontologists could validate the rules on their list is an issue for them to discuss. The question for virtue ethics is whether, and how, we can validate particular views about which character traits are the virtues. Can we hope to achieve a justified conviction that certain views about which character traits are the virtues (and which not) are objectively correct?[2] That is the problem with which I am concerned.

My answer to this question will be a (highly qualified) 'Yes' but, in order to avoid raising false expectations, I should say at the outset that philosophers set different standards for what counts as sat-

---

[2] I take this formulation, slightly adapted to views about the virtues, from Wiggins, 'Eudaimonism and Realism in Aristotle's Ethics: A Reply to John McDowell' (1995), 229.

isfactory in this area, and some may well think I set them too low. For I follow McDowell in supposing that the validation must take place from within an acquired ethical outlook, not from some external 'neutral' point of view.

The worry about such 'validation' is that it cannot provide rational justifications at all, but is merely circular, doomed to be a mere rationalization of one's personal or culturally inculcated values. And this, we might say, is the standard dilemma which confronts any attempt to say anything substantial about the rationality, or objectivity, of ethics. If, speaking from within our ethical outlook, we seek to validate our ethical beliefs, we shall merely be re-expressing that outlook, not subjecting it to any kind of genuine reflective scrutiny. (That we are not really scrutinizing it will become glaringly obvious when someone points out that a mafioso drug baron or a pleasure-pursuing egoist or 'the moral sceptic' could object in a certain way.) So, it seems, our only alternative is to speak from outside our ethical outlook, from 'the neutral point of view'; nothing short of that will do. And many philosophers believe either that that is impossible or that it can at best yield very little.

But, as McDowell has argued in a number of papers,[3] there is a path between the horns of this dilemma—a Neurathian procedure in ethics which mirrors the Neurathian procedure Quine endorsed.

Writing in relation to the very broad issue of subjecting our whole conceptual scheme to rational appraisal, Quine said:

we must not leap to the fatalistic conclusion that we are stuck with the conceptual scheme that we grew up in. We can change it bit by bit, plank by plank, though meanwhile there is nothing to carry us along but the evolving conceptual scheme itself. The philosopher's task was well compared by Neurath to that of a mariner who must rebuild his ship on the open sea. We can improve our conceptual scheme, our philosophy, bit by bit, while continuing to depend on it for support; but we cannot detach ourselves from it and compare it objectively with an unconceptualized reality.[4]

Now once we have the Neurathian 'There's no basing knowledge on an *independent* foundation' image firmly in mind, we can see the possibility of *radical* ethical reflection, the critical scrutiny of one's ethical beliefs which could be genuinely revisionary and not merely

---

[3] Most illuminatingly (in my view) in 'Two Sorts of Naturalism' (1995).
[4] W. V. O. Quine, 'Identity, Ostension, and Hypostasis' (1950), 78–9.

a reiteration of an acquired ethical outlook, despite proceeding from within it.

The worry about proceeding from within an acquired outlook is that, for all we know, the one we have acquired through our particular upbringing in a particular culture at a particular period of human history might be 'all wrong'. Foundationalists in ethics think that the only way out of this problem (if there is a way) is a sort of modified Cartesian method of doubt. What I must do is throw out every ethical belief I have, take what I am left with as certain knowledge (facts recognizable from 'the neutral point of view', science, logic) and try to reinstate my ethical beliefs on those foundations. In the course of this attempt I will discover what in my acquired ethical outlook was right (if anything) and what was wrong (if anything).

But the Neurathian approach allows for the same worry—that our acquired ethical outlook might be all wrong. All it denies is that we could either find this out or fix up a new correct one *quickly*. For, in theory, Neurath's boat might, over many years, become like Theseus's ship, without a single plank of the original remaining. And then, in a manner of speaking, we, or our descendants, could look back at the ethical outlook within which we started and condemn it in retrospect as all wrong.[5]

In what follows, I shall assume, without argument, that McDowell is right to claim that, in the abstract, there is a way between the horns of the above dilemma. That is, I assume that he has shown that there is a space within which the rational validation of beliefs about which character traits are the virtues could proceed, unhampered by either the excessive demands of ethical foundationalism or the bogy of being nothing better than mere rationalizations of one's personal or culturally inculcated values. The particular judgements that emerged, bit by bit, from reflective scrutiny, within one's ethical outlook, might well represent a change in that outlook rather than expressing it. And those that were part of the outlook and survived the reflective scrutiny would not merely re-express it; they would now express, so to speak, that they had survived the scrutiny.

---

[5] I say 'in a manner of speaking' because there is some question as to whether we, or our descendants, with our new outlook, could understand the original one well enough to describe it as 'all wrong'. We might just find it completely incomprehensible, and thereby neither right nor wrong.

However, to establish the existence of a space is not to say anything about how it is to be filled. The general idea is that I take one of my beliefs—say, that courage is a virtue—and, holding the rest of my ethical outlook intact, put it up for question. Is it true? But where do I go from there? How do I set about trying to validate it? The neo-Aristotelian virtue ethics answer with which we began is that I turn to the second premise of the theory, namely

A virtue is a character trait a human being needs for *eudaimonia*, to flourish or live well.

I still stand by this claim, but now is the time to point out that it is much more complicated than is usually supposed—and than I supposed when I first asserted it.[6] (This is hardly surprising when one thinks of how much *weight* these second premises have to carry. If one remembers how much work is still going into discussions of what is involved in claiming that a correct moral rule is one that can be willed as a universal law, or of what decisions rational agents would come to behind Rawls's veil of ignorance , or even of what utilitarianism's second premise should be, one can expect any second premise virtue ethics comes up with to generate dispute and to call for more elaboration.) I now regard it as encapsulating something that I will dub (but not describe as) 'Plato's requirement on the virtues'.[7] This, I shall say, is made up of three theses.

(1) The virtues benefit their possessor. (They enable her to flourish, to be, and live a life that is, *eudaimon*.)

(2) The virtues make their possessor a good human being. (Human beings need the virtues in order to live well, to flourish *as* human beings, to live a characteristically good, *eudaimon*, human life.)

(3) The above two features of the virtues are interrelated.

---

[6] See *Beginning Lives*, ch. 6.

[7] Since I am far from being a Plato scholar I do not want to claim that these three theses, let alone interpreted as I am going to interpret them, are actually in Plato. But I owe the idea of them to a conversation with Julius Moravcsik, in which he attributed something very like them to Plato. And, in what follows, I have benefited greatly from Julia Annas's subtle positioning of Plato's argument for justice in a space 'which is widely regarded as untenable by both sides in a great many modern discussions of justice'. See *An Introduction to Plato's Republic* (1981), particularly under the index entries for 'consequentialist arguments'.

By way of very crude illustration, consider two significantly different sorts of answers that a fairly honest philosopher might give to the self-addressed question 'What's good about the character trait of honesty?'

(i) It's so much easier than being dishonest; you don't have to keep a constant guard on your tongue and worry about the details of what you should say—mostly you just tell the truth. Lying is usually so pointless and silly. People know and you just look a fool, trying to pretend that you never make mistakes or are admirable when you're not. It's such an essential part of good relationships that there should be trust between you; as Bacon says, 'A principal fruit of friendship is the ease and discharge of the fulness of the heart . . . No receipt openeth the heart but a true friend, to whom you may impart whatsoever lieth upon the heart to oppress it.' And who would want to be loved and respected for a façade one presents rather than what one is? And it's essential to doing philosophy and teaching it well; there's no joy in trying to arrive at views that are fashionable, only in the pursuit of truth, and you don't inspire the students if you can't convince them that you care about the truth more than anything else.

(ii) It plays such an important role in human life; it enables human beings to rely on each other, trust each other and form intimate relationships, learn from each other, do science, run various beneficial and/or worthwhile institutions efficiently. Think how much in human life hangs on the simple fact that you can ask a stranger the time or how to get somewhere in the reasonable expectation of getting an honest answer.

I hope it is clear that the significant difference between these two answers is that the first might well be construed as an answer to the question 'What is good, *for me*, about my being honest?' or even 'What do I like or enjoy about being honest? Why am I happy to be that way?' while the second might well be construed as an answer to 'Why does honesty make its possessor a good human being?' The first answer pertains to thesis (1), the second to thesis (2). And concerning thesis (3), I hope it is also clear that, despite their difference, the answers (i) and (ii) are interrelated. Answer (ii) implicitly makes some claims about what is important in human life—trusting each other and forming intimate relationships, running various institutions such as universities where we learn from each other—which (i) implicitly endorses as personal views about what is part of *my* flourishing. If only wildly eccentric human beings would hold the personal views expressed in (i), (ii)'s claims about what is important in human life would be implausible. And (i) relies on (ii)'s claims about how human life works. It assumes that honesty *is* needed in close human relationships; it assumes that it is needed for human beings to learn from each other and pursue research (at least in philosophy).

And I hope it is also clear that (i), at least, is a collection of remarks that could come only from someone with a certain ethical outlook, one according to which the exercise of honesty (at least towards one's nearest and dearest and in the pursuit of philosophy) is partially constitutive of what the speaker thinks of as flourishing or living well.

I said above that I thought the neo-Aristotelian virtue ethics approach has something distinctive and largely unrecognized to contribute to the enterprise of cracking the problem of 'the rationality of morality', but in one way it is not true that it is unrecognized. Many people familiar with Philippa Foot's 'Moral Beliefs' recognize that one thing it offers as a contribution is something along the lines of thesis (1), and Williams, most notably amongst others,[8] has made familiar the idea that Aristotelian naturalism offers something along the lines of thesis (2). What I think is largely unrecognized is that either (1) or (2) can even get off the ground, and that virtue ethics can offer *both*, in an interrelated way.[9] The view I aim to make plausible in the following chapters is that *both*,

[8] Amongst the others, see especially Gary Watson, 'On the Primacy of Character': 'Living a characteristically human life (functioning well as a human being) requires possessing and exemplifying certain traits, T. T are therefore human excellences and render their possessors to that extent good human beings.'

[9] Foot repudiates (1) in the footnote added to 'Moral Beliefs' in *Virtues and Vices*, pp. 130–1, and Williams describes (2) only to repudiate it and say that we cannot get back to Aristotle's normative view of nature. At the time of writing, Foot, in her published work, is still repudiating (1) and vigorously defending (2) (in her Hart lecture 'Does Moral Subjectivism Rest on a Mistake?' (1995), and in 'Rationality and Virtue' (1994)). McDowell, on my reading of him, has eventually come to a qualified recognition of (2) (in 'Two Sorts of Naturalism'), but remains implacably hostile to (1) as any kind of criterion of a character trait's being a virtue.

in their interrelated way, can get off the ground; that, not independently, but in combination, they provide us with the framework within which we can set about trying to validate our beliefs about which character traits are the virtues.

So the programmatic thesis is this. When, in reflective philosophic mode, we ask ourselves 'Is it true that A is a virtue, and thereby that what an A person would characteristically do is right or good action (barring tragic dilemmas)? Do I have rational grounds for believing this, and thereby for believing that what I should do is what an A agent would characteristically do?' we should bring both theses (1) and (2) to bear. 'We should' bring them to bear because this looks like a genuinely promising track to follow. The thesis is programmatic because, as I said above, no one has yet tried to work it out in any detail, and in advance of any detailed attempts, no one, myself included, can have any certainty that its promise will not fail.

Having stressed at the outset that theses (1) and (2 ) are interrelated, I am now going to discuss them separately, and bring them together again later. The topic of the remainder of this chapter is thesis (1).

## OBJECTIONS TO THE VERY IDEA

The claim that the virtues benefit their possessor because they enable her to flourish, to be, and live a life that is *eudaimon*, is standardly taken as intended to provide a motivating reason, perhaps to most, perhaps to everyone, for being virtuous (or indeed, moral) in accordance with the standard list of the virtues. It is important for me to emphasize that that is not primarily how I intend it. I am thinking of it as a starting point in an enterprise of critical reflection on the standard list—on whether one's views about which character traits are the virtues are correct.

However, in order to fulfil this role, the claim must have at least a *prima facie* plausibility with respect to the standard list,[10] so I need

---

[10] I agree with Sarah Conly, 'Flourishing and the Failure of the Ethics of Virtue' (1988), to this extent, that if one aims to offer a justification of the virtues as we (take ourselves to) know them, one had better not begin with something that immediately promises to validate cruelty, selfishness, dishonesty, disloyalty . . . as virtues.

to defend it against those who, construing it as a claim about the standard list, think that it is obviously false.

The first essential step towards getting clear about what is at issue is to recognize that 'the' question 'Does being virtuous (honest, just, charitable, etc.) benefit the one who is?' is ambiguous. It can mean 'Does doing what is virtuous, being virtuous on a particular occasion, always benefit the agent?' (Call this 'the particular question'.) Or it can mean 'Does possession and exercise of the virtues benefit the one who has them over all?' (Call this 'the general question'.) A plausible answer to one version of the question might well be an implausible answer to the other.[11]

The second essential step is to recognize that the question 'Do the virtues (on the standard list) benefit their possessor?' can be considered in very different contexts. We may feel compelled to disavow it in the philosophical context of considering what we could say to the wicked or the moral sceptic without noticing that we accept it in other contexts such as considering how to bring up our children.

Failure to take these steps has bedevilled much of the discussion. Let me begin with the ambiguity of 'Does being virtuous (according to the standard list) benefit the one who is?'

Precisely the same ambiguity infects the question 'Why should I be moral (or virtuous)?' in terms of which this issue is usually discussed. And it should be immediately obvious that the answer to the particular question 'Does doing what is virtuous (what is, say, honest or courageous or charitable) on a particular occasion always benefit the agent, enabling her to flourish etc?' is 'No'. Here is an occasion where, say, if I speak out as I should, I am going to be shut in an asylum and subjected to enforced drugging; here is another where doing what is courageous maims me for life; here is another where if I do what is charitable I shall probably die. The answer to the particular question, on these occasions, just cannot be 'If you want to be happy, lead a successful, flourishing life, you should do what is honest or courageous or charitable *here*—you will find that it pays off'. (Within, that is, a secular morality. Of course it makes a difference if I have the possibility of a 'life' after this one. And I

---

[11] Cf. Foot: 'The reason why it seems to some people so impossibly difficult to show that justice is more profitable than injustice is that they consider in isolation particular just acts.' 'Moral Beliefs', 129.

shall discuss later those who, even within a secular morality, deny that I am harmed when my virtuous action brings about my death or disablement.)

So, putting the particular question to one side for the moment (it will rapidly return), let us concentrate on 'the general question' of whether the virtues (on the standard list) benefit their possessor, enabling her to flourish over all. Here too, many people think the answer must be 'No', for two reasons. One is the claim that virtue is not sufficient for happiness or *eudaimonia* and the second is the claim that it is not necessary. It is not necessary, since it is generally acknowledged that the wicked may flourish like the green bay tree. And it is not sufficient because of those nasty cases that came up in consideration of the particular question. (I said it would rapidly return.) As soon as it is admitted that exercising virtue on a particular occasion may lead to my life's being cut short, or to its ruin, the claim that virtue is sufficient for *eudaimonia* is undercut.

The brisk response to the first claim is to deny that 'The virtues benefit their possessor, enabling her to flourish' was ever supposed to provide a guarantee or a sufficient condition.[12]

Suppose my doctor said, 'You would benefit from a regimen in which you gave up smoking, took regular exercise, and moderated your drinking.' Her grounds are that that's the way to flourish physically, to be healthy, to live a long, healthy life. But she does not thereby offer me a guarantee of a long healthy life. If, despite following her advice, I develop lung cancer or heart disease or my liver fails, in my youth or middle age, this does not impugn the correctness of what she said; I can't go back to her and say, 'You were wrong to tell me I should give up smoking, etc.—look, it hasn't worked.' She and I both know that doing as she says does not guarantee perfect health; nevertheless, if perfect health is what I want, the only thing to do is to follow her advice and hope that I shall not be unlucky.

Similarly, the claim is not that possession of the virtues guarantees that one will flourish. The claim is that they are the only reliable bet—even though, it is agreed, I might be unlucky and, precisely because of my virtue, wind up dying early or with my life marred or ruined.

---

[12] In committing myself to defending 'Plato's requirement', I have committed myself to defending the claim as stated at the outset of this chapter, not Plato, according to whom virtue is supposed to be sufficient for *eudaimonia*.

It is a puzzle, to which I shall return in a minute, why the mere threat of virtue leading to one's downfall (as though vice did not carry a similar risk) should be thought to undermine the claim that it is one's only reliable bet as far as a flourishing life is concerned. But, for the moment, let us press on and note that the health analogy, with its claim that acquiring and exercising the virtues is the only reliable bet, seems to lay us open to the second objection. Why should we accept that 'the only thing to do' is to acquire and exercise the virtues, as if, despite not being a sufficient condition of happiness, virtue was necessary? Given the acknowledged threat of the possibility that one's life will be cut short or ruined, shouldn't we, if we have any sense, be looking for an alternative? And don't the wicked, flourishing like the green bay tree, offer one?

There is a brisk response to this objection too which, once again, exploits the medical analogy. Does my doctor's right answer to my question about how I should live claim that following the regimen she outlines is necessary for a long healthy life? No, because if it did, it would be readily falsified; the newspapers regularly describe the lives of people who have achieved remarkable longevity and are in as healthy a state as anyone of their age could possibly be expected to be, despite flouting at least some of the requirements she laid down. (As I write, a splendid old lady in France has clocked up 120 years—and gave up smoking at 115.) To claim that the virtues, for the most part, benefit their possessor, enabling her to flourish, is not to claim that virtue is necessary for happiness. It is to claim that no 'regimen' will serve one better—no other candidate 'regimen' is remotely plausible.

As with the appeal to the possibility that my virtue may lead to my downfall, there is something odd about the way in which the appeal to the wicked who flourish operates in this debate. Given the medical analogy, the mere fact that some wicked people flourish— for example, some of the Nazis who ran concentration camps and then escaped to South America and lived (and perhaps, in a few cases are still living) the life of Riley, benefited materially by their past wickedness, and happily unwracked by any remorse—should be neither here nor there. Logically, their existence no more impugns the correctness of 'The virtues benefit their possessor' than the existence of the few centenarians who have regularly smoked and consumed remarkable quantities of alcohol impugns the correctness of my doctor's saying, 'A regimen of not smoking,

moderate alcohol intake, regular exercise, etc. benefits those who
follow it.' What is needed, to discredit the answer, is not just a few
cases, but a clearly identifiable pattern. The objection should be not
'What about those few Nazis and murderous bank robbers in South
America?' but 'What about this pattern that we can all perceive in
life, the pattern according to which the evil regularly triumph and
the good get done down?'

Now someone might bring this claim about a pattern in life as
an objection to the view that the virtues benefit their possessor, and
it is one I shall mention later. But it is not the one that is usually
made in the philosophical literature. It is just the few cases of the
wicked who get away with it that present themselves as the stumbling block, and that this is so is a second puzzle.

At least a partial explanation of both puzzles lies, I believe, in the
following: those who draw attention to the fact that my virtue may
lead to my downfall and/or the fact that the wicked sometimes
flourish like the green bay tree are, perhaps unconsciously, thinking
of these as the obvious responses that would be made by the wicked
or 'the moral sceptic' if we were to recommend the life of virtue to
them on the grounds of the benefit that it will bring. They foresee
that, if we tried to convince them that the life of virtue was worth
the risk, whereas the life of vice (which clearly carries its own risks)
was not, we shall fail. They will just laugh at us and go their merry
wicked way, finding our answer completely implausible.

At this point of the discussion, we need to make what I claimed
was 'the second essential step' and consider different contexts in
which we might consider the view that the virtues benefit their possessor.

## DIFFERENT CONTEXTS

It is too readily assumed that a failure to convince the wicked or the
moral sceptic that the virtues benefit their possessor (because possessing virtue is the only reliable way to lead a happy life) discred-
its the claim, showing it to be generally implausible and a
non-starter. But once that assumption is made manifest, it does not
look clearly true. Few of us (by which I mean myself and you, my
readers) are likely to be steeped in vice or to be genuine moral sceptics. Thereby we believe many things we know we couldn't convince

them of, but we do not reject those beliefs as implausible just because of that. We should look at what we think about the virtues benefiting their possessor in other contexts before abandoning it as a non-starter.

R. M. Hare perceptively considers what we think about it in the context of bringing up our children and, as we say 'preparing them for life' and beginning their moral education.[13] Why do we go in for the moral education of our children—what is our motivation? One answer might be that we think that our own lives will be easier if we bring our children up to be virtuous rather than undisciplined selfish egoists; we try to bring them up to be virtuous for our sakes. Another might be that we are ourselves so impartially high-minded that we are thinking in terms of how we can turn our children into altruists who will be useful to other people's children when they have grown up; we try to bring them up to be virtuous for the sake of others, or society.

But if we are good parents, neither of these answers will do. Although, no doubt, there is a grain of truth in each of them, they do not identify what chiefly motivates good parents. Good parents have their children's interests at heart. They want to do what is best or good for *them*, the individual children, to enable them to live well, be happy, make a success of their lives. But, having their children's interests at heart, it does not occur to most of them to bring them up to be entirely self-interested and immoral. On the contrary, they see the natural childish impulses to self-gratification and self-indulgence as impulses that need to be modified and redirected, and their natural impulses to love and generosity and fairness as impulses that need to be developed; they see the naturally self-centred perspective of children as something that has to be enlarged—for the child's own sake.

And thereby, good parents start inculcating the virtues—developing the character traits on the standard list—in their children from a very early age, in the belief, conscious or unconscious, that this is indeed preparing them for their lives, laying the foundations that will enable them to live well.

This is something that we should find striking. Never mind, for the moment, about irresponsible parents who do not bother about

---

[13] R. M. Hare, *Moral Thinking* (1981), ch. 11.

their children's upbringing; never mind about the fact that some parents may have very corrupt ideas about what is involved in the exercise of some or even all virtues. If we just concentrate on the fairly virtuous parents who are fairly conscientious about their children's upbringing, is it not a striking fact, in this context, that (a) they try to inculcate virtue in their children despite (b) having their children's interests at heart and wanting to prepare them for life? Perhaps in philosophic or reflective mode they might profess sincere doubt as to whether acquiring and exercising the virtues is the best way to achieve a good life; perhaps they might even deny it. But, I would say, the way they bring up their children manifests their belief that it is so.

I am not, of course, offering this point as an abstract argument for the truth of the view that the virtues on the standard list benefit their possessor. It is, rather, an *ad hominem* argument addressed to any reader who is inclined to profess the belief that the view is obviously implausible. It amounts to my asking you the question, 'Are you quite sure you believe that? If you think about what is involved in bringing up children to prepare them for life rather than imagining yourself trying to convert the wicked or convince the moral sceptic, don't you find that actually you do believe that virtue is the most reliable bet?'

It might be objected that, in so far as we believe it, we recognize it as a very local view. 'We may believe that virtue is the only reliable bet for *eudaimonia* here and now,' it may be said, 'living as we do, fairly easy and protected lives. But wouldn't we think differently if circumstances changed in such a way that virtue was likely to lead to our downfall?'

Suppose our lives were to change horribly; we fall under a vicious regime in which, it might be said, to be virtuous is not merely to run the risk of dying young or spending one's life in misery, but to court it. Under these circumstances, would we not have to admit that virtue is far from being the only reliable way to achieve *eudaimonia*? And would we not have to give our children, for their sakes, something very different from a moral education which began inculcating the virtues, to prepare them for the hard lives they were going to lead?

In neither case, I believe, is the answer a simple 'Yes.' In times of great evil, it can indeed cease to be true that those who have and exercise the virtues characteristically achieve *eudaimonia*, and thereby, virtue can indeed cease to be a reliable way to achieve it. So, to that extent, the answer to the first question is 'Yes'. But, even in such times, it is still not the case that there is some *other* reliable way. In evil times, life for most people is, or threatens to be, nasty, brutish, and short and *eudaimonia* is something that will be impossible until better times come. And in the hope that better times will come, and that their children, at least, will live to enjoy them, many parents, living under the most oppressive and dangerous regimes, have still tried to inculcate some version of virtue in their children. No doubt they have taught them versions tailored to the extreme circumstances in which they live; no doubt they have to lay great emphasis on prudence, to teach a caution about, and detachment from, others that would count as lacking trust and being callous in a better society. But teaching a tailored version is a far cry from abandoning the whole idea and bringing them up to hope for nothing better than survival at the expense of others.

Just as we may be surprised by the realization that good parents, who have their children's interests at heart, try to inculcate virtue in them, for the children's own sake, we may be surprised by the realization that, personally, our answer to the question 'Why should I be virtuous/moral?' may be 'I want to be—that's the sort of life I want to live, the sort that I think is a good and successful and rewarding one.'

Contemplating the lives of, say, those who are wealthy and powerful, and, apparently at least, perfectly happy, but who lie and cheat and ruthlessly sacrifice some others when it suits them, we may find that we do not regard them as enviable or desirable at all. The wealth and influence might be nice to have, but not at the cost of living like that. And contemplating our own lives, we may find many sources of dissatisfaction, but quite possibly none that we attribute to our possession of such virtues as we have. On the contrary, we may find ourselves inclined to attribute some of them to the imperfection of such possession. 'If only I could be less selfish and self-centred, more thankful for what I have, more concerned with the good of others and the good *in* them, how much happier I would be,' is not an uncommon thought. Considered in the context of reflection on one's own character and life, the view that the virtues on the standard list benefit their possessor looks as plausible as it does in the context of bringing up our children to which Hare directs us.

## NO NEUTRAL VIEWPOINT

So suppose that the very idea that the virtues on the standard list benefit their possessor is not obviously false. There is still the question of whether we can give any grounds for it. Well, Hare not only states his conviction, which I share, that for our own children's sakes, we should bring them up to possess the character traits on the standard list; he gives grounds for it, many similar to those Foot had given in support of the view that justice, in particular, benefits its possessor.[14] Where I depart from him is not so much over these grounds, with which I mostly also agree, but over the status he assigns to them.

He says that it would not be in the child's interest to bring him up to be a (cautious) immoralist because human beings are, for the most part, incapable of getting away with this. One would have to be 'an exceptionally talented devil' and we have no way of knowing in advance that a child has this 'talent'. He says:

> successful crime is for nearly everyone an impossibly difficult game and not worth the candle. If it is alleged against this that in the past people have amassed large fortunes in business careers which were far from unspotted, I reply that the money did not on the whole bring them happiness, and that with their talents they could have done better for themselves by making less money in a more socially beneficial career. If there are exceptions, they are rare enough to be unpredictable by an educator.

He says that 'by far the easiest way of seeming upright is to be upright'. Referring (we may suppose) to virtues such as charity, generosity, loyalty, honesty and justice as 'the dispositions which make possible mutual cooperation and affection', he says that without them, 'all our endeavours would miscarry, and all the joy and warmth in life would disappear. Those who do not love their fellow men are less successful in living happily among them'. He even says that 'it does look as if people who set themselves higher moral standards which are within their capacity, or not too far outside it, are in general happier than those who do not set their sights so high'.[15]

With these claims I basically agree. But he describes all of them as 'empirical' claims about the way human life works ('the way the

---

[14] Foot, 'Moral Beliefs'.
[15] *Moral Thinking*, ch. 11 *passim*.

world goes') and regards them as providing reasons 'of a non-moral sort' for not choosing to be an amoralist 'from the point of view of an egoist', and I do not agree with him that they have this status. When Hare makes these claims he does not, it seems to me, speak from a neutral point of view he might share with an egoist, but from the point of view of the humane, high-principled man that he is, the man who regards Albert Schweitzer and Mother Teresa as 'very saintly' (rather than cranks or deluded fools who wasted their lives) and Oxfam as doing 'wonders' (rather than tipping good money down the drain).

The trouble with supposing (as I take it Hare does) that these claims about human nature and the way life works are 'empirical' and thereby recognizable by anyone, is that we can all so readily imagine the immoralist/egoist disagreeing with them. The immoralist may deny that exceptional talent is called for—just a reasonable amount of *nous*, which he, of course, has. Valuing wealth and power as he does, he denies that successful crime is not worth the candle; not only does Hare overestimate the risks, but the really big rewards at stake justify a high-risk strategy anyhow. Of *course* large amounts of money 'on the whole' bring people happiness, he says, though it is true that some people are foolish enough to throw this happiness away by getting too involved with some of their fellow human beings instead of sensibly making sure the ones you associate with are always in your control. There is nothing particularly difficult about seeming upright when it is necessary; you can fool most of the people most of the time. And so on.

And this, it may be said, is inevitable rather than surprising. There is no possibility of 'justifying morality from the outside' by appealing to anything 'non-moral', or by finding a neutral point of view that the fairly virtuous and the wicked can share. We may say, with Hare, that the greedy and dishonest are not *eudaimon*, not truly happy, that they are missing out on 'joy and warmth', but when we do, we are not making a merely empirical remark, based on the observation that all of them go round with long faces saying, 'Oh, woe is me.' We are, in part, saying, 'That's not the sort of life *I* count as *eudaimon*, because it does not involve the exercise of the virtues.'

However, note the qualification 'in part'. For although I accept that there is no neutral point of view from which morality can be justified, I want to disagree with the construction that D. Z. Phillips

and John McDowell (both responding to the Foot of 'Moral Beliefs'
rather than to Hare) have put on that claim in this context.[16] Unlike
them, I think that the sorts of claims Foot and Hare make in support of their view that the virtues on the standard list benefit their
possessor are worth making and have a role to play. For, briefly
sketched as they are, I think that their grounds do provide some
rational support for our belief that the standard list of the virtues is
the correct one. Although they must be regarded as only programmatic (for, in theory, each individual candidate virtue would have
to be thus grounded in detail and at length), they certainly look
promising. Agreed, they are promising only as a way in which we
might validate our beliefs about the standard list from within the
ethical outlook we share with Hare and Foot, not from a neutral
point of view common to us and the immoralist or egoist. But, once
that point is made clear, there is, I shall argue, no reason to deny
that they are exactly the sorts of considerations that can, indeed,
play a role in validating our belief that the character traits on the
standard list are, in truth, the virtues.

Let me emphasize again that I do not regard their role as providing a motivating reason for being virtuous. Phillips and
McDowell are both concerned to stress the familiar point that virtuous action is to be chosen for its own sake, for the right reasons,
and both seem to suppose that any attempt to provide grounds of
the sort Foot and Hare do for their belief that the virtues on the
standard list benefit their possessor must, somehow, be ignoring
that point. But one can, as a fairly virtuous person (such as Hare
and Foot are), be adequately motivated to perform virtuous actions
for the right reasons and, as a quite separate issue, give justifying
grounds for one's belief that the virtues on the standard list benefit
their possessor. So I put the motivation question aside here as a red
herring.[17]

Phillips and McDowell, as I understand them, maintain the following:

---

[16] D. Z. Phillips 'Does It Pay to be Good?' (1964); John McDowell, 'The Role of
*Eudaimonia* in Aristotle's Ethics' (1980).

[17] As Michael Slote notes, there is a distinction between seeking reassurance
about whether morality pays (which shows lack of virtue) and treating the question
'as a purely philosophical issue', *Goods and Virtues* (1983), 113, n. 9. One of the few
people who manages to do the latter is Brad Hooker, in 'Does Moral Virtue
Constitute a Benefit to the Agent?' (1996).

(1) It is only from within the outlook of the (at least moderately) virtuous that the truth of 'the virtues benefit their possessor' can be discerned.

(2) From the perspective of this outlook it is necessarily or infallibly true that the virtues benefit their possessor, because

(3) The virtuous have a conception of *eudaimonia*, of benefit, advantage, harm and loss, of 'profit' and 'what pays' such that nothing gained by action contrary to virtue pays or is a genuine advantage or benefit, and no sacrifice necessitated by virtue counts as a loss. In virtuous action one 'accomplishes all', achieves 'moral benefit', and since the virtues, uniquely, enable one to act virtuously, and never fail to do so, they are, indeed, guaranteed to benefit their possessor, enabling her to achieve *eudaimonia*, namely, a life lived in accordance with the virtues.

In the light of these conceptions, there is no room for questions about whether virtue or vice is a more reliable bet, whether someone particularly cunning might live a successful life of crime, whether wealth 'on the whole' brings happiness, whether the easiest way of seeming upright is being upright, whether human beings need other human beings and cannot 'beat them into reliable submission like donkeys'.[18] All these putative facts, yea or nay, are simply irrelevant to the question of whether the virtues benefit their possessor, because, from within the outlook of the virtuous, no such question can arise; it is already settled. And, if they are not relevant to whether the virtues benefit their possessor, what is the point of asserting the yeas or nays? Surely it can be nothing but the misguided attempt to justify morality from the outside.

But Phillips and McDowell always limit the raising of questions about whether virtue or vice is a more reliable bet and suchlike to the context of the immoralist or egoist. They never consider whether the putative facts Hare and Foot appeal to might not figure not only properly, but quite essentially, in what the virtuous say to their children as they are bringing them up, and to themselves, in reflective mode.

---

[18] Foot, 'Moral Beliefs', 129.

I shall argue that they do.

Phillips and McDowell are obviously right that the virtuous and the immoralist are going to have distinctively different views on what counts as, for example, benefit and advantage, harm and loss. I find a full purse lying in the street; to the immoralist, this is a beneficial windfall; to me it's a nuisance because I'll have to take it to the police station and I'm trying to catch a train. Someone points out in public that I have not done something I promised to do. The immoralist regards himself as having been put at a disadvantage; now he will have to keep the promise or come up with an excuse. I regard myself as benefited, because I had clean forgotten and can now make sure I keep the promise. And we certainly have different conceptions of *eudaimonia*. Whether he thinks of it as the life of wealth, power, pleasure, or the discovery of scientific truth, he thinks that achieving these ends is all that counts, not by what means they are achieved, whereas I think that, whatever my personal ends, they are not to be pursued by means contrary to virtue; that *eudaimonia* cannot be achieved that way.

But to say that we differ is not to say that we have no overlap at all, and yet this is what Phillips and McDowell seem to want to say, insisting that to the virtuous, 'no sacrifice necessitated by the life of excellence . . . can count as a genuine loss' (McDowell) and that no disaster that the virtuous bring upon themselves through their virtue *is* a disaster (Phillips). So if virtue necessitates your losing all your possessions and becoming destitute, or losing your limbs, or eyes, or freedom, indeed your mental faculties or your life, this is no loss and no disaster to the virtuous.

To insist on such a view is surely to deny the possibility of resolvable tragic dilemmas discussed in Chapter 3,[19] and although such a harsh, Stoicized view can hardly be described as painting a rosy picture of life, it can be described as unrealistic.

It may be that both Phillips and McDowell have simply overlooked the sorts of examples that I would count as being paradigm

---

[19] McDowell may have modified his position somewhat, since he now acknowledges the possibility of tragic cases in which 'no available action can count as doing well by the light of one's conception of doing well' (34, n. 15 of 'Deliberation and Moral Development'). But it is not clear. If he is thinking of irresolvable rather than resolvable tragic dilemmas, as seems quite likely, he has still not retracted the claim that 'no sacrifice necessitated by the life of excellence . . . can count as a genuine loss', for it is only in resolvable tragic dilemmas that what is done is *necessitated* by virtue.

examples of tragic resolvable dilemmas. Nothing either says so much as hints that they have considered, for example, dying not to serve some noble cause but only because you have fallen into the hands of a mad tyrant and, despite his threats, refused to do something wicked,[20] or having to leave one of your children to die in a fire because, though willing to lose your life to save hers, you are physically capable of saving only the other one. (No loss? No disaster?) They both seem to have in mind laying down one's life or sustaining great 'loss' for a noble cause.

This, to my ears, smacks of a masculine yearning for the ideal of 'the short life with glory'.[21] At least part of the reason why death or complete destitution or loss of one's limbs or one's mental faculties should be regarded as a harm, loss, or disaster by the virtuous is that they render you entirely or relatively incapable of doing anything further for anyone else, and cause great grief to those who care about you. These things can all be regarded as losses and disasters by the virtuous without their losing sight, for a moment, of the fact that, in *these* circumstances, one just has to risk bringing them upon oneself, or, indeed, courting them as a certainty.

That last distinction—between risking and courting as a certainty—brings me back to the question of whether the sorts of claims Foot and Hare make have any role to play. According to Phillips's and McDowell's picture, virtue (from the point of view of the virtuous) is bound to benefit its possessor simply because it enables its possessor to act well and thereby 'accomplish all', never sustaining thereby any loss or disaster. But is this what we teach, or could teach, our children?

It is one thing to bring up children to recognize that the life of virtue is not guaranteed to be a rose-garden, to prepare them for the idea that it may call for sacrificing one's life, and to inculcate the idea that this may be well worth doing. It is quite another to attempt to do so without stressing the fact that people do not always lose

---

[20] David Wiggins notes something strained in McDowell's willingness to leave unquestioned Aristotle's claims that the courageous always act for the sake of the noble or acting well (*eupraxia*), pointing out that although acting to avoid the base is related to acting for the sake of the noble, they are not the same. 'Compare,' he says, 'the audible difference between being glad you're not dead (after a near miss at a crossroads) and being glad you are alive.' 'Eudaimonism and Realism in Aristotle's Ethics', 223, n. 2.

[21] Unsurprisingly, there is more than a hint of this Homeric idea in Aristotle himself. See *Nicomachean Ethics* 1169a20–6.

their lives when they put them on the line and that people who are unwilling to risk their lives frequently lose out. If we brought them up exclusively on stories in which the virtuous lost their lives when they risked them, and those who aimed to save their own skin always survived, if those were the only cases in the newspapers to which we drew their attention, I doubt that (again within secular households) we would succeed in instilling virtue in them.

Of course the grosser children's moral tales tend to foster the idea that virtuous action brings gross rewards. The hero saves another, or shares his last loaf of bread in the desert, or tells the truth, putting his life on the line, and lo and behold! it has just been a test, for the passing of which he is lavishly rewarded; the anti-hero behaves badly, fails the test, and loses out on the princess and the kingdom. But others foster a picture of how life works which is not unrealistic; the heroine risks her life and *survives*, her life unmarred; the anti-hero behaves badly and comes to a sticky end. Surely, along with teaching children that helping others in need is a good reason for doing something and that the fact that something is the truth is a good reason for speaking it, it is essential to teach them that if they risk danger in acting well they do not thereby court certain death or disaster.

More generally, we encourage them to believe that, if they act well, things will go well. When the child acts well, in the way we have urged, and things do go well, we point this out and stress it as something to be expected, in contrast to when they act badly and receive ill-treatment in return. ('You can't expect him to be nice to you if you're not nice to him.') When the child acts well and gets kicked in the teeth for its efforts, we emphasize that they *did* act well, we say we are proud of them—but it would be an odd parent who always simply left it at that, as if this consequence was only to be expected and did not call for comment. Don't we sympathize, say how terrible, perhaps condemn the ingratitude or meanness of the other person involved, perhaps say it was well worth a try and what bad luck, and in general convey the idea that this is *not* a pattern in life that the child simply has to put up with if it is to go on getting our praise? As before, it is one thing to bring up children to seek the good of others, to be generous with their possessions, to tell the truth, to be fair, for virtuous reasons, not for the sake of immediate returns. It is quite another to attempt to do so without stressing the fact that decent returns can reasonably be expected from ordinary people as a pattern in life. (How could we bring them up to be good friends, charitable, loyal, even just, rather than censorious, self-righteous, and deeply misanthropic, if we didn't stress that?)

So, contrary to Phillips and McDowell, I do not think that we have conceptions of *eudaimonia*, benefit, harm, disaster, etc. such that no sacrifice necessitated by virtue counts as a loss, nor do I think that this is because we are all imperfect in virtue. I think our conceptions of loss, harm, disaster, the conceptions we began to form in our childhood, though distinctively different from those of the immoralist, overlap with his with respect to such things as death, physical injury, suffering, and helplessness. But one way in which we differ from him is that we do not think that the exercise of virtue characteristically brings these things in their train, or is more likely to do so than the exercise of egoism (except, as noted above, in evil times). We think that (for the most part, by and large), if we act well, things go well for us. When it does not, when *eudaimonia* is impossible to achieve or maintain, that's not 'what we should have expected' but tragically bad luck.

Our conceptions overlap with those of the immoralist in another respect too. That the life of virtue can be represented as enjoyable and satisfying is not solely a matter of a special employment of the terms 'enjoyable' and 'satisfying' that only the virtuous can understand. Although, if we are fairly virtuous, we and the immoralist do not enjoy, or take delight in, or find satisfying many of the same things, it is a fact, observable by the immoralist, that we really do enjoy ours. He may (if he bothers to think about it) find it strange or risible that our lives manifestly contain 'joy and warmth', and that we are manifestly 'living happily', in Hare's words. He may despise us for being content with, from his point of view, so little, but we do not need to tell him that we are enjoying ourselves in some arcane sense that he does not grasp—he can see and hear that we are, in a sense he grasps perfectly well. (I need a shorthand description for the indications of enjoyment—that things are done with zest and enthusiasm, anticipated and recalled in certain tones of voice with certain facial expressions, and in a certain vocabulary, and so on—so I shall call them 'the smile factor'.)

There is a charming Thurber cartoon which depicts a riotously drunk woman who is clearly having a whale of a time being contemplated with frosty disapproval by a dour man in a dog-collar who is saying, 'Unhappy woman!' Now part of what makes this

funny, I take it, is not so much that describing this obviously cheer-
ful woman as unhappy is completely inappropriate, for it makes
good sense to pity people who habitually get very drunk, no matter
how much they may enjoy themselves at the time. What is inappropriate is that the man who calls her unhappy so clearly never
enjoys himself, by the criterion of the smile factor, at all. If she may
truly be described as unhappy, so may he, and in vain might he
protest that his life is supremely happy because it is the life of virtue
and that he delights (in his own strange way that only the virtuous
can understand) in his virtuous actions. If he never enjoys himself in
the straightforward way evidenced by the smile factor then, though
his life may be the life of continence, it cannot be the life of virtue.

And this, once again, is an important factor in our bringing up
of our children. We can, and do, represent the life lived in accordance with the virtues to our children as (for the most part) enjoyable and satisfying, as containing the benefit and advantage of
enjoyment and satisfaction. True, we have to 'train them from
infancy to feel joy and grief at the right things',[22] amending, developing, complicating, and enriching their desires, but we should find
striking the fact that the upshot of such training can *be* the enjoyment of virtuous activity. We can represent giving pleasure to others, helping, co-operative activity, companionship, harmony rather
than strife, truth-telling, even the conquering of (some) fear and the
endurance of (some) pain and discomfort, to our children as enjoyable in themselves, as well as being good or praiseworthy or having
to be done, in the full confidence that they will indeed come to find
them enjoyable, as we have.

This is not to renege on the qualifications I put on the claim that
'virtuous conduct gives pleasure to the lover of virtue' in Chapter 4,
nor is it to suggest, absurdly, that we bring up our children to do
things for and with others solely with a view to enjoying themselves.
We urge proto-virtuous actions *for X reasons* on them, not for
immediate gratification; but it is no mere accident that we present
some of them, such as going to the dentist without making a fuss,
as things that have to be done, that will please us, that will be over
quickly, that won't be so bad, and that will be rewarded by a treat
afterwards, and others, such as giving other people nice Christmas
presents, simply as rewarding in themselves.

---

[22] Aristotle, *Nicomachean Ethics* 1104b10–11, alluding to Plato.

McDowell, rightly, wants to deny that the life of virtue can be shown to be maximally desirable by canons of desirability available from the neutral point of view, that is, available to the virtuous and the vicious alike. Phillips, rightly, wants to deny that something similar can be shown about the life of virtue on the basis of facts about human good and harm available from the neutral point of view. But one can maintain this position without going to the implausible lengths of claiming that the virtuous and vicious share no views about death and suffering as, in general, undesirable and harmful, and enjoyment as, in general, desirable and a human good.

It is as though McDowell and Phillips construe the claim 'Morality can't be justified from the outside—from the neutral point of view', as something that has to be made true by insisting that any facts recognizable by the virtuous and vicious alike would necessarily be irrelevant. But why so? As things are, it is true that morality can't be justified from the outside. But if things were otherwise—if, for instance, our nature was such that virtue was healthy and vice unhealthy, so that virtue characteristically yielded long life and vice was fatal—would it not then be true that 'morality could be justified from the outside'?

It might be thought that this is a dangerous idea. For does it not allow that if, contrariwise, it were vice that yielded long life and virtue that dropped you in your tracks at thirty, it would be immorality and wickedness that were justified? For reasons that I hope will emerge in the following chapters, I would say 'No', because the latter is not a coherent supposition. If we had, by nature, been like that, the whole history of our ethical thought would be unimaginably different, for amongst the natural facts that underlie our concept of virtue are the following: the fact that virtue is not unhealthy, nor vice healthy, that the virtuous are no strangers to enjoyment, and those facts that Foot and Hare appeal to in support of the claim that the virtues on the standard list benefit their possessor.

## FACTS WITHIN AN ETHICAL OUTLOOK

The (observable, empirical) fact that the virtuous are no strangers to enjoyment (by the evidence of the smile factor), and the sorts of claims Foot and Hare make, fall well short of justifying morality from the outside. For, as I have noted, the immoralist who recognizes that the virtuous are enjoying their lives may dismiss their enjoyments and satisfactions as paltry, or pathetic, or despicable, or, at the very least, not for him; from his point of view, that is how they look in contrast to the sorts of things he enjoys and finds satisfying. The virtuous may claim that he is wrong about this, that their enjoyments and satisfactions are better than his—more readily come by, safer, longer lasting, less subject to the vagaries of luck. (Here Hare, without resorting to his virtuous conception of *eudaimonia*, may point to the many known examples in which the materialistic, intemperate, and profligate wind up on the psychiatrist's couch saying, 'Woe is me, my life is dust and ashes, lacking joy and warmth.')[23] But it is all too readily imaginable that he will either dismiss these claims as irrelevant, or the examples as atypical, as we can imagine him disagreeing with all of Hare's and Foot's other claims. The virtuous point out that someone who is generous and charitable is likely to enjoy the benefits of being liked and loved, which the selfish and callous miss out on. The immoralist says— what? Perhaps that he regards this as no loss because he is strong and independent and doesn't need close personal relationships; perhaps that he *is* loved and is surrounded by friends. The virtuous say they are no true friends and cannot be relied on; he says the virtuous can't rely on theirs either; the virtuous point to occasions when their friends have treated them with outstanding generosity and charity; he says they had ulterior motives, or that the virtuous can count themselves astonishingly lucky. The virtuous point to the occasions when people who live like him are stabbed in the back by their so-called friends; he points to the occasions when the virtuous bring disaster and loss on themselves, the virtuous say this was just bad luck, he says it's only to be expected, and so on and so forth.

Now the interesting thing about these sorts of disagreements, and the imagined disagreements over Hare's and Foot's claims, is not that we have, as far as I know, no idea at all how to set about resolving them at a philosophical level (or, if we take this as different, at the level of rational debate), but rather that we do not have any clear idea of how to *classify* what they are about.

---

[23] For a practising psychotherapist's account of the view that vice leads to unhappiness and virtue to happiness, see the long-term bestselling *The Road Less Travelled* by M. Scott Peck (1978).

Our picture of empirical facts is that they are facts accessible from 'the neutral point of view'. Those who subscribe to a form of moral realism can also form a picture of 'evaluative' or 'moral' facts that are only accessible from within a well-formed ethical outlook, but are facts nonetheless, such as that, in these circumstances, it is rational to do so-and-so because it is virtuous, that doing it would bring one, or would constitute, a benefit, that it would be acting well. And those who reject this picture of moral facts can still produce an analogue of it in terms of evaluative beliefs or projected attitudes. But the beliefs and putative facts about who can and cannot be relied on, about whether you can fool most of the people most of the time, or whether they can easily be manipulated, about what can be discerned to be a pattern in life, what is to be attributed to good or bad luck and what is 'just what is to be expected'— about, in short, human nature and the way human life works—do not fall tidily under either classification. Neither side believes what they believe about how life works on the basis of even local, let alone worldwide, observation or statistical analysis. The beliefs are part and parcel of their ethical (or immoralist) outlook, and the (imagined) disagreements surely count as ethical disagreements. But they are far from being *obviously* part of an ethical outlook, and far from being obvious candidates for 'evaluative beliefs'. It is hardly surprising that Hare took his to be empirical/non-moral, and that Phillips regards Foot's arguments as having an 'empirical character', for very few of them can be regarded as being about values.

For want of anything better, I suppose we could classify them as 'ethical but non-evaluative beliefs about human nature and how human life goes'. But if we do classify them thus, the parameters of the contemporary debate about the rationality or objectivity of morality shift. The debate ceases to be (what is quite problematic enough) solely a debate about what should be said about *evaluative* beliefs or whether there are *evaluative* states of affairs such as 'that certain things are better than others, that a certain thing is the thing to do on a certain occasion and so on'.[24] It will have to encompass these other sorts of beliefs too.

---

[24] As Barry Stroud puts it, in the context of discussing what would be involved in giving a non-reductive account of ethics (a reductive account being one that seeks 'an understanding of evaluations as built up out of non-evaluative ingredients alone'). 'The Charm of Naturalism' (1996), 54.

Now from the perspective of neo-Aristotelian virtue ethics, this is not particularly surprising—albeit no less problematic. For *phronesis*—moral or practical wisdom—is, we virtue ethicists say, a form of knowledge, and something that, characteristically, is not to be found in the young and inexperienced. And what do we—not just virtue ethicists, but anyone who employs the concept of moral wisdom—say about the young and inexperienced? Not just that their values are wrong or crude—in fact, sometimes their values are very fine—but that they do not understand human nature or the way human life works. Getting *those* things right is, speaking very generally, what moral wisdom is all about. Getting them wrong is the folly from which, sadly, so much human wickedness springs, and the folly we try to correct in our adolescent children, and the young people who fall under our sway, when we see them being tempted by fantasies about how they might reap the advantages of virtue and vice simultaneously (because they fancy themselves to be particularly clever, or insightful, or charming, or strong).

I said, at the beginning of this chapter, that my aim was programmatic, that I wanted to show that virtue ethics had something distinctive to offer to the current debate about the objectivity or rationality of morality. My conclusion, in this chapter, is that it offers a distinctively unfamiliar version of the view that morality is a form of enlightened self-interest, a version *so* unfamiliar that probably, as things are at the moment, that is a dangerously misleading way to describe it. For within the parameters of the current debate, that description connotes one of only two things. It can connote the view that morality is a form of 'enlightened self-interest' specified from the neutral point of view—and I deny that. Or it can connote the view that morality is a form of 'enlightened self-interest' specified in a 'value-laden' way, from within an ethical outlook. I have not disassociated myself entirely from this latter view—I agreed with Phillips and McDowell that the virtuous and the immoralist have some different views about what counts as advantage, and loss, and *eudaimonia*—but I have stressed the point that the extensions of 'value-laden' and 'from within an ethical outlook' do not coincide. These peculiar beliefs that Hare and Foot and I and (my supposition is) most of my readers share about human nature and the way human life works, which the immoralists we imagine do not share, are part of our ethical outlook all right, but are not 'value-laden' or 'evaluative' according to any current understanding of those terms.

The idea that morality is, provably from a neutral point of view, a form of enlightened self-interest has some currency. Hare supports it. David Gauthier supports it.[25] Peter Singer seems to be a recent convert to it.[26] It's around and it has its critics as well as its supporters. Its critics (apart from those who complain that it is improperly attempting to provide the wrong sorts of reasons for acting well) focus on ways in which various immoralists might disagree, and locate the source of disagreement in the different *values* (or desires or projects or ends) they suppose their immoralist to have. But the idea that we have to interpret the claim in terms of parameters that import the idea of *phronesis*—of an understanding of human nature and how human life works in a way that is not a matter of adverting to facts available from within a neutral point of view—is, as far as I know, quite unrecognized in the current literature.

[25] D. Gauthier, *Moral Dealing* (1990).
[26] Singer, *How Are We to Live?*

# 9

# Naturalism

In this chapter I turn to the second thesis of what I called 'Plato's requirement on the virtues' (p. 167 above), the thesis that the virtues make their possessor good *qua* human being. As in the preceding chapter, the aim is to show that the thesis can get off the ground as a criterion for a particular character trait's being a virtue. Virtue ethics, or at least any form of it that takes its inspiration from Aristotle, is usually taken to be a form of ethical naturalism—broadly, the enterprise of basing ethics in some way on considerations of human nature, on what is involved in being good *qua* human being—and a fundamental doubt about whether this could possibly work has been well described by Gary Watson. He says:

Many of our modern suspicions can be put in the form of a dilemma. Either the theory's pivotal account of human nature (or characteristic human life) will be morally indeterminate, or it will not be objectively well-founded. At best, an objectively well-founded theory of human nature would support evaluations of the kind that we can make about tigers—that this one is a good or bad specimen, that that behaviour is abnormal. These judgements might be part of a theory of *health*, but our conception of morality resists the analogy with health, the reduction of evil to defect. (This resistance has something to do, I suspect, with a conception of free will that resists all forms of naturalism.) An objective account of human nature would imply, perhaps, that a good human life must be social in character. This implication will disqualify the sociopath but not the Hell's Angel. The contrast is revealing, for we tend to regard the sociopath not as evil but as beyond the pale of morality. On the other hand, if we enrich our conception of sociality to exclude Hell's Angels, the worry is that this conception will no longer ground moral judgement but rather express it.[1]

He encapsulates the doubt in the question,

---

[1] 'On the Primacy of Character' (1990), 462–3.

Can an objective theory really establish that being a gangster is incompatible with being a good human being?

but, rather than answering 'No' or 'Surely not', concludes that this is one of

the main worries and issues that must be faced before we can determine the prospects for an ethics of virtue. There is much to be said about what an objective account of human nature is supposed to be, as well as about the supposed disanalogies with health.[2]

That there is 'much to be said about what an objective account of human nature is supposed to be' in the context of ethics is an understatement. In this chapter, I aim to say some of it. But first, a reminder about what an 'objective account of human nature', in the context of ethics, is *not* supposed to be, reiterating some points from the previous chapter.

Watson's dilemma can be seen as a particular version of the general one I discussed at the beginning of the last chapter. Ethical naturalism hopes to validate beliefs about which character traits are virtues by appeal to human nature, and this may seem a vain hope. For either we speak from the neutral point of view, using a scientific account of human nature—in which case we won't get very far—or we speak from within an acquired ethical outlook—in which case we will not validate our ethical beliefs, but merely reexpress them.

Now, as in the preceding chapter, I shall assume, without argument, that McDowell is right to claim that the Neurathian procedure in ethics provides a way between the horns of this dilemma. The pretensions of an Aristotelian naturalism are not, in any ordinary understanding of the terms, either 'scientific' or 'foundational'. It does not seek to establish its conclusions from 'a neutral point of view'. Hence it does not expect what it says to convince anyone whose ethical outlook or perspective is largely different from the ethical outlook from within which the naturalistic conclusions are argued for. (So the mafioso drug baron, or whatever other wicked character we imagine being unconvinced, is largely irrelevant.) But, for all that, it may serve to provide rational credentials for our beliefs about which character traits are the virtues, not merely reexpress them.

[2] Ibid. 464.

The second, related, point to be reiterated from the previous chapter is that *this* is what it is supposed to be doing. The naturalistic conclusions are *not* intended to produce motivating reasons. They are not supposed to be providing motivating reasons for the mafioso drug baron even if, *per impossibile*, we did convince him, so to imagine him saying 'Well, I don't care about being a good human being, I want to be a good drug baron' is simply irrelevant. And they are not supposed to be providing motivating reasons for those within the ethical outlook either. Secure within the outlook according to which the life I want to lead *is* the life lived in accordance with honesty, temperance, courage, charity, justice, etc., I am not in any need of motivating reasons, and when I explore the claims of ethical naturalism, such motivating reasons are not what I am looking for. I'm looking to see whether my beliefs about which character traits are the virtues can survive my reflective scrutiny and be given some rational justification.

But—the third point from the previous chapter—to establish the existence of a space within which such validation could proceed is not to say anything about how it is to be filled. As we saw, McDowell does not think it can be occupied by considerations of how the virtues on the standard list benefit their possessor. But he does seem to think it can be filled by ethical naturalism.

However, that still needs to be shown, and to show it, quite a bit more needs to be said about what the naturalism is supposed to be like. This chapter aims to 'say more' by giving some fairly specific details of how, in naturalistic terms, I might set about finding the rational credentials for my beliefs about which character traits are the virtues. Virtue ethicists *must*, I believe, consider some detailed ideas about how the naturalistic project might proceed before we commit ourselves to the naturalism embodied in thesis (2), the thesis that the virtues make their possessor good *qua* human being. This is because, in advance of looking at them, we do not know that the thesis is not a non-starter—that it can indeed occupy some of McDowell's space. For all that he has said, it is still quite possible that it may yield disappointingly sparse results. Or, at the other extreme, it may yield far too many horrific ones for us to count it as validating *ethical* beliefs at all. In advance of looking at any details, what grounds do we have for thinking that it will not take us too far, endorsing anything natural as good, like some supposedly Darwinian versions of sociobiology?[3] Moreover, without any details about what the naturalism is supposed to be like, we cannot even begin to consider in what ways the evaluations of ethical naturalism might be analogous or disanalogous to evaluations of health. So some details are what is needed, and they take quite a bit of space to lay out.

I have taken over many of the details which follow, and the whole idea of ethical naturalism, from Philippa Foot, so I must begin with some account of what she has already done.

The starting point is an idea that she has never lost sight of, and which figures in her early attack on Hare. It is the idea that 'good', like 'small', is an attributive adjective.[4] What that entails is that, although you can evaluate and choose things according to almost any criteria you like, you must select the noun or noun phrase you use to describe the thing you are calling good *advisedly*, for it determines the criteria of goodness that are appropriate. Hare can call a cactus a good one on the grounds that it is diseased and dying, and choose it for that reason, but what he must not do is describe it as a good *cactus*, for a cactus is a living thing. He can describe it as a good 'decorative object for my windowsill' or 'present to give my detestable mother-in-law', but not as a good *cactus*. And it was part and parcel of what used to be thought of as Foot's 'naturalism' in ethics that, following Anscombe in 'Modern Moral Philosophy', she denied that this grammatical feature of the word 'good' and its related terms suddenly underwent a mysterious change when we started doing ethics. What goes for 'good cactus', 'good knife', 'good rider', also goes for 'good human being' even when we use that phrase in ethics. Hence her early animadversions against the fact–value distinction and the corresponding idea that 'good' was

[3] In 'Two Sorts of Naturalism', McDowell argues not for the claims of Aristotle's naturalism, but for a proper understanding of it. Martha Nussbaum, in 'Aristotle on Human Nature and the Foundations of Ethics' (1995), also argues powerfully for an understanding of Aristotle's conception of human nature as 'internal and evaluative' rather than external and 'scientific' in the modern sense—and none the worse for being so. But neither of them, as far as I can see, pretends to show that Aristotle validated his beliefs about which character traits were the virtues by appealing to human nature. (They certainly do not think that the *ergon* argument does that.)

[4] Though note that this formulation of the idea comes from Peter Geach, 'Good and Evil' (1956).

purely descriptive in non-ethical contexts but somehow quite different and 'evaluative' in ethical ones.[5]

Over the last ten years or so, Foot has been exploring something
that is also called naturalism in ethics, namely the Aristotelian naturalism which seeks to ground ethics, in some way, in considerations of human nature. And she has, brilliantly, yoked together her
early thoughts about the evaluation of living things such as cactuses
and the Aristotelian naturalistic project. She began her (alas)
unpublished Romanell lecture[6] with the riveting remark, 'In moral
philosophy, it is useful, I believe, to think about plants', and went
on to talk about the use of evaluative words such as 'good', 'well',
'defective', and so on in relation to plants (harking back to the early
discussion of good roots in trees),[7] then to non-human animals, and
finally to human beings. In her most recent publications on this
topic,[8] she dispenses with the plants and starts straight in on the
other animals. Her idea is that, just as 'there is something wrong
with a free-riding wolf, who eats but does not take part in the hunt'
and 'with a member of the species of dancing bees who finds a
source of nectar but does not let other bees know where it is', there
is something wrong with a human being who lacks, for example,
charity and justice. 'These "free-riding" individuals of a species
whose members work together are just as *defective* as those who
have defective hearing, sight, or powers of locomotion. I am,' she
continues 'quite seriously likening the basis of moral evaluation to
that of the evaluation of behaviour in animals.'[9] She concludes:

---

[5] Anscombe says (29), 'The terms "should" or "ought" or "needs" relate to good
and bad', illustrating the claim in relation to what a machine or a plant needs, or
ought to have, or should have, and continues, 'According to this conception, of
course, "should" and "ought" are not used in a special "moral" sense when one says
that a man should not bilk.' (Nor, she might have added, is 'bad' used in a special
'moral' sense when one says that a man who goes in for bilking is a bad man.) In
'Goodness and Choice' (1978, 134), Foot argued that 'if Hare's account of the "good"
in "good man" were correct, then this use of the word would seem to be different
from all other cases in which we speak of a good such-and-such', with the strong
implication that it would be extremely odd if there were a special, 'moral', 'evaluative' use of 'good' exclusively reserved for our evaluations of ourselves and utterly
distinct from our evaluations of all other things.

[6] A public lecture delivered at the American Philosophical Association, Pacific
Division Conference, in 1989.

[7] 'Goodness and Choice', 145.

[8] 'Rationality and Virtue' and 'Does Moral Subjectivism Rest on a Mistake?'.

[9] 'Does Moral Subjectivism Rest on a Mistake?', 9.

In my view . . . a moral evaluation does not stand over against the state-ment of a matter of fact, but rather has to do with facts about a particular subject matter, as do evaluations of such things as sight and hearing in ani-mals, and other aspects of their behaviour. Nobody would, I think, take it as other than a plain matter of fact that there is something wrong with the hearing of a gull that cannot distinguish the cry of its own chick, as with the sight of an owl that cannot see in the dark. Similarly, it is obvious that there are objective, factual evaluations of such things as human sight, hear-ing, memory, and concentration, based on the life-form of our own species. Why, then, does it seem so monstrous a suggestion that the evaluation of the human will should be determined by facts about the nature of human beings and the life of our own species? Undoubtedly the resistance has something to do with the thought that the goodness of good action has a special relation to choice. But, as I have tried to show, this special relation is not what noncognitivists think it, but rather lies in the fact that moral action is rational action, and in the fact that human beings are creatures with the power to recognize reasons for action and to act on them.[10]

It can be seen that Foot is stressing ways in which ethical evalu-ations are analogous to evaluations of tigers (or wolves or bees) as good, healthy, specimens of their kind, in the way Watson described. And that is the idea that I have taken over from her wholesale in what follows. I depart from her published papers in reinstating her original idea of beginning with the plants, because it makes it easier to discern the development of the particular struc-ture that I claim to find in our evaluations of living things.[11]

## EVALUATING PLANTS AND ANIMALS

Living things can be chosen and evaluated according to all sorts of criteria. We may evaluate them as potential food, as entries in com-petitive shows, even as 'decorative object for *my* windowsill given *my* preferences', and each noun or noun phrase brings its own cri-teria of goodness with it. In the context of naturalism we focus on evaluations of individual living things as or *qua* specimens of their natural kind, as some well-informed gardeners do with respect to plants and ethologists do with respect to animals.

[10] Ibid. 14.
[11] It should be noted that, although most of the examples I give in illustration of the structure I outline below are hers, I find more structure than she thinks is there.

An individual plant is a good (or bad/poor) specimen of its species (or sub-species), a good rose or nettle, according as (i) its parts and (ii) its operations (including reactions under this heading where relevant) are good or not. By a plant's parts, I mean such things as its leaves, roots, petals; by its operations such things as growing, taking in water, developing buds, dying back, setting seed; by its reactions, such things as sunflowers and pansies turning towards the sun, and some plants' leaves drooping and curling inwards as a moisture-conserving measure.

An individual plant's parts and operations are evaluated as good in the light of two ends; they are good according to whether they are contributing, in the way characteristic of such a member of such a species, to (1) individual survival through the characteristic life span of such a member of such a species and (2) continuance of the species. So, evaluating parts with respect to individual survival, we find, for example, that a tree (of species $x$) should have certain sorts of roots, the sort that, in this species, help it to survive, by keeping it anchored and taking up nourishment. And, perhaps, its leaves should curl when it is short of water (operations with respect to individual survival). Evaluating operations with respect to continuance of the species, we find, say, that it should produce seeds at a certain time of year (the time members of that species characteristically do produce them), which themselves should be good seeds, namely seeds which ripen and are fertile.

So, in the evaluation of individual plants, we find that we evaluate *two* aspects—parts and operations—in relation to *two* ends. A good $x$ is one that is well fitted or endowed with respect to its parts and operations; whether it is thus well fitted or endowed is determined by whether its parts and operations serve its individual survival and the continuance of its species well, in the way characteristic of $x$s.

What happens when we, as we say, 'ascend the ladder of nature' to animals? We continue to evaluate individual animals as members of their species or sub-species; we continue to do so by evaluating the same two aspects in relation to the same two ends; but, somewhere along the ladder, two further aspects and two further ends become involved.[12]

---

[12] This is the point at which I start introducing more structure than Foot. But most of the examples are still hers.

First, there is some indeterminate point at which we have to go beyond talking about mere reacting (as pansies and sunflowers react to the sun) and start talking about acting or doing. Even fish and birds 'do' things in a way that no plant 'does' things. So, in evaluating animals which act, we consider not only whether they operate well but also whether they act well with respect to the two ends of individual survival and continuance of the species.

So, animals of a certain level of sophistication are evaluated as good or bad/defective specimens of their kind according to whether they act well, in the way characteristic of their species, as well as according to whether they have good parts and good operations.

Naturally (*sic*), with more complex living things which can act, we get more complex ways of realizing the two ends. One thing both good birds and plants 'do' is absorb nourishment, but birds have to act to get nourishment as no plants do. For an owl to be good at getting nourishment, it needs not only its good parts and operations—its eyes and wings and talons and a functioning digestive system—it needs to be able to hunt well. An owl that can't hunt well in the way characteristic of its species is, in at least that respect, a bad or defective owl.

Moreover, in animals that do things, 'the continuance of the species' involves a great deal more than just, so to speak, the scattering of seed. So the evaluation of the individual animal, with respect to the end of the continuance of the species, is based upon whether they do this 'great deal more' that is necessary for that end—in the way characteristic of their species. So a king penguin who abandons his mate's egg is thereby bad or defective. A lioness who does not suckle her cubs, and then feed them, and then teach them to hunt is thereby defective.

So much for the third aspect—acting—on the basis of which we evaluate many animals. Now let us consider a third end, beyond individual survival and continuance of the species. Somewhere along the ladder of nature—once again, quite possibly somewhere indeterminate—we start ascribing pain, and somewhere—perhaps at the same point, perhaps not—pleasure. Animals that can feel pain and that are capable of pleasure or enjoyment are evaluated in relation to not only the first two ends, but a third one, namely characteristic freedom from pain and characteristic pleasure or enjoyment.[13]

[13] See the first part of Foot's 'Euthanasia' for the different, but related, point that

The emphasis on 'characteristic' is important. As ethologists rejecting utilitarian approaches to animal suffering are wont to point out, much of the pain that animals undergo is, far from being an evil, an important survival mechanism. A dog that feels no pain when the pad on its foot is cut is not *better* than the usual run of dogs, but defective. In a species of animal that feels pain in a damaged part, freedom from pain in a damaged part is, in an individual member of such a species, a defect. Characteristic freedom from pain *is* what is found in the characteristic life of members of such a species. So, for example, a ram with a twisted horn would, probably, just have an abnormality, but if it twisted in such a way that it grew into his cheek and caused him constant pain, then it would be a defect. An animal whose teeth had grown in such an abnormal way that it couldn't chew without pain would be thereby defective.

So there is our third end—characteristic freedom from pain and (where appropriate) characteristic pleasure or enjoyment. It brings to our attention a fourth aspect of animals which we evaluate in evaluating them as good or defective. Closely associated with the ascription of pain and pleasure to the more sophisticated animals is the ascription of a certain, at least minimal, psychology, of emotions and desires. Animals capable of such a psychology are evaluated as good or defective not only with respect to the three other aspects but also with respect to some emotions and desires. They are defective—something is wrong with them—when they do not want to eat or reproduce. (There are few things more sad than the notice that used to appear on the cages of certain animals in zoos, 'Does not breed in captivity'.) A species is, say, characteristically frightened of some other species and not others; a member of such a species that does not feel fear in the right way thereby has a defect.

So now we have, for the more sophisticated animals, four aspects—(i) parts, (ii) operations/reactions, (iii) actions, and (iv) emotions/desires—and three ends with respect to which they are evaluated—(i) individual survival, (ii) the continuance of the species, and (iii) characteristic pleasure or enjoyment/characteristic freedom from pain. If we now move onto another rung, and con-

---

'what is beneficial to a plant may have to do with reproduction [as well as its] survival' (38), and that, when we turn to animals that can feel pain, 'new things count as benefit' such as comfort or the relief of suffering (39).

sider, specifically, social animals, we find that a fourth end comes in, namely (iv) the good functioning of the social group.[14]

I do not know enough animal physiology to be sure of any examples of their parts being evaluated with respect to this fourth end. The obvious example for operations/reactions is the capacity of a member of a social group to recognize its fellow members, lack of which would clearly be a defect and, for all I know, might be caused by a defective part. It might be said that a bee that is defective in lacking a sting is defective with respect to the end of its hive's surviving and functioning well rather than the continuance of the species. But the bulk of examples come in relation to the aspects of action and emotion/desire.

Wolves hunt in packs; a 'free-rider' wolf that doesn't join in the hunt fails to act well and is thereby defective. Social groups of wolves, elephants, and horses have leaders; an animal of such a species that doesn't defer to the leader's authority is defective (unless it is, in the manner characteristic of the species, challenging the leadership). Some species of social animals go in for play; a member of such a species that doesn't join in is thereby defective, and, more strongly, a member that tries to join in but doesn't do so appropriately—that doesn't obey the rules of the game—thereby has a defect. Some species of ape go in for mutual grooming; an ape that doesn't groom others is defective. There are characteristic patterns of fear and anger which differentiate between other members of the group and members of the same species which are not members of the group; a social animal whose emotional reactions are out of line and disrupt the functioning of the group is thereby defective.

What is 'the good functioning of the social group'? Or, in other words, what is it for such a group to function well? The function of such a group is to enable its members to live well (in the way characteristic of their species); that is, to foster their characteristic individual survival, their characteristic contribution to the continuance of the species and their characteristic freedom from pain and enjoyment of such things as it is characteristic of their species to enjoy. And all this involves its fostering the development of its members'

---

[14] Social creatures such as bees and ants cause a hiccup in this smooth progress, since we do not ascribe pain, let alone pleasure, to them and hence they are not evaluated in the light of the third end, but are in the light of what I have called 'the fourth'. I will stick to the terminology of 'the fourth' even in relation to them, rather than complicating the discussion with qualifications.

characteristic capacities. That is what a social group should do. So if it is doing it well, it is functioning well.

Considering the social animals, we see that the four ends interconnect. This feature of connection is not lacking in the other cases—an animal needs to survive to maturity in order to reproduce (even a plant needs to do that) and beyond maturity to nurture the young while they need nurturing—but becomes particularly striking in the case of the social animals.

The individual survival of social animals is in general served by their sticking with the group, if it is functioning well. The continuance of the species depends on the group's functioning well. Moreover, individual pain and pleasure, in the more sophisticated social animals, can be group related. Such a social animal, deprived of companionship, pines and suffers; correspondingly, it enjoys the companionship and mutual activity of the group. Or rather, if that's what members of its species characteristically do, it is defective in so far as it doesn't; so an ape (of the mutual grooming sort) which does not enjoy being with its group, or being groomed, or playing, is in that respect defective.

So, summing up, a good social animal (of one of the more sophisticated species) is one that is well fitted or endowed with respect to (i) its parts, (ii) its operations, (iii) its actions, and (iv) its desires and emotions; whether it is thus well fitted or endowed is determined by whether these four aspects well serve (1) its individual survival, (2) the continuance of its species, (3) its characteristic freedom from pain and characteristic enjoyment, and (4) the good functioning of its social group—in the ways characteristic of the species.

There are several points worth noting about the evaluations of living things as just outlined which we will need to bear in mind when we turn to considering evaluations of ourselves as good human beings.

First, the truth of such evaluations of living things does not depend in any way on my wants, interests, or values, nor indeed on 'ours'. They are, in the most straightforward sense of the term, 'objective'; indeed, given that botany, zoology, ethology, etc. are sciences, they are scientific.[15] Readers unfamiliar with such evalua-

---

[15] In fact, if John Dupré is right, this is not quite true, for he argues that there is no unique way of dividing up the biological world and that different modes of classification are in part determined by different interests of ours. See *The Disorder of*

tions, or inclined to think that they necessarily have something to do with approval or praise, should take note of the many excellent gardening and nature programmes available on television. The former are filled with diagnoses of 'What's wrong with/defective about this plant?' (or 'Why are these damned nettles doing so well?') and the latter, in a way beautifully captured by Michael Thompson,[16] with 'The (non-defective) $x$s have this, do that (in the spring, when hunting, etc.)'. Farmers, and people concerned with domestic animals, have always had a special kind of vested interest in arriving at a subset of such evaluations correctly; botanists and ethologists are now just interested in arriving at true ones for their own sake.

Second, notwithstanding their objectivity, indeed their scientific status, such evaluations are true only 'for the most part' and, moreover, riddled with imprecision and indeterminacy. They are judgements about individuals as members of a certain species or subspecies, and species terms have fuzzy edges and a fair amount of arbitrariness about them.[17] Should we classify this plant here as an $x$, in which case it is a poor stunted specimen of its kind, or should we classify it as an excellent specimen of the dwarf form of $x$, the subspecies $x$ *nanus*? A species' 'characteristic way of operating, etc.' is identified by how it characteristically operates in its natural environment, or natural habitat, and those terms are as awkward as species terms. (Indeed, that a subset of $x$s has adapted well to what is a hostile environment for $x$s can be a ground for reclassifying it as a subspecies.) Hence a botanist's or ethologist's initial judgement that there is something wrong with that $x$ or those $x$s might be withdrawn with hindsight, if it was decided that the species $x$ needed to be subdivided, or if it looked as though its members were developing a new characteristic way of going on.

The overall summing-up evaluation—that this individual $x$ is a good $x$, a good specimen of its kind—supervenes on the evaluations of its relevant aspects. A good $x$ is well fitted or endowed with respect to its parts, operations, etc.; it is a good $x$ in virtue of its good parts and operations, its acting, feeling, and desiring well. The aspects are evaluated in relation to the relevant ends (frequently interconnected, as we noted). And, given all this complexity, it

*Things* (1993). However, although I am sure he *is* right, I think that, in this context, allowing the more common picture of the biological sciences is harmless.
[16] 'The Representation of Life' (1995).
[17] For an extended defence of this view, see Dupré, *The Disorder of Things*.

should be obvious that an individual $x$ might be perfect in this way, defective in that, fairish in another, and eventually best described as 'an almost perfect specimen apart from such-and-such', 'a superlative specimen given its age', 'rather a poor specimen given its environment', and so on.

In some cases, it will be quite indeterminate whether an individual $x$, particularly well-endowed in some aspects but mildly defective in others, is, overall, a good $x$ or not, and whether, if good, it is as good or better than another $x$ which is fairly but not particularly well endowed in all relevant aspects. In some cases it will be indeterminate whether an $x$ is a good $x$, given how remarkably well it is doing in an unnatural and hostile environment, or whether it should be described as defective because of the ways in which it is different from the good ones in their natural habitat.

The ends in relation to which the aspects are evaluated can conflict, and when they do, the truth or falsity of the overall summing-up judgement is not always clearly determined. But, significantly it often is—and by what is characteristic of members of the species. Consider some of Foot's most notable cases; the (perhaps imaginary) free-riding wolf, the worker bee without a sting, the lioness who does not defend her cubs. Here it might initially appear that the individual was endowed well with respect to one or both of the first and third ends but less well, or even ill, with respect to one or both of the other two. But the overall evaluations of them as good or defective $x$s—with the consequent evaluation of them as living or failing to live good $x$ lives—overrules that initial appearance by stressing the species' characteristic ways of going on and characteristic enjoyments or freedom from pain. An infertile female cheetah, unusually free from pain as her life may be, is not well endowed with respect to *characteristic* freedom from pain, nor the free-riding wolf with respect to characteristic enjoyment of available food, nor the stingless worker bee with respect to the characteristic way of attaining its natural life span. Birds whose members try to distract predators from nests of their chicks are defective if they do not do so, notwithstanding the fact that they, and the lioness, are thereby better endowed with respect to individual survival and freedom from pain.[18]

---

[18]  Cf. Foot: 'the evaluation of an individual—of its features and operations—may depend on harm, public or private, which threatens others than itself.' 'Rationality and Virtue', 209.

Third, good *x*s do not necessarily have all the same characteristics but may have to be evaluated as good *fx*s or good *gx*s. Even amongst some species of plants there is female and male; a good female skimmia produces berries and one that does not is thereby defective, but a male skimmia does not and is not thereby defective. It is good worker bees that dance, not the drones or the queen. Wolves are not defective in virtue of not being leaders of the pack, but the one who is the leader is defective if it is not a good one, and so on.

Fourth, the overall summing-up evaluation—that this *x* is a good specimen of its kind—identifies it as an *x* that is as ordinarily well fitted or endowed as an *x* can be to do or live well, to thrive or flourish (in a characteristically *x* way). What living things *do* is live; quite generally, a good living thing lives well—unless prevented by something outside itself. However, even a perfect *x*, perfectly endowed in every relevant aspect, may still not live well. Its environment may be poisoned; it may be eaten or accidentally killed before its time. Moreover, through chance, it may fail to live well in its characteristic way, precisely *because* of being a good specimen of its kind, as, for instance, when capable of feeling pain in its characteristic way, it sustained such damage that it suffered for the rest of its life. An animal that never felt pain in a damaged part might, by chance, survive undamaged to a ripe old age and be individually benefited by its defect, in its last months, when it sustained a serious injury. But it would be defective for all that, and fail to live a good characteristically *x* life.[19]

And fifth, the truth of the overall evaluation depends in part upon the needs and (as we ascend the ladder of nature) the interests and desires of the kind of *x*s in question.

## EVALUATING OURSELVES

If Anscombe, Geach, and Foot are right that 'good' is attributive and does not suddenly change its grammar when we start evaluating

---

[19] Compare Foot's early version of this point, in connection with the claim that human beings need the use of their hands and eyes ('This is not to say that an injury might not bring more incidental gain than necessary harm; one has only to think of times when the order has gone out that able-bodied men are to be put to the sword', 'Moral Beliefs', 123), with the new version in the context of naturalism: 'it is the way

ourselves ethically, then the criteria of goodness in human beings must be related to what human beings are and/or do, as such. There is, of course, room for disagreement over what we are. It might be said, for example, that what human beings *are* are possessors of an immortal soul through which they can come to know and love God for eternity. But 'ethical naturalism' is usually thought of as not only basing ethics in some way on considerations of human nature, but also as taking human beings to be part of the natural, biological order of living things. Its standard first premise is that what human beings *are* is a species of rational, social animals and thereby a species of living things—which, unlike 'persons' or 'rational beings', have a particular biological make-up and a natural life cycle.[20]

If all the above is basically right, then, if there is any truth in ethical naturalism, our ethical evaluations of ourselves ought to exhibit at least a recognizably similar structure to what we find in the botanists' and ethologists' evaluations of other living things. More particularly, we would expect the structure of our ethical evaluations of ourselves to resemble that of a sophisticated social animal with some differences necessitated by our being not only social but also rational. This is the first question we have to look at in order to see whether ethical naturalism can even get off the ground as a possible occupant of McDowell's space.

The preceding evaluations are all concerned with good *x*s as *healthy* specimens of their kind. And one very obvious way in which our ethical evaluations are a bit different is that we hive off overall evaluations that supervene on our evaluations of our physical

---

of life of the species that determines what the better or worseness of (features and operations such as) sight consists in for an individual . . . , rather than the circumstances it itself happens to be in. For an individual put into a special environment, like a wild animal in a zoo, may have what is no less a defect because it happens to fit its special life. Expressions such as "good sight" have reference to a species in their meaning. If we want to talk about the kind of sight that happened to be advantageous to a particular individual in a special environment, or even in its own, we can always do so, but then we are not talking not of good sight but of something else.' 'Rationality and Virtue', 208.

[20] In my view, an excellent reason for keeping the word 'person', used as a deliberate contrast to 'human being', out of ethics is that it is usually so thinly defined that it cannot generate any sense for 'good person'. If what a person *is*, is just a self-conscious being, what would count as being a good or a bad one? Having a very good, as opposed to a rather poor, conception of oneself as a being with a past and a future?

aspects—our parts and operations, at least—into human biology and/or medicine. The evaluation of someone as a good, physically healthy, specimen of humanity is, for us (as it was not, perhaps, for the ancient Greeks) quite distinct from those evaluations we call 'ethical'.[21] That granted, let us consider whether our ethical evaluations exhibit what remains of the structure when the merely physical has been thus hived off.

That would leave the aspects to be evaluated as reactions that were not merely physical, actions and emotions and desires, and our rationality makes for one obvious addition to this list, analogous to the addition that came with the move from plants to the less primitive animals. If we were simply transferring our talk about the other social animals to us, we would be evaluating 'actions' only in the limited sense in which the other animals (and small children) act—'from inclination', not 'from reason', as I put it in Chapter 4. But it is quite certain that it is primarily our acting from reason, well or ill, rather than those occasional actions we do 'from inclination', that make us good or bad human beings in the ethical sense. So that would be a further aspect to be added.

Now we have some details, we can ask, 'How plausible is this thesis? Does it look like a starter?' We need to consider this question first in relation to the proposed aspects, and then in relation to the proposed four ends.

Is it plausible in so far as it claims that we are ethically good (or bad) human beings according to whether we are well (or ill) endowed with respect to reactions that are not merely physical, our (occasional) actions from inclination, our emotions and desires, and our actions from reason? *Are* those, in short, our ethically relevant aspects? As a list that has emerged from a consideration of plants and animals and then had the merely physical hived off and actions from reason added on, it may look like rather a rag-bag. But viewed from another perspective it has a notable unity; it is a list of just those aspects of us that manifest our ethical character, for well or ill.

To possess the virtues is, as we have seen in previous chapters, not only to be well disposed with respect to actions from reason but

---

[21] The possibly distinct third sort of evaluation occurs in the field of human psychology, but it would need a book on its own to discuss the issue of whether the evaluation of a human being as a good, mentally healthy, specimen can be clearly separated from ethical evaluations.

also with respect to emotions and desires. Notwithstanding the enormous importance of our actions from reason, our emotions are also morally significant, and being well disposed with respect to them involves being well disposed with respect to the occasional impulsive actions from inclination, and the emotional reactions which are not merely physical, to which they give rise.[22] Virtuous action also involves 'reactions which are not merely physical' in the form of perceptions of what is relevant in a situation, which, as we saw in the first three chapters, is indispensable. Hence the concept of a virtue emerges as apparently tailor-made to encapsulate a favourable evaluation of just those aspects which, according to the naturalism here outlined, are the ethically relevant ones. To be a good human being is to be well endowed with respect to the aspects listed; to possess the human virtues is to be thus well endowed. The human virtues make their possessor good *qua* human being, one who is as ordinarily well fitted as a human being can be in not merely physical respects to live well, to flourish—in a characteristically human way.

Note that, so far, this leaves entirely open the question of whether temperance, courage, generosity, honesty, justice, etc. *are* human virtues. And that brings us to the other half of the question about whether the proposed ethical naturalism looks like a starter, namely, is it plausible in so far as it tells us to evaluate our aspects in the light of the four ends appropriate to social animals? The other social animals were well fitted or endowed according as their parts, actions, etc. served the four ends of individual survival, continuance of the species, characteristic enjoyment and freedom from pain, and the good functioning of the social group. Are we ethically well endowed according as our character traits serve just those same four ends? Or would any attempt to establish which character traits were the virtues by means of such naturalistic criteria produce a bizarre and unrecognizable characterization of a good human being? The discussion of a few examples suggests that the naturalistic criteria serve us rather well.

Is it not plausible to say that, for example, courage plays much

---

[22] It is worth recalling, in this context, my claim (p. 106 above) that even when we adults act 'from inclination', such actions are not just like those of the other animals, because we do not act from the same state as them. Our state includes our knowledge that such actions are up for assessment as innocent or deplorable, unjustifiable or justifiable in the circumstances, and so on.

the same sort of role in human life as its analogue does in that of, say, wolves? Good wolves defend themselves and their cubs and each other, and risk life and limb as the pack attacks the prey, thereby fostering their individual survival, the continuance of the species, and the particular way the members of the social group co-operate in order to secure food for the group and protect themselves from danger. Human beings who are good in so far as they are courageous defend themselves, and their young, and each other, and risk life and limb to defend and preserve worthwhile things in and about their group, thereby fostering their individual survival, the continuance of the species, their own and others' enjoyment of var-ious good things, and the good functioning of the social group. I have read that, amongst the social animals, both wolves and ele-phants have patterns of action that resemble our charitable or benevolent acts, and again it seems plausible to say that the patterns play similar roles in the different forms of life. Charity directed to the young and helpless particularly serves the continuance of the species; directed more widely it serves the good functioning of the social group by fostering the individual survival, freedom from pain, and enjoyment of its members, and also by fostering its cohe-sion. (Charity, unlike courage, does not serve the end of individual survival directly, but, like worker bees' stings, indirectly. An indi-vidual worker bee's functioning sting, unlike a wolf's sharp teeth, is not a good part because it fosters its individual survival; when a worker bee uses its sting it promptly dies. But given that bees have stings, predators learn to avoid bees because they sting, and that fosters the survival of individual bees.[23] Charity does not, by and large, foster the individual survival of its possessor (though, as we saw, it may do), but given that members of a social group living together have charity, they can often live longer, avoid some suffer-ing, enjoy more, because someone else helps them.) And other virtues which perhaps have no analogue amongst the other animals still serve some of the four ends (without being inimical to the oth-ers). Without honesty, generosity, and loyalty we would miss out on one of our greatest sources of characteristic enjoyment, namely lov-ing relationships; without honesty we would be unable to co-operate or to acquire knowledge and pass it on to the next

---

[23] This excellent point about bees' stings was originally made by Geach in *The Virtues.*

generation to build on. And it has long been a commonplace that justice and fidelity to promises enable us to function *as* a social, co-operating group.

All this seems to me not only plausible but also not entirely unfamiliar. It is not so far removed from Hume's claim that the virtues are those characteristics that are useful and/or agreeable to their possessor and/or to others, nor from modern attempts to evaluate actions or principles of action as right in the light of their tendency to promote the greatest happiness and freedom from suffering or as necessary for our living together in a society. True, modern discussions, being mostly by non-virtue ethicists, tend to emphasize right action rather than the virtues or good human beings, but most will readily accept that good human beings are those who have the virtues and that the virtues are those character traits that tend to produce what they identify as right actions. And although the ends of individual survival and the continuance of the species do not look as familiar as the other two, I think one can usually discern their influence too. Accounts that turn out to require widespread self-sacrifice or the fatal turning of the other cheek are criticized on that score and usually amended accordingly so that good human beings—the ones who tend to produce right actions—have a reasonable expectation of individual survival.[24] The continuance of the species is a much trickier issue as far as reproduction is concerned (to which I shall return), but in so far as it involves the nurturing and education of our children (like the lioness suckling her cubs and then teaching them to hunt), I would say that, though rarely mentioned, it is almost universally presupposed. No moral philosopher knowingly attempts to rationalize actions or principles of action which foster general happiness or 'persons' living together in society at the *expense* of the nurturing and education of children; one can see that most of them are just assuming that the existing babies are going to survive and become adults like them and their readers in the future, even if they have overlooked what a great deal

---

[24] All accounts that emphasize the 'agent-neutrality' of goods such as life—roughly, the idea that my life's being *mine* should not give it any additional practical importance to me—have a bit of a problem about allowing me to devote any especial efforts to preserving and defending my own life. But their proponents do characteristically regard this as a problem and try to get around it to some extent—they do not just accept that the individual survival of the agent is an end irrelevant to ethics.

of deliberate human activity has to go into ensuring that this happens. So I think there is enough similarity for us to expect that, if this naturalistic project were to be pursued, there is no reason at the moment to suppose that it would yield a bizarre characterization of a good human being.

And, of course, that is important. If, as soon as we embarked on the naturalism project, it looked as though the character traits of charity, justice, courage, honesty, etc. were not going to turn out to be good-making characteristics of human beings then, I would say, we had better give up on naturalism entirely. That is why I said at the outset that McDowell's creating a space for it is no guarantee that it is not a non-starter; we have to look at some details and see.

However, to say that it looks as though it may pass the test of yielding the virtues rather than the vices is still not to show it is a starter. There may be many other things that are implausible about it, and I will now discuss some fairly straightforward candidates, leaving deeper worries to the next chapter.

One worry is that the naturalism project will yield far too determinate a specification of what it is to be a good human being, one in which all good human beings are, in some important way, supposed to be the same, living the same 'characteristically human life', like *this*, from day to day, as the other animals do.

The first point that needs to be made to dispel this worry is a reminder that the ethical naturalism in question is supposed to be something that provides a criterion for a particular character trait's being a virtue, *not* a criterion of right or good action, except indirectly; it is not just 'natural law' theory. Suppose we satisfied ourselves that temperance was indeed a virtue according to naturalism. Then, taking this conclusion back to the first chapters, we would indeed be able to satisfy ourselves that (barring tragic dilemmas) a particular action which was what a temperate agent would, characteristically, do *in those circumstances*, was, indeed a good or right action. But that is a far cry from producing a law to the effect that, for example, all good human beings always refrain from immoderate eating. Establishing, in so far as it can be established, that a particular character trait is a virtue is one thing; working out how to apply that virtue term correctly in particular cases in order to determine whether doing this, in these circumstances, for these reasons, would be right or not, is, I have tried to show in the earlier chapters, largely something that does indeed have to be done case by case. When, from within my acquired ethical outlook, I consider whether, for example, temperance is a virtue, on naturalistic grounds, it is my own conception of temperance that I scrutinize, just as it is my own conception of, say, charity, with its associated conception of what it is to aim at another's *good*. The reflective scrutiny might lead me to give up my view that these are virtues. Or it might lead me to alter my conception of them somewhat, in such a way that some of my views on particular right and wrong actions change somewhat. But the considerations drawn from naturalism are not suddenly going to reveal to me how this character trait which I have now reassured myself is truly a virtue, is to manifest itself on each and every occasion, in every conceivable circumstance and cultural setting, in good human beings' lives. Temperate human beings might well comport themselves in very different ways in different circumstances.

Moreover, just the little examples of the division of labour in other animals is enough to undercut the idea that naturalism will entail that all good human beings 'live the same life', *as* the other animals do. For, as we have seen, the other animals do *not* all 'live the same characteristically *x* life'. The third point I noted concerning evaluations of other living things (p. 205 above) was that good *x*s do not necessarily all have the same characteristics. In evaluating an individual member of a species as good or defective, sometimes we can stick at the species level, but sometimes we have to go through a more specific move, assessing the individual as, say, a good or defective leader-of-the-pack wolf, or next-leader-of-the-pack wolf, to get back to good or defective wolf. For human beings there is indeed a much greater diversity of roles or lives than we find in any other animal, but given that that *is* how we are, there is nothing about the naturalistic judgements which suggests that considerations of human nature are going to yield conceptions of *good human being* that are even more determinate than that of *good wolf* or *good bee*.

But doesn't the project aim at a conception of a good human being which is such that all good human beings are the same at least in so far as they all possess and exercise the virtues? Well, with a few exceptions to which I shall return below, yes, and to that extent it claims that all good human beings live 'the same sort of life'—a life in accordance with the virtues. But that still leaves room for a great diversity of lives—including those in which the exercise of at least one virtue figures much more largely than, and even at the expense of the exercise of, at least one of the others. It may well be that being particularly well endowed with respect to some virtues inevitably involves being not very well endowed in others, and the kind of naturalism I am endorsing does not rule that out.

Indeed, one might say that it anticipates the possibility. The second point I noted in relation to evaluations of other living things was that in some cases it will be quite indeterminate whether an individual *x*, particularly well endowed in some aspects but mildly defective in others is, overall, a good *x* or not, and whether, if good, it is as good or better than another *x* which is, say, fairly but not particularly well endowed in all relevant aspects. Now when we come to ethical evaluations we may be inclined to think that, in theory, there *must* be determinate answers, that in every case we *must* be able to compare and rank human beings in respect of their ethical goodness. But far from promising, or threatening, to provide all such answers, naturalism strongly suggests that they are not always available. Why should they be in our case, when they are manifestly not so for other living things?

I mentioned above the possibility of 'a few exceptions' to the view that all good human beings have and exercise *the* virtues, that, if a character trait is a virtue then a good human being must have it to at least some minimal degree. This view is such a commonplace and so deeply rooted in our tradition that it is easy to overlook the fact that it might be denied without sacrilege and that even Aristotle himself does not hold it.[25] True, to lack entirely any one of the virtues on the standard list is necessarily to be on the way to possessing a corresponding vice, but it may be that there are some less familiar ones of which this is not true. Is there, for example, a virtue of being a good parent, which one can be bad in lacking because one is well on the way to possessing the vice of being a bad parent, or can lack consistently with being a good human being because one is not a parent at all?

Our concept of a character trait does not seem sufficiently sharp

---

[25] In *Nicomachean Ethics*, Book 4, ch. 2, Aristotle distinguishes liberality on an ordinary scale from 'magnificence' which involves expenditure on a grand scale as two different virtues, noting that although 'the magnificent man is liberal, the liberal man is not necessarily magnificent'. For all the snobbery that his discussion of 'magnificence' reflects, I cannot find any clear suggestion that anyone who lacks the resources necessary for that virtue is thereby not as good a man as one who has it.

at the edges to settle this firmly one way or the other. We might say that what is involved in being a good parent just is the possession and exercise of the familiar virtues on the standard list specifically in relation to one's children, in which context they have to be exercised in special ways. Or we might be struck by the fact that it is not unknown for people to be rather good parents but very limited in virtue outside their immediate family circle, and conversely, for fairly virtuous people to have a strange blind spot where their own children are concerned, showing them little of the charity, generosity, loyalty, and compassion they show to others, unable to judge them justly or deal with them honestly as they do with others. And that might lead us to say that being the sort of person who is a good parent needs to be distinguished, as a character trait, from being the sort of person who is charitable, generous, just, etc. *If* we say the latter, then the character trait in question looks likely to be assessed as a virtue in the light of the four naturalistic ends, but it would be a virtue that one could lack entirely without thereby failing to be a good human being. And, given the point about division of labour made above, it might be that there are other role-dependent virtues, such as being the sort of person who is a good leader or a good thinker or even a good artist. Possession of such a virtue would count towards an overall assessment of an individual human being as a good one, but the lack of it in a different individual would not necessarily count against their being good.

Even when it is made clear that the naturalism we are considering would not readily yield the conclusion that a good human being must *ipso facto* be a good parent (and hence a parent), the presence of the end of the continuance of the species continues to worry people. Does it not, they wonder, guarantee that, according to this form of naturalism, practising homosexuals are all, in that respect at least, bad, defective human beings? The answer is that it does not, or at least, not without the addition of a hefty premise or two.

It must be recalled again that what is at issue is not a particular form of sexual activity or orientation, but character traits, and by long-standing tradition we have words for the sort of character who pursues sexual gratification as an end in itself, regardless of other considerations, who chafes at all abstinence, whose enjoyment is unaffected by the wishes of his partner, and the sort of character who, while not insensible to sexual pleasure, pursues it and enjoys it in a much more restricted and discriminated way. The former is licentious, the latter temperate (with respect to sex). Like the other virtues on the standard list, temperance (with respect to sex) looks as though it, rather than licentiousness, might well emerge as a virtue when evaluated in the light of the four ends. (Temperance with respect to sex is not inimical to reproduction and, in contrast to licentiousness, fosters the nurture and education of the young. The temperate enjoy themselves as much as the licentious do, albeit in different ways, going by the evidence of the smile factor, and it is temperance that helps to protect us and the good functioning of society from the violent passions that, in human beings, sexual activity tends to give rise to. Nowadays and perhaps for the foreseeable future, it also fosters our individual survival by helping us to avoid fatal sexually transmitted diseases.) So let us suppose that, according to naturalism, temperance with respect to sex is a virtue. Then any human being who lacks such temperance is, in that respect at least, bad *qua* human being.

But clearly, any further step towards the conclusion that practising homosexuals were, in respect of their homosexuality, ethically bad or defective human beings would require a substantial premise about what practising homosexuals were like, or one about temperance and/or licentiousness. It would have to be said, for example, that practising homosexuals were all wildly, wilfully, promiscuous (and thereby licentious and thereby lacking in temperance). Or it would have to be specified that anyone who went in for sexual activity with their own sex was *thereby* lacking in temperance or *thereby* licentious (albeit not in the usual way). And wherever such premises come from, they do not come straightforwardly from the naturalism. (The former, I take it, comes from prejudiced ignorance, the latter from the further premise that homosexuals pursue sexual satisfaction in wilful defiance of the recognizable function of sexual activity ordained by God.) In particular, they do not come from its reliance on the end of the continuance of the species as forming part of the criterion for a character trait's being a virtue.

To underline this point, let us consider the practice of celibacy. Given the naturalistic ends of continuance of the species and the good functioning of the social group, does it follow that being a monastic contemplative is incompatible with being a good human being? Surprising as it may seem, it does not—or, at least, not obviously or directly.

The naturalism project, *if* it can be carried through, will go some way towards validating certain beliefs about which character traits are the virtues. Let us assume that it validates pretty much the standard list. Take this list back to the life of a monastic contemplative and ask whether the human being in question is leading a life in accordance with the virtues (i.e. *the* sort of life that good human beings live if nothing external to them prevents it). Well, according to my conception of the virtues on the standard list, that is an open question, and whether or not it were so would all depend on the details. Some monastic contemplatives might lack charity, honesty, and courage; in some societies, or in some circumstances, leading such a life might be a sustained act of folly, or selfishness, or irresponsibility. And then they would be bad *qua* human beings and not living well. But some others, differently situated, with different reasons for their choice of life, and different ways of living it, might turn out to be good human beings, leading good human lives. As I noted above, a life lived in accordance with the virtues can take a great variety of forms, including those in which the exercise of at least one virtue figures much more largely and even at the expense of the exercise of others.

# Naturalism for Rational Animals

In this chapter and the next, I continue the discussion of the particular form of ethical naturalism outlined in the preceding one,
exploring some of the very deep issues it involves and eventually
pushing it to the point where it connects back to Plato's first requirement—that the virtues benefit their possessor.

## WHAT DIFFERENCE DOES OUR
## RATIONALITY MAKE?

When we moved from the evaluations of other social animals to
ethical evaluations of ourselves, there was an obvious addition to
the list of aspects which are evaluated. The other animals act. So do
we occasionally, but mostly we act from reason, as they do not, and
it is primarily in virtue of our actions from reason that we are ethically good or bad human beings. So that is one difference that our
being rational makes. But, it may be said, surely that sole difference—just one further aspect—is nothing like enough to register the
huge gap that exists between us, rational creatures that we are, and
the rest of the animal kingdom. Either ethical naturalism is a non-
starter or our rationality has to make much more difference than
has hitherto been recognized here. I agree, and, continuing to
defend it as a starter, will now turn to the ways in which our rationality does make a difference .

It was a noteworthy feature of the structure of evaluations of living things that, as species acquired significant new capacities, two
corresponding new ends appeared in the structure in the light of
which aspects of individual members were evaluated. The aspects
of creatures capable of pain (and perhaps pleasure) are evaluated in

the light of the third end of characteristic freedom from pain and enjoyment; the aspects of social creatures in the light of the good functioning of the social group. So we might expect that, having reached creatures who are rational, their aspects would be evaluated in the light of some fifth end which relates to this new, transforming, capacity.

But what could this fifth end be? Tradition offers us a few alternatives. We might say that the fifth end was the preparation of our souls for the life hereafter, or that it was contemplation—the good functioning of the theoretical intellect. But to adopt the first is to go beyond naturalism towards supernaturalism, and even philosophers have baulked at following Aristotle and endorsing the second. I am not in a position to assert that there is no fifth end peculiarly appropriate to our rationality, but no plausible candidate suggests itself and I will suggest instead that the genuinely transforming effect of our rationality on the basic structure adequately registers the 'huge gap' that exists between us and the other animals.

Looking back at the evaluations of other living things, we should be struck by the extent to which they depend on our identifying what is *characteristic* of the species (and/or special members of it.) The other sophisticated social animals have a characteristic life expectancy, characteristic ways of continuing their species, characteristic pleasures, sufferings, and freedom from suffering, characteristic ways of going on in their social group, and it is in the light of what is characteristic of them that they are evaluated. If they are good *x*s, they will, with a bit of luck, be thriving or flourishing in their characteristically *x* way, living well, as *x*s, unless something external to themselves is preventing it. But what, in an *analogous* way, is characteristic of human beings? We have a characteristic life expectancy, but do we have anything else?

Well, we might note that, as a species, we are like many species of birds and unlike fish or quite a lot of mammals in that we continue our species by (a) producing a rather small number of offspring which (b) need a fair amount of time devoted to their protection and nurturing in their early stages in order for the species to continue. But do we have a characteristic way of going in for this sustained protecting and nurturing, as the king penguins have theirs, and the cuckoos have theirs, and the polar bears have theirs? And if so, what is it?

We might say that, like the other higher mammals, we characteristically enjoy food and suffer when physically damaged; like some of the other sophisticated social animals, we characteristically enjoy company and play, and suffer when solitary or confined. But we do not seem to be pained by and enjoy these things in just the same way as the other animals do (except perhaps for physical damage) because, with us, what we think about the food or company, play, solitude, and confinement can make such a difference; none of them as such is a characteristic pleasure or source of suffering for human beings.[1] (Recall the dire influence of a racist upbringing.) Moreover, when we think of the great range of things that human beings can enjoy—art, music, literature, sports, mountain climbing, making things, gardening, the acquisition of knowledge (anything from astrophysics to finding out how people live in other countries or what their food is like), trying to solve problems, being with other animals, to say nothing of hunting, killing, wielding power over other people, inflicting pain and humiliation, rape, pillage, and destruction—how can we retain the idea of *characteristic* pleasures? Are they everything on this list and more? Some subset? The range of things we can be pained by, if not as wide, is wide enough to make the idea of characteristic pain and suffering equally problematic.

Human beings are characteristically social, *ex hypothesi*, but as with the fact that we characteristically nurture our young, this does not take us far enough. Do we have a characteristic way, or ways, of functioning as a social group, as the wolves have theirs, and elephants theirs, and chimpanzees theirs? If so, what is it, or are they? Well, it might be said, we characteristically communicate with each other by means of language, and there is something very significant about that fact about us as a species. But it is not easy to see what the significance is.

So if ethical naturalism depends on identifying what is characteristic of human beings as a species in the way their pleasures and pains and ways of going on are characteristic of the other species, it looks doomed to failure. 'The way' human beings live varies enormously from place to place, from time to time, from one to

---

[1] Cf. Foot, noting 'a feature of the operation of human beings to which Aquinas drew attention, when he said that while animals perceive things that are good and go for them, human beings go for what they *see as good*', 'Rationality and Virtue', 210.

another. When we look at the other species, although we do find regional and temporal variety (for instance, between the town-dwelling and country-dwelling members of those species of crea-tures that have fairly recently taken up doing both) and some idiosyncrasies, the variation in us is of quite a different order.

Moreover, we regard this variation as the unsurprising upshot of that very rationality that distinguishes us from the other animals. The other animals live 'the way' they do because it is in their nature to do so; we do not. They cannot contemplate alternatives and decide to change things, or choose to try a new way as we can; they are biologically determined, we are not.

This thought that we have about the variation, the absence of characteristically human ways of going on, is more important than the variation itself. For, as Watson noted, it is what makes us resis-tant to the idea that ethical evaluations can be strictly analogous to the biological/ethological evaluations of good (healthy, well-functioning) animals. Nature determines how they should be, but the idea that nature could be normative with respect to us, that it could determine how we should be, is one we will no longer accept.

It is true of all other living things that (for the most part) if xs don't, then they can't.[2] And since (amazingly enough) the familiar truth expressed in the slogan 'ought implies can' is true of all living things, it makes no sense to say that, for example, a male polar bear is a bad/defective polar bear because, far from defending its young, it has to be prevented by their mother from killing them. Nor is an exceptional male polar bear that hangs around its cubs offering food anything other than defective. There is no sense to be attached to saying that polar bears would be better fitted to flourish in a char-acteristically polar bear way, to live well, as polar bears, if the males were different, or indeed, if males and females banded together to hunt. Polar bears just *don't* act that way and thereby cannot—

---

[2] There is an obvious putative counterexample—chimpanzees and orang-utans do not 'talk', but we have managed to teach some of them to do so after a fashion. So some can, even though they, as a species, do not. But they can only because we have interfered with the ways of life that are characteristic of their species. I have read conflicting reports on whether the ones we have taught are passing on the teach-ing to their young without further intervention from us. Suppose they do, and the next generation does too, and it persists. Then that would be what they, now, *do* do; we would have changed their nature, as we have, wittingly or unwittingly, changed the natures of many living things.

unless they mutate—and that is all there is to it. Nor does it make sense to say that, for example, male cheetahs flourish more, live better lives as cheetahs, than female cheetahs, or drones than worker bees. Our concepts of 'a good member of the species $x$', and 'living well as an $x$', in relation to the other animals, are completely constrained by what members and specialized members of the species in question actually do.

But in virtue of our rationality—our free will if you like—we are different. Apart from obvious physical constraints and possible psychological constraints, there is no knowing what we *can* do from what we *do* do, because we can assess what we do do and at least try to change it. Suppose that, as far as human ethology goes, human beings do have a 'characteristic' way of going in for the sustained protection and nurturing of their young—the biological mothers of the offspring do it. Thereby human beings resemble a large number of other species in which (to coin a phrase) stepfatherly nature bears much harder on the females than it does on the males. With those other species, this is (unless we are mad enough to interfere) necessarily so, but with us it is not, and it has been one of the most illuminating aspects of feminism that it has made us see this. It is in the nature of things—in the nature or 'essence' of cheetahs and thereby of female cheetahs—that, speaking anthropocentrically, female cheetahs are bound to have a rotten life in comparison with male cheetahs.[3] Part of what feminists are after, and right about, when they deny 'essentialism', is that, for us, it is not in our nature or essence that female human beings are bound to do whatever they have, so far, done. We can do otherwise. Our concepts of 'a good human being' and 'living well, as a human being' are far from being completely constrained by what members and biologically specialized members of our species actually, or, at the moment, typically, do; we have room for the idea that we might

---

[3] I once saw a nature documentary which followed a cheetah in the wild through her pregnancy and managed to capture in full the extraordinary sight of her trying to bring down a small deer (on her own, of course, because cheetahs are solitary) when very near to her term. Apart from the pregnancy, she was nothing but skin and bone and sinew, and although she started off with the characteristic gravity-defying bounds, she couldn't keep it up, and collapsed. According to the documentary, she had been, in the last few weeks, a little unlucky in the availability of prey, but only a little; near starvation and exhaustion after attempts at hunting during pregnancy are, it was said, pretty much the female cheetah's lot.

be able to be and to live *better*. (Hence (pending some further discussion at the end of the next chapter) the irrelevance to ethical naturalism of the human ethological fact that human beings (male
human beings?) are characteristically aggressive.)

This is a major part of the genuinely transforming effect the fact
of our rationality has on the basic naturalistic structure.

But has it transformed the structure beyond recognition? I said
that ethical naturalism looks to be doomed to failure *if* it depends
on identifying what is characteristic of human beings as a species,
in the way their pleasures and pains and ways of going on are characteristic of the other species. By and large we can't identify what
is characteristic of human beings as a species in this way—there is
too much variety. And even if we could, it looks as though we would
not allow anything we identified to carry any normative weight if
we thought it was something we could change. So is ethical naturalism, after all, a non-starter?[4]

Not yet, for there is a standard claim to the effect that there *is*
something characteristic of human beings, that we *do* have a characteristic way of going on, but not in the way that is true of the
other animals. Their characteristic ways of going on are many and
have to be described in detailed terms, specifically related to such
things as the acquisition of nourishment, mating, feeding the young,
hunting, selecting leaders, etc., and are discovered by observation.
Our way of going on is just one, which remains the same across all
areas of our life. Our characteristic way of going on, which distinguishes us from all the other species of animals, is a rational way. A
'rational way' is any way that we can rightly see as good, as something we have reason to do. Correspondingly, our characteristic
enjoyments are any enjoyments we can rightly see as good, as something we in fact enjoy *and* that reason can rightly endorse.

Now as 'a characteristic way' for members of a species to go on,
this is manifestly very different from all the others, and not just in

---

    [4] Bernard Williams, who is Aristotelian naturalism's most subtle and penetrating
critic, has made a number of attempts to pin down what he thinks is wrong with it,
and that we do not have a characteristic or 'appropriate' way of going on has been
one of his persisting worries: 'The idea of a naturalistic ethics was born of a deeply
teleological outlook, and its best expression, in many ways, is still to be found in
Aristotle's philosophy, a philosophy according to which there is inherent in each natural kind of thing an appropriate way for things of that kind to behave.' 'Evolution,
Ethics and the Representation Problem' (1983), 109.

virtue of being general rather than particularized. The notion of 'in the way characteristic of the species' is, perhaps, not just a statistical notion even in the case of the other animals.[5] But to maintain, as I am recklessly doing, that 'our characteristic way of going on' is to do what we can rightly see we have reason to do, is to give up with a vengeance any idea that most human beings do what it is 'characteristic' of human beings to do. The notion is avowedly normative, and is clearly going to yield judgements to the effect that many human beings are *not* going on 'in the way characteristic of the species' and are thereby defective human beings.[6]

But isn't this exactly what we should expect a plausible ethical naturalism to yield? Does anyone think that most human beings are good human beings? Does anyone think that, regarding ourselves as a collection of social groups or as one global one, we are flourishing, living well, as human beings? Surely not. We know that, ethically, many of us are rather poor ethical specimens, and when 'we'—human beings living in the kind of circumstances that enable us to write and read this sort of book—think about how life is for the majority of other human beings, 'we' know that our (human beings') aspirations to live well even as healthy animals, let alone as human beings, are still, in general, but unrealized hopes. Perhaps it is irrational to have such hopes (a point I shall return to later) but, while we have them, we should not be surprised if ethical naturalism yields the conclusion that they are not realized *because* so many of us are ethically defective.

Moreover, if ethical naturalism is not going to be just a branch of biology or ethology, if, as I took as a premise from McDowell at

---

    [5] Against the idea that it is a statistical notion, see Dupré, *The Disorder of Things*, and Thompson, 'The Representation of Life'.

    [6] Annas, *The Morality of Happiness*, is most illuminating on the ways in which the idea that human beings are 'naturally' rational is played out not so much in Aristotle as in the Stoics: 'The Stoics are the first to produce an ethics that appeals to nature and is prominently a *developmental* one; this enables them to take as primary the points that human nature is developing and rational. Thus we get a more sophisticated use of nature which combines the idea of nature as the inevitable aspects of ourselves with nature as indicating a goal of development, one that can be corrupted.' 'This', as she notes a couple of paragraphs later, 'is the part of ancient ethics which modern readers are apt to find most unsympathetic. Partly this is because the claim is manifestly a normative one, whereas we expect the appeal to nature to be to non-normative "fact". Partly it is because the ancient claims are so plainly revisionary, whereas we expect nature to be an empirically specifiable notion' (215).

the outset, it has no pretensions to establishing any conclusions from scientific foundations accessible from a neutral point of view, we might expect it to be avowedly normative.

But, it may be objected, if we introduce a normative notion of 'a characteristic way of going on', how have we preserved any vestige of naturalism? Well, we have preserved the structure; it is still the case that human beings are ethically good in so far as their ethically relevant aspects foster the four ends appropriate to a social animal, in the way characteristic of the species. And the structure—the appeal to just those four ends—really does constrain, substantially, what I can reasonably maintain is a virtue in human beings. I cannot just proceed from some premises about what it is reasonable or rational to do to some conclusion that it is rational to act in such-and-such a way, and hence that a good human being is one who acts that way. I have to consider whether the corresponding character trait (if such a thing could be imagined) would foster or be inimical to those four ends.

Consider, by way of illustration, the claim that completely impersonal benevolence, conceived of as, perhaps, Peter Singer would conceive of it, is a virtue.[7] This would be a benevolence that knows no species-boundaries and recognizes no special bonds of family or friendship. To someone who is convinced that we have no reason to take any account of animal suffering, that animals are just here for us to use, in any way we choose, including torturing them for amusement, this is bound to seem an utterly implausible claim. To someone whose ethical outlook includes the view that charity and compassion extend to animals, and are virtues, that cruelty and vanity are vices, and that much of our current treatment of animals is the product of such vices, the claim is not immediately implausible. But could it be maintained, within the terms laid down by the naturalistic structure?

To consider this question fairly we would have to take seriously the point that the impersonal benevolence is being considered as a

---

[7] It is, inevitably, difficult to get a virtue-ethics-cum-ethical-naturalism way of talking to engage with Singer's utilitarianism-cum-anti-speciesism. But given the standard claim that 'utilitarianism is the ethic of benvolence' because of its concern with the interests of those affected by one's actions, and Singer's claim that we should always give *equal* consideration to the interests of all sentient beings thus affected, and nothing else, I hope that what I give is an attributable conception. See, especially, Singer, *Practical Ethics* (2nd edn., 1995).

*virtue*, not merely as a reliable tendency to churn out actions determined by Singer's non-speciesist utilitarianism. So it is not to be dismissed out of hand on the grounds that our individual survival
might fare rather poorly if we did not, prudently, sometimes put our
own life first. (Our standard conception of benevolence (or charity)
sometimes requires self-sacrifice, but certainly not invariably.) But,
thinking of benevolence as a character trait, we do have to think of
its possessor as someone who does not think of 'That's a fellow
human being' or 'She's my child/parent/friend/ partner' as an X reason for seeking another's good; we have to think of her as someone
whose emotions, being in harmony with her reason, do not particularly engage with her fellow human beings or her own children or
parents, as someone who does not have close emotion-involving
attachments to other individual human beings that would make it
difficult for her to act from this putative virtue.

Such a character trait might well not be inimical to individual
survival or enjoyment (of a 'characteristic', rationally informed
sort); vegetarianism certainly is not, and the possibility that human
beings could, by and large, live out their natural life span, by and
large in harmony with the other animals, is perhaps something we
could hope for. It does seem certain that we could make a better job
of it than we are currently doing. But it is when we consider the
other two ends, the continuance of the species and the good functioning of the social group, that the insistence that the benevolence
be impersonal in the way Singer would require both comes into play
and into question.

Could impersonal benevolence, as a character trait of human
beings, foster these two ends? The question is, admittedly, wildly
speculative, but on the face of it, it rather looks as though the
species and familial bonding that are part of our biological, animal
nature, and make us 'partial' to our own species and children, play
an essential role in sustaining these two ends.[8] This is *not* to lapse
back into resting content with our nature as we find it, *not* to deny
that we could reshape our nature in such a way that we no longer

[8] In this connection, Annette Baier argues that society could not be sustained and
continued without the relation of trust and trustworthiness that occurs between loving parents and their children. See 'What do Women Want in Moral Theory?' (1985).
Mary Midgley emphasizes the importance of familial (and thereby species) bonds in
the sustaining of our lives and discusses it illuminatingly in her defence of a moderate 'speciesism'. See ch. 10 of *Animals and Why they Matter*.

cared particularly about our own species and children. Maybe we could. It is to draw attention to the fact that, with respect to the continuance of the species and the good functioning of the social group, our natural tendency to bond to other human beings and our children seems to be serving us rather well. The onus is on those who recommend impersonal benevolence as a virtue to provide at least a speculation about how a species of rational animals who had brought themselves to care naught for their own children or each other's company might still be a species of *social* animals who, moreover, nurtured their young—and, indeed, went to the trouble of giving them a moral education and bringing them up to be impersonally benevolent in their turn.

So despite relying on a normative notion of 'our characteristic way of going on', ethical naturalism does not cease to be naturalism; the four ends appropriate to us just in virtue of our being social animals really do constrain what will pass reflective scrutiny as a candidate virtue.

## ANALOGIES AND DISANALOGIES

Let us pause to consider where we have got to. Ethical naturalism, in the context of virtue ethics, aims to capture Anscombe's and Foot's idea that, when we talk about ethically good human beings, we have not suddenly started to use the word 'good' in a totally new 'moral' or 'evaluative' way. There is a structure (not necessarily of the sort I have outlined, but some structure) in the botanical and ethological evaluations of other living things as good or defective specimens of their kind, which supervenes on evaluations of their parts and behaviour as good or defective in the light of certain ends, and this carries over (*mutatis mutandis*) into evaluations of ourselves as ethically good or bad as human beings in respect of our characters. Moreover, in preserving the structure (and hence the four ends appropriate to social animals), the particular subject matter has been kept 'natural'; we evaluate ourselves as a natural kind, a species which is part of the natural biological order of things, not as creatures with an immortal soul or 'beings' who are persons or rational agents. And, so far, the ethical and the non-ethical evaluations are analogous.

However, they are also disanalogous. For a start, according to

the form of ethical naturalism I am defending, what is particularly
evaluated are character traits, not, directly, actions or lives. (I have
found, in discussion, that this is a point that can hardly be emphasized too often.)

Consider the ethical issue of whether one should be vegetarian.
As with homosexual activity, neither being vegetarian nor being
omniverous is a character trait, it's a practice. I myself incline to the
view that most of 'us'—that is, people in the circumstances that
make it possible for them to write or read this sort of book—act as
we should when we refuse to eat meat and as we should not when
we do not (in most, but by no means all, circumstances). And I do
so (oversimplifying) on the grounds that (i) temperance (with
respect to the pleasures of food) is a virtue, and (ii) that for most of
'us', eating meat is intemperate (greedy, self-indulgent). And ethical
naturalism bears primarily on (i), *not* on (ii). I do not try to get to
my ethical view about vegetarianism by starting with claims about
how things are with respect to human beings *eating meat* (or not
doing so). I start with (i)—a claim about how things are with respect
to human beings being temperate, which, as it stands, says nothing
about meat-eating at all, and it is *that* claim that (if ethical naturalism can fulfil its promise) I hope that it can help to justify. But, if it
can, it would thereby have done most of its work; what can (if anything) justify (ii) will not, by and large, be drawn from ethical naturalism.

I insert the qualifications 'most of' its work, and 'not by and large
drawn from', because the issue of vegetarianism is a particularly
instructive example of the kind of holism that the Neurathian procedure in ethics involves. An upshot of this is the subtle interplay
between the possible validation of a particular character trait as a
virtue and a modification in one's detailed conception of that virtue.
Subjecting my belief that temperance (with respect to food) is a
virtue to reflective scrutiny, I might have an indeterminate or a very
determinate conception of temperance's bearing on 'our' meat-
eating. Either may well survive the scrutiny, as things actually are
with respect to human beings. But *if* things were as a number of
people (remarkably ignorant of (at least) the lives of millions of
Hindus and Buddhists) think they are, namely, that human beings
need to eat meat, that, without it, their life expectancy and their
capacity to produce healthy progeny is seriously impaired, then a
determinate conception that had already ruled meat-eating out

would not survive intact; it would have to be abandoned as a candidate virtue or modified.

Turning now to lives, let us return to Watson's question of whether ethical naturalism could establish that 'being a gangster is incompatible with being a good human being'. If the programme can, when pursued in detail, fulfil its promise, then the answer is, 'Yes, it could (with the addition of some plausible extra premises)'—but it would not do so by moving from the premise that 'a good human life must be social in character' as Watson suggests. A gangster is bad *qua* human being, if he is, because a gangster is, as such, callous, unjust, dishonest, reckless, and thereby lacks charity, justice, honesty, and courage (at the very least). The first move is to validate charity, justice, etc. as virtues—which, I have claimed, looks at least possible. The next move, which comes not from the naturalism but from (putative) knowledge of what sorts of characters gangsters are, is to establish that gangsters are callous, unjust, etc. (the plausible extra premises). These moves together would establish that a gangster was bad *qua* human being, and thereby unable to live a good human life. No mention need, nor indeed should, be made of 'a good human life's being social in character' for, as we saw in the case of the virtuous monastic contemplative, a human being might live a good human life—a life in accordance with the virtues—notwithstanding the fact that the life in question was not social.

A related disanalogy is that we do not have characteristic ways of going on in the same way that the other animals do. Our single characteristic 'way of going on' is in a rational way, i.e. in any ways we can rightly see as something we have reason to do. Ethical evaluation cannot be a branch of biology or ethology because neither we, nor our concepts of 'a good human being' and 'living well as a human being', are completely constrained by nature. With the other animals, it is (almost) guaranteed that overall, there are good, healthy members of the species, who, with a bit of luck, will be living well, for what counts as being good and living well is determined by the standard that, so to speak, nature has laid down for them.[9] But for us it is an open question whether *any* human being

---

[9] I say 'almost' in the light of two possibilities. Every member of a particular species might, at one period of time, be defective (perhaps because they had all been poisoned). But then they would all be defective in comparison with the good ones that had been around before. And if they are currently all defective by that standard

is good, or living well, given what we could be, not something that has already been determined by nature.

A further disanalogy is that the ethical evaluations are made from within an ethical outlook, an outlook which already has its own conceptions of the virtues, and related conceptions of what is good, beneficial, advantageous, worthwhile, important, enjoyable (and their opposites), and of what we have reason to do. It is from within some ethical outlook that one considers whether, e.g. charity or temperance or impersonal benevolence is a virtue; those character traits cannot be given a neutral, scientific, specification. And if one decides that it is (or is not), in the light of the four ends, one's consequent judgement that someone is a good human being in so far as she possesses this character trait, or is not a bad one despite lacking it, will issue from a mixture of constraints imposed by nature and by the ethical outlook.

On a further point, it is unclear whether we should say that the ethical and the non-ethical evaluations are analogous or disanalogous.

In the last chapter (pp. 202–5 above) I listed five points 'worth noting' about the evaluations of other living things. The first was that the truth of such evaluations did not depend in any way on my wants, interests, or values, nor indeed on 'ours'. They are 'objective' in the most straightforward sense of the term. Indeed, I added, given that botany, ethology, etc. are sciences, they are scientific. The fifth was that the truth of the overall evaluation depends in part upon the needs and (as we ascend the ladder of nature) the interests and desires of the *x*s in question. Do these two claims remain true of our evaluations of ourselves?

Clearly, the additional remark in the first point no longer applies; the ethical evaluations are not scientific. But, unless natural science exhausts the realm of the objective, which, following McDowell, I am assuming is not so, that does not show that the ethical evaluations are not objective as long as the beginning of the first point

---

because they have all been subject to radiation, it might be indeterminate for a time whether the radiation has produced a new mutation which will have its own standard of goodness or whether the original species is still going through a bad period in which all its members are defective. The other rather remote possibility is that perhaps some very simple living things are just too simple to have defects without immediately dying from them. So with them there would be no contrast between good/defective, healthy/unhealthy, and it would be indeterminate which they were.

holds good—that the truth of such evaluations does not depend in any way on my wants, interests, or values, nor indeed on 'ours'. But, if that holds good, it seems clear that the fifth point has to go.

However, the fifth point certainly stands. If 'A good human being is one who possesses charity, justice, honesty, courage, etc.' is true, its truth depends upon facts about human needs, interests and desires, just as 'A good elephant is one which has good tusks, follows the leader, does not attack other elephants, looks after the young, is not frightened of water, etc.' depends upon facts about elephant needs, interests and desires. How could the truth of evaluations of living things with interests and desires not depend in part upon such facts?

So must we say that it is the first point that has to go, almost *in toto*? True, the truth of the ethical evaluations does not depend on *my* wants, interests, and values—that much still holds. But not only are they are not scientific, their truth does depend in part on 'our'—human beings'—interests and desires. So must we conclude that they are not objective and that this is a further disanalogy?

Clearly, our difficulty here is with the awkward (and over-used) phrase, 'truths that depend on our interests and desires'. For, in the context of *ethical* naturalism, we think of this as, yet again, raising the spectre of merely re-expressing our ethical outlook. 'The conclusions of ethical naturalism can be arrived at only from within an acquired ethical outlook, not from a scientific account of human nature. They are *thereby* dependent on our interests and desires and merely serve to re-express our outlook.' But, as the above remark about the elephants should remind us, the conclusions of ethical naturalism do not depend on our interests and desires *because* they are arrived at from within an ethical outlook. They depend on our interests and desires because their subject matter is us, namely, animals that *have* interests and desires, just as the true judgements about the psychology or practices of human beings do. It cannot be that judgements whose truth is in part, or even wholly, dependent upon human interests and desires are thereby not objective—how could the truth of a judgement be independent of all or part of its subject matter? So, so far, we have no reason to conclude that the ethical evaluations naturalism yields are not objective. *That* much of the first point can (pending further argument) still stand, and count as an analogy that holds between the ethical and the non-ethical evaluations. But two things seem disanalogous.

One is that we seem somewhat stuck for any articulation of the way, if there is a way, in which the ethical evaluations are objective. They are analogous in many ways to the non-ethical ones and we have not (yet) got a reason for saying they are not objective—but in their case, more needs to be said. The second disanalogy is that, objective though they may be in some sense, they do seem to be 'necessarily practical'. I will return to the objectivity issue in the final chapter; but consider the second issue now.

## ETHICAL EVALUATIONS AS NECESSARILY PRACTICAL

The claim that ethics, or morality, is 'necessarily practical' is standardly, and correctly, ascribed to Hume but might equally well be ascribed to Aristotle, to whom we owe the distinction between the theoretical and the 'practical' in the sense in which Hume used the latter term. He did not mean that ethics was necessarily down-to-earth and pragmatic rather than airy-fairy, but that it was necessarily concerned with action (*praxis* being the ancient Greek word for 'action' and *praktike* the associated adjective, from which we have 'practical').

Hume glossed his claim by saying, amongst other things, that morals 'serve to produce and prevent action'. At first sight, this seems obvious enough, but it has proved extraordinarily difficult to understand it in a way that enables it to be modified by 'necessarily' and remain plausible. If morals, or ethical judgements, necessarily provide reasons or motives for action (or refraining from action), how come there are so many wicked people who are indifferent to them? But a beautifully precise sense which captures its truth has been given to it by Simon Blackburn, who says, 'it is difficult to imagine . . . that we could rightly translate a society as making ethical . . . judgements, if there were no inclination to take them into account in the business of practical reasoning'.[10]

This could be helpfully contrasted with the same claim made about the judgements of human medical science. We, as it happens, are interested in these in a not merely theoretical but also practical way. There is, for us, a significant difference as far as our actions

---

[10] S. Blackburn, 'The Flight to Reality' (1995), 48.

are concerned between 'X causes cancer in mice' and 'X causes cancer in human beings'; the latter sort of judgement is one we are strongly inclined to take into account in the business of practical reasoning. But it is possible to imagine rightly translating a society as making such judgements even if there were no such inclination amongst them—if, for example, we knew that they had all become Christian Scientists but continued to pursue medical research out of merely theoretical interest.

Now clearly none of the evaluations of other living things are necessarily practical in this sense. Nor are our medical evaluations of ourselves. If our ethical evaluations are, how has this come about? The answer lies in the normative sense attached to 'our characteristic way of going on'. The very substantial effect of claiming that our characteristic way of going on is in a *rational* way, that is, 'in any way or ways that we can rightly see we have reason to do', is that it connects ethical evaluations, in our own mouths, with our own views about what there is reason to do.

Let us imagine an atheist considering whether piety (conceived as a character trait) to the Judeo-Christian God is a virtue. (This is the plank she is considering, her other views about the virtues, which we will take to be those on the standard list, not being called into question at this point.) An open-minded atheist will bring a tolerant conception of such piety to such an enquiry. She will not, for example, assess it as the character trait whose possessors murder people they suspect of performing abortions, or persecute Hindus. That would be like assessing charity or benevolence as the character trait whose possessors sometimes commit involuntary euthanasia, or honesty as the character trait whose possessors never remain discreetly or charitably silent. Our open-minded atheist would assess it as the character trait that some distinctly admirable people, past and present, possess, and she can then hardly fail to recognize that, in them, it is inseparably intertwined with, and positively reinforces, their other virtues (as, given even the limited unity of the virtues, they tend to intertwine with and reinforce each other). So it might seem that she should conclude that, viewed in the light of the four ends, it is a virtue, since it fosters all of them to the very extent that charity, justice, courage, honesty, etc. do.

But do those who act from piety act in the way characteristic of human beings, i.e. in a rational way? Well, in so far as their piety is inseparable from, say, their charity, our atheist may say that they do.

But in so far as their piety prompts them to pray, to refrain from blasphemy, to go to church, to spend time thinking about God and trying to get closer to an understanding of Him, the atheist, by her own lights, must think that they are not acting rationally, because the right reasons they think they have (as *pious*, not merely conventional or Pascal's wager people) for doing these things, are no reasons at all. Though the character trait indeed fosters the four ends, it does not do so in the way characteristic of our species, namely in a rational way. Moreover, although by the evidence of the smile factor I mentioned in Chapter 8, piety undoubtedly brings great joy and serenity to its possessors, no atheist can regard such joy as 'characteristic of human beings', that is, as something that reason can endorse. For, although it may be both supremely satisfying to those who have it, and perfectly harmless, from the atheist's standpoint it is based on a complete illusion; reason cannot endorse it. Hence, employing the normative idea of 'our characteristic way of going on', our atheist will conclude that piety is not, after all, a virtue.

Contrast this with another case. Suppose that, though no stranger to virtue in general, I have, under various influences, lost my conviction that loyalty is a virtue. Drifting happily around the world, dropping in and out of transitory friendships, it comes to seem to me that loyalty and related gratitude—that obsessive clinging to old relationships and institutions ('the old boy network', I sneer), which always harks back to the past, the misplaced trust involved—are a mistake. Each case should be considered afresh; one should stand up for someone here and now because here and now he is a pleasant chap you have just spent some pleasant hours with, not because you happen to have known him for twenty years. Thinking or speaking ill of people who are not present does not matter; the people you are with at the moment are the only ones that matter, and keeping the conversation with them friendly and amusing. The things I used to see as reasons for doing or not doing certain things—he's my friend, he'll be expecting me to (we go back a long way), it's an institution that has done a lot for me, he would be shattered if he heard me say that (I know he couldn't possibly hear, but that's not the point), it would be disloyal—now seem to me, in one way, to be no reasons at all. (Of course, I can still see that they are reasons people give, just as the atheist knows what reasons the pious give.)

And now suppose someone points out to me how loyalty fares

as a virtue in the context of ethical naturalism. Young, footloose, and foolish as I am, I may well have overlooked the fact that not many human beings are living the way I am, that their different ways of living are sustaining mine, and that theirs are in part sustained by loyalty and gratitude. I am passing through settled communities of people who have established long-standing networks of personal and business relationships many of which are working well and working, in part, because the people involved act for the sorts of reasons that I have lost sight of. I may well too have overlooked the fact that some old people are rejoicing in relationships that go all the way back to their youth, and that the age of the relationship and the serene confidence each party to it has in the loyalty of the other has enabled it to develop into something that looks worth having.

This I might come to believe if it (and more) were pointed out to me. But in coming to believe it, in coming to recognize that loyalty and gratitude foster the good functioning of social groups and the sort of personal relationships which can be one of our greatest sources of joy, I recover my grasp of the reasons loyal people give for acting loyally *as* reasons. Loyalty isn't a silly thing; I now see; those loyal people who give those sorts of reasons for what they do, *are* going on in a rational and not a silly way; their reasons really are reasons.

And thereby reasons for me. To believe (as we suppose I now do) that loyalty is a virtue is to believe that people who act loyally are acting in a rational way, exercising practical rationality. But to believe that when someone, say, sticks by a friend because he *is* a friend he is exercising practical rationality is to believe that if I were to do the same, in the same circumstances, for the same reason, I would be exercising practical rationality. To recognize a character trait as a virtue, on the grounds of ethical naturalism, is to recognize the X reasons for acting people with that character trait characteristically have *as* reasons, to recognize them as reasons for oneself.[11] (This is why the atheist cannot judge piety to be a virtue without abandoning her atheism.)

A few points about this claim should be noted. The first is mere repetition with emphasis. What are recognized as reasons for act-

---

[11] Foot also includes this as part of her account of 'the way in which morality is necessarily practical: it serves to produce and prevent action, *because the understanding of reasons can do that*'. 'Does Moral Subjectivism Rest on a Mistake?', 10.

ing are the reasons people with the relevant character trait do, or would, give—X reasons, the range associated with the character trait in question—*not* the fact that the character trait in question sustains any of the four ends. Loyal people do not stick by their friends, continue with the business that has treated them generously and has now fallen on hard times, and refuse to mock their partners behind their back *because* they think doing so fosters good relationships and the good functioning of the social group. They do so for the X reasons and, as we have seen, 'because they think it's right'. Seeing the point of a character trait, V—seeing what is good about it in the life of human beings and thereby endorsing it as a virtue—is seeing the point of human beings' doing what is V 'for its own sake', not doing what is V because it does play that role in human life.

The second point is that recognition of reasons cannot be expected to work miracles or, more prosaically, to unseat well-established habits. We have no reason to expect that an individual who lacks a particular character trait, and comes, through the considerations of ethical naturalism, to the conclusion that the character trait in question is a *virtue*, to leap transformed from their bed the next morning. For one thing, as we noted in Chapter 7, a virtuous character trait is not acquired overnight, even with the best will in the world; for another, the will may be weak. Every smoker recognizes that she has not just reason, but overriding, compelling, reason to stop smoking, but weakness of will rules; she wants this cigarette here now, and the next, and the next. Moreover, the difficulties of acquiring a character trait one did not hitherto possess—of actually coming to enjoy its exercise—may well prove sufficiently arduous to tempt one into lapsing back into one's old ways. The young drifter I imagined above is not likely to find it easy to start doing what is loyal if he decides to throw up his present way of life and go home to his long-suffering, loyal parents, and his first attempts at serious long-term relationships may prove discouraging failures. So he might well lapse back into his own, easy, going-for-short-term-pleasures ways (many of which, we are supposing, are quite consistent with virtue), not bothering to think about whether he has reason to do otherwise.[12]

---

[12] As Foot says, 'I suppose one can evade either "endorsing" or not "endorsing" morality, or part of morality, by simply refusing to think about it; and I suppose that most of us do that at times.' 'Does Moral Subjectivism Rest on a Mistake?', 11.

The third point is that the example of the drifter is nothing more than a single example. It represents him as a quick and willing learner, whereas if he were more of a stranger to virtue than I initially supposed he might prove much more recalcitrant. And this brings me to a further question.

It might be thought that, in connecting ethical evaluations in our own mouths with our own views about what there is reason to do, I have reneged on my earlier claim (p. 194 above) that the naturalistic conclusions are not supposed to be providing motivating reasons for the mafioso drug baron, nor for, say, me, when I engage in reflective scrutiny of my ethical outlook and conclude that, say, loyalty is a virtue. For have I not just made it clear that, if someone were to conclude, on the grounds of ethical naturalism, that loyalty is a virtue, they would thereby acquire motivating reasons for doing what is loyal (if they had not had them before)? And, in theory, would the same not be true of the mafioso drug baron?

I made the earlier claim in the context of forestalling an objection to the naturalism project that many people are inclined to make before they even look at how it might work. The objection springs from the correct insight that it is wildly implausible to imagine a mafioso drug baron going through the naturalistic reasoning, coming to the conclusion that e.g. charity, justice, and honesty are virtues, and promptly becoming a reformed character. It is equally implausible to imagine him listening patiently and sympathetically to any one of us going through the same reasoning for him, and coming to agree with us,[13] as the (basically quite decent) young drifter did, and I wanted to make it clear that I was not, in defending the naturalistic project, denying that these are anything but implausible.

I have not reneged on the earlier claim, but it now needs a little qualification. Someone *may* support the view that such-and-such a character trait is a virtue on naturalistic grounds with the intention of producing motivating reasons. The usual context for this is in the bringing up of children when we are trying to inculcate the virtues in them. As I noted in Chapter 8, in urging certain character traits (and hence acting for certain reasons) on them we not only say things that relate to the thesis that the virtues benefit their posses-

---

[13] As Aristotle says, such a man 'would not listen to an argument to dissuade him, or understand it if he did', *Nicomachean Ethics*, 1179b25.

sor, but also to the thesis that they are the good-making characteristics of human beings—that they play a particular role in human
life. Alongside teaching children the personal benefits they can
expect to derive from being e.g. honest, we point out some of the
things in their social life that honesty sustains such as (depending
on their age and circumstances) their being able to leave things in
their school desks, getting reliable directions, the school library
(with its amnesty day for returns), acquiring qualifications and references. In such a context we are indeed aiming to get them to recognize the reasons appropriate to various virtues as reasons for
them, as motivating reasons. And we may take an interest in someone who, somehow, has rather lost sight of some range of reasons
appropriate to a particular virtue, like the young drifter, and think
it worth trying to reanimate his recognition of that virtue so that he
would find the reasons appropriate to it motivating again. We might
even, as a very long-term project, take on trying to reform a bad
character from scratch, and then, as we sought to re-form his character we could no doubt use naturalistic arguments, along with
much else besides, as we do when forming our children's characters.

So I do not deny that, in various contexts of moral education,
appeals to ethical naturalism may be intended to produce motivating reasons, in those who are being educated, by having those conclusions urged upon them. I shall not even deny that I might,
possibly, go through a piece of naturalistic reasoning to a conclusion about a particular character trait with the intention of beefing
up my own motivation in that area, of reminding myself, vividly,
that e.g. refraining from lying because it *is* lying really is a rational
way for human beings to go on. But important as the former contexts are, there is clearly a distinguishable context for ethical naturalism wherein it is not directed towards producing motivating
reasons. That is the context in which it is directed towards the discovery of truth—to the validating, or discrediting, of particular bits
of an ethical outlook, in a Neurathian way—and it is this context
which is our present concern.

In this chapter I have been responding to a range of objections
that can be made to the very idea that such a project could be
remotely considered as feasible. Most of these have been objections
to the effect that ethical naturalism would be too analogous to non-
ethical naturalism—imposing too much uniformity, resting too
content with nature as we find it, threatening to come up with

unpalatable conclusions, failing to represent the huge gap our
rationality makes between us and the other animals, or the indubitable point that ethical evaluations are necessarily practical.
Many of them could also be regarded as versions of an objection
which points to a disanalogy: the non-ethical evaluations all involve
reliance on species' characteristic ways of going on, which are determined by nature, but human beings do not have characteristic ways
of going on that are determined by nature.

Without supposing for a moment that I have now established
that the project should be considered feasible, I will suppose that I
have met such objections to the extent that I can here. For some
space must be reserved for what many may regard as the most serious issue of all, namely the issue of objectivity that I put to one side
above (p. 231). I admitted there, as a disanalogy between the ethical and the non-ethical evaluations, that we cannot say that the former are objective either on the grounds that they are scientific, or
on the grounds that their truth is independent of our interests and
desires. So do we have other grounds for saying that they are?

# Objectivity

A large part of the difficulty in discussing 'the objectivity of ethics' springs from the fact that this issue is, in the literature, discussed by so many philosophers who start from such very different bases. Consider, for instance, J. L. Mackie, who argues that ethics is not objective but subjective.[1] His view is that 'This action is right/wrong' presents the grammatical appearance of ascribing a property (rightness/wrongness) to a certain sort of event in the world; it does not look like a judgement whose truth depends in any way at all on human interests and desires, nor even, necessarily, on anything to do with human beings at all. But if we take the surface grammar seriously, supposing that, for example, 'This action is right' is like 'This action moved a piece of matter' or 'This action took five minutes', we are making a mistake or error; the truth of the judgement does depend in some way on human interests and desires.

But with *all* of that, virtue ethics agrees. The truth of 'this action is right' is dependent on the truth of 'This is what a virtuous agent would characteristically do in the circumstances'; the truth of that is dependent upon (i) what an agent with a certain character trait would do in the circumstances and (ii) whether that character trait is a virtue. The truth of (ii), whether the character trait in question is a virtue, depends on whether the character trait conduces to the four naturalistic ends (in a rational way) and the truth of that depends in part on human interests and desires, as I noted above.

However, it is clear that Mackie has not envisaged the virtue ethicists' way of glossing his claim. For, on the one hand, he is, apparently, happy to say that we are not in error if we construe the surface grammar of 'This action is cruel' as ascribing a genuine property to

[1] *Ethics: Inventing Right and Wrong.*

the event (that an action is a piece of deliberate cruelty is a 'natural fact', he says) and, on the other, he assumes that we can move straight from his position about 'this action is right/wrong' (which, unbeknownst to him, he shares with virtue ethicists) to the conclusion that 'Morality is not to be discovered but made: we have to decide what moral views to adopt . . .',[2] to 'invent' right and wrong. But, on the naturalistic virtue ethics account, 'we', whoever we may be, can no more decide what it is for a human being to be a good human being than we can decide what it is for a cactus to be a good cactus.

Now virtue ethics certainly denies one sort of objectivity to ethics, namely the sort of objectivity that Kant aspires to.[3] In the version I am defending, it denies another sort too. The sorts of facts it appeals to are not all 'empirical' and accessible from 'a neutral point of view'. The long-term naturalistic project of validating the standard list of the virtues is Neurathian, and proceeds from within our ethical outlook. It is not a matter of reading the standard list off the book of nature as if human nature and our characteristic ways of going on were brute givens. But neither is it a matter of deciding in advance that our standard list is the correct one. Whether it is correct will be discovered when we discover the extent to which we can give a coherent account of the roles the character traits on the list play in our lives, an account that coheres not merely with our ethical outlook but with all the empirical and other facts that we bring into play. This seems to me to be enough to count as objectivity—not *a priori* or scientific objectivity—but a kind of objectivity appropriate to the subject matter.

However, I do not mean to dodge the issue by leaving matters just there; certainly more needs to be said—but not, I think, specifically in terms of 'objectivity'.

Williams says:

---

[2] Ibid. 106.

[3] As Williams points out, 'Kant's theory offers an *objective grounding* of morality that is not (as one might say) realist. Moral claims are objectively correct or incorrect, but when one gives a general explanation of what makes them so, that explanation does not run through the relation between those statements and the world, but rather through the relation between *accepting* those statements and practical reason.' 'Ethics and the Fabric of the World' (1985), 175. The disagreement between the new Kantians and the virtue ethicists may by now arise *only* at the point when the former want to go one step beyond facts about human nature to the sort of objectivity Williams describes.

Many different things have been discussed as the question of objectivity [in ethics], but they all tend either to come to nothing, or to come back to one issue: the proper understanding of ethical disagreement. Some philosophers have been very exercised, for instance, with the question whether moral judgements can be true or false. But work has to be done to find what, and how much, that question means. Indisputably, remarks about the morally good and bad, right and wrong, are called 'true' or 'false': the question is how much follows on that use. The concepts of truth and falsehood carry with them the ambitions of aiming at the truth and avoiding, so far as we can, error; the question must be, how these ambitions could be carried out with regard to ethical thought. I see no way of pursuing that question which does not lead back to questions such as these: if an ethical disagreement arises, must one party think the other in error? What is the content of that thought? What sorts of discussions or explorations might, given the particular subject matter, lead one or both of them out of error? It is only in the context of such questions, as it seems to me, that issues of objectivity in ethics acquire any content.[4]

With a couple of provisos, I am sure Williams is quite right about this. The fundamental issue concerning 'objectivity' in ethics is whether ethical disagreements, when traced painstakingly to their source, turn out to be rooted in disagreements about facts, or differences in values about which nothing can be said. The first proviso concerns the universality of the claim that *all* discussions of objectivity in ethics which do not come to nothing come back to the proper understanding of ethical disagreement. Might one not say that, even if everyone agreed on some particular ethical judgement, there would still be room for the thought, 'Why do I/we believe this? Can I/we give any grounds for it, and, if so, what are they? Might I/we be wrong, and, if so, how could I/we find out?' (In my experience, what leads many beginning students to despair of any objectivity in aesthetics is not a worry about people who might disagree with their belief that Shakespeare's or Mozart's productions are great works of art (for they are often sitting in classes where everyone does agree), but the discovery of their own inability to say anything about *why* they believe this, beyond 'Oh, but the plays/the music are just so wonderful!') Nevertheless, one might plausibly redescribe a worry about whether one could find any grounds for oneself as a worry about what, if anything, one could say to some

---

[4] 'Saint-Just's Illusion' (1991), 145.

imaginary interlocutor who disagreed, and reinstate Williams's claim.

The second proviso concerns the scope of 'ethical disagreement'. Professional moral philosophers manifest a degree of ethical disagreement amongst themselves that is rarely, if ever, encountered in ordinary life, some maintaining, for instance, that unless infanticide infringes the rights of a baby's parents, or some other interested parties, it is morally innocuous and calls for no justification. Some of these disagreements can doubtless be described as merely theoretical—there is reason to doubt that the proponents of infanticide really believe what they say in a practical sense—but not all of them are. Moral philosophers often take their theories to heart and put some of their conclusions into practice. But this sort of disagreement that we have amongst ourselves, though we do think the other party is in error, does not seem to me to have much to do with the question of objectivity in ethics. We think that it is objectively the case that their ethical theory or approach is rotten, that the premises it provides are false, or that their arguments are bad or their position inconsistent, whereas our theory or approach or premises or arguments are better—but however much better we think our own ethical theory is, we still have the same worries about whether ethics is objective.

So (in so far as it is possible) I want to put ethical disagreements that arise from philosophical disagreements to one side and consider only those that might arise within the constraints of the virtue ethics and ethical naturalism I have outlined.

## ETHICAL DISAGREEMENTS

Let us begin by considering ethical disagreements between people whose ethical outlook is pretty much the same—not us and the mafioso drug barons, but, say, you and me—and consider whether the source of the disagreement is to be located in disagreements about facts or about values.

Some of the most obvious examples come from disagreements whose penultimate source is differences in religious belief, which is consistent with a very great degree of agreement in ethical outlook. One of Hume's most instructive mistakes is his conviction that he can dismiss 'celibacy, fasting and the other monkish virtues' without making any assumptions about 'the end of man'. Of course he cannot. He can dismiss them only if he assumes that human nature is as conceived by atheists and that thereby 'the end(s) of man' are given by ethical naturalism rather than supernaturalism. For the monkish virtues (supposing them to be agreeable neither to their possessor nor to others) are not shown to be useless *tout court* by showing that they are of no use to their possessor or to others in *this* life, on the assumption that there is no God. They are traditionally recommended as being 'useful' for bringing one closer to God in this life and as preparing one's soul for the life hereafter.

Now for all that the belief in, for example, the Christian God's existence surely counts as part of a believer's ethical outlook, both it and related beliefs about the immortality of the soul are not what we usually think of as evaluative beliefs or moral opinions; they are beliefs or opinions about supernatural or metaphysical facts. And we know that this is an area where 'argument breaks down' at least in the sense that intelligent and even philosophically very sophisticated people exist on both sides of the debate, fully conversant with each others' arguments and completely unshaken by them. All the Christians and atheists I know think that the people on the other side are just plain wrong, but that there is no 'sort of discussion or exploration which might, given the particular subject matter', lead either side out of error. So where the source of ethical disagreement definitely lies in disagreement over religious beliefs, both sides may recognize that there is no available way of resolving the disagreement—but we do not say, 'Oh well, that is only to be expected, because ethical disagreements are, at bottom, disagreements about values about which nothing can be said.' They are, at bottom, disagreements about metaphysical facts about which (as far as we can see at the moment) there is nothing more to be said than has been said many times already.

Many of our ethical disagreements are over whether a particular action was or is right or wrong. According to virtue ethics, it is not invariably, but usually, going to be the case that one (or possibly both) parties to such a disagreement are going to be in error and what being in error will involve is an incorrect application of a virtue or vice term, or an incorrect judgement as to what a virtuous agent would do. The sorts of things that might lead one or both parties out of error would be just those things that are relevant to a correct application of such terms or a correct judgement about what the virtuous agent would do in relation to the action under dispute. These could range from something as simple as an overlooked or misidentified feature which will eliminate the disagreement on the spot, to something as complicated as the ongoing ways in which we try to keep our adolescent children from straying into the paths of folly and vice, which could take a lifetime to sort out. Given the range, it is not to be expected that many such disagreements will actually be resolved in practice, since the parties to them may well not have the time, or patience, or humility, or mutual respect to go through the painstaking discussion of the particularities of the case that may be required. But that is not to say that such a discussion, *if* it occurred, would be bound to break down in a conflict of values.

The above will not invariably be the case because the virtue and vice terms, and the concept of 'a virtuous agent' itself, allow for a certain amount of indeterminacy and degree. It may be that both parties are in error because they are assuming more determinacy than there is, and the sort of thing that might lead them out of that would be to show them that that was so. It also might be the case, if the disagreement is explicitly expressed in terms of 'right' and 'wrong', that it can be dissolved simply by discarding that vocabulary. Perhaps what is at issue is a distressing irresolvable dilemma, or a tragic one, or a case in which someone did what a virtuous agent would do for vicious reasons, and all that the parties to the disagreement are doing is emphasizing different aspects of the situation with 'right' and 'wrong'. Then the ways out of it would include moving to more discriminatory descriptions, such as 'What was good about it was this, but what was bad about it was that'.

Consider, next, something much more wholesale; the ethical disagreements we know we would have with our sexist forebears. To a large extent, we still share their ethical outlook; we think many of them were fairly virtuous human beings—given the sexism they acquired from their upbringing. Many of our disagreements with them would be about the application of various virtue terms to many of their actions. They said this was just, we say it was monstrously unjust; they said this was charitable or benevolent, we say it was not only paternalism, but also not charitable because harmful; they said this was just common sense (one can't fight nature), we say it was pusillanimous or folly. But part of the reason why we would disagree with them about the application of our shared virtue terms is that they had other virtue terms in play—and they drew distinctions between masculine and feminine virtues. To be a good human being, a man had to have the masculine virtues and a woman the feminine ones.

The major source of our ethical disagreements with them is a set of disagreements about human nature, most particularly about the nature of female human beings. And, as I think we now know, our forebears were just plain wrong about a lot of facts about female human nature accessible from a neutral point of view. I do not mean that these facts were accessible to them at the time. I mean that they are accessible now and *not* merely from within a modern, Western, ethical outlook which embraces 'liberal ideals of individual auton-omy'.[5] Whether female biology (for the most part) severely con-strains women's capacity to do logic and mathematics, as used to be believed, was not something we could know about until we had seen the results of teaching girls to do them—and also ensured that we had eliminated impeding social factors. It was our 'modern lib-eral ideals' that led us to try (and to identify the likely impeding social factors), but the results are available now to anyone who cares to look. True, diehard sexists, both male and female, still con-tinue to deny the existence of some of them, but this we attribute to wilful or culturally induced blindness to facts accessible from the neutral point of view.

By way of contrast, consider a minor but illuminating disagree-ment about whether temperance with respect to sex is a virtue within the context of naturalism. I think it is, others think it is not, and that the relevant virtue is self-control with respect to sex.[6] So what is the source of our disagreement? Is it a disagreement about facts accessible from a neutral point of view? Well, possibly. Some

---

[5] In 'Aristotle on Human Nature and the Foundations of Ethics', 94, Nussbaum argues that Aristotle's conception of human nature is avowedly evaluative. Replying, Williams, I think rightly, complains that 'Nussbaum could not let it stand that accounts of human nature [are] "evaluative"'. For, as he says, if the Aristotelian (pur-suing the naturalism project) is to avoid vacuity, 'she must surely provide some con-straints on what can count as the best understanding of human powers, and these constraints must be, to some degree, independent of distinctively ethical demands and hopes'. Williams, 'Replies' (1995), 200. And the facts we now have about the powers of female human beings are independent in just this way.

[6] It should be recalled, from Chapter 4, that this involves acting as the temperate agent would act, and for the same X reasons, but without one's desires being in har-mony with one's reason. Williams dismisses temperance as 'a substantive and tedious Aristotelian ideal, which we can ignore' in 'Acting as the Virtuous Person Acts', 18.

people do think (or believe they think) that, in human beings, the physical appetites are totally insulated from reason. If the disagreement can be traced to that source, we know that that is just a mistake. The very well-known facts of cultural variety in what is found immensely enjoyable and utterly disgusting show, from a neutral point of view, that our appetites can be trained in such a way that they are somewhat harmonized with judgements about whether eating, or drinking, or having sex with, *this* in *these* circumstances would be an innocent pleasure or a bad (terrible, degrading, dirty, undignified, or childish) thing to do. If that is all there is to it, the disagreement can be cleared up very quickly. If we disagree about whether people can (characteristically) refrain from licentious sexual activity gladly and without effort, once again matters are easily settled. The evidence of the 'smile factor' with respect to enjoyment that I mentioned in Chapter 8 makes it obvious, even from a neutral point of view, that some people who have remained faithful to their partners for decades have done so gladly, without more than the most transient twinges of temptation, and have also maintained a zesty and enjoyable sex life. But from here on, things become more difficult, for we may start to disagree about human nature in a way that is not so readily resolved.

Those who dismiss temperance with respect to sex as an impossible ideal may give a special account of those few who, manifestly, enjoy their temperate way of going on. They may say that it is only possible for human beings naturally underendowed with sexual drive, or only for human beings who have been led to, or contrived to, starve, or cripple, or misdirect their sexual drive, or only at the cost of advanced self-deception, and so on. I, believing that temperance is a virtue, a feature of good human beings, do not agree. Our disagreement is clearly one about human nature—but is it about facts that are or could be accessible from the neutral point of view? It is hard to say.

True, one may imagine, rather vaguely, that it might be possible to do some sort of statistical survey of the level of sexual drive in the temperate and the merely self-controlled and determine whether there was a systematic disparity. Or perhaps that this would be possible 'in theory' (though not in practice, given how people lie and deceive themselves about sex) just as 'in theory' the ideal observer might monitor every private action and impulse of the temperate and settle whether or not they went in for advanced self-deception.

But how, even 'in theory', could it be established from a neutral point of view that the temperate have 'starved, crippled, or misdirected' their sexual drive? If the temperate, characteristically, dropped dead in their fifties of what we have reason to suppose are stress-related diseases, we would have something to go on, but we know there is no available fact like that.

However, it still seems to be a disagreement about facts all right; each party to the disagreement must think the other is in error, not merely digging in their toes about what they personally value or desire. But it also seems as though the only sort of 'discussion and exploration' that might lead either side to change would have to be a very prolonged one, one that explored, in exhaustive detail, how coherent an account either side could give of facts about human beings both parties agreed on. It seems too as though it would usually have to be pretty personal, for the one who believes that temperance is an impossible ideal is unlikely to be temperate himself. So according to one side, the other party still has intemperate reactions and desires and thoughts which he claims, perhaps sincerely, but mistakenly, he can do nothing about, being constrained, in this respect, by nature, and is hence indulgent to (although he controls them). According to him, his idealistic interlocutor either, by nature, has them too and is deceiving herself about her corrective attempts, or has managed to eliminate them and in some way starved or crippled her sexual drive. Such discussion would, inevitably, be very rare, but if it did take place—within a good marriage say, or between a therapist and her patient—the one who is not bothering to aim for temperance because it is an impossible ideal might well be led out of error.

## THE THIRD THESIS: HUMAN NATURE AS HARMONIOUS

With disagreements over these sorts of facts about human nature we reach, at last, the third thesis of what I called 'Plato's requirement on the virtues' (p. 167). This is the claim that the two features of the virtues already discussed—that they benefit their possessor and make their possessor good *qua* human being—are interrelated. For, pursuing disagreements that might arise within the constraints of ethical naturalism, we have reached the area I was discussing at the end of Chapter 8: the area of 'ethical beliefs about human nature and how human life goes on' in relation to what can be said in support of the view that the virtues benefit their possessor. The sorts of facts that the advocate of temperance would, eventually, have to get the advocate of mere self-control to recognize to lead him out of error are the very sort that (we can all too readily imagine) the sexy immoralist would disagree with if we tried to convince him that temperance benefits its possessor.

Now when we look again at the four ends in the light of which the relevant aspects of social animals are evaluated, this should come as no surprise. Notwithstanding the fact that they are interconnected, we can see that two of them (individual survival and individual enjoyment/freedom from pain) manifestly and directly relate to what benefits the individual, and the other two (continuance of the species and the good functioning of the social group) do not. (I mean 'not manifestly and directly'.)

The disagreement over temperance and self-control with respect to sex I have been envisaging *is* minor because the parties to it agree on so much; the advocate of the latter is no licentious immoralist. Given that both temperance and self-control give rise to the same actions (and omissions) from reason, they agree, we may suppose that each is a plausible candidate for being a virtue in so far as each conduces to all four ends, and thereby to its possessor living well as a human being. Their disagreement, it seems, is only over the *extent* to which either character trait endows one well with respect to, particularly, the third end—characteristic enjoyment and/or freedom from pain.

The advocate of self-control presumably thinks that his candidate virtue is our best available option, *given* the constraints of human nature. True, it has to involve some irksome self-restraint and perhaps painful regret; like courage, its exercise is not often enjoyable. But, as with courage, our animal nature does impose some constraints; we cannot completely transfigure our sexual desires any more than we can completely transfigure our fears of death and pain. If we try, and think we have succeeded, we are either not going on in a rational way (but deluding ourselves) or have starved and crippled our sexual drive in such a way that we are not well-endowed with respect to the third end at all—and thereby defective. Human nature constrains the extent to which any candidate virtue in the area of sexual activity can conduce to the third end. It enables us to get as far as self-control (and thereby such characteristic enjoyments in human life as long-term sexual relationships), but at *that* point we are as stuck as the female cheetahs.

And the advocate of temperance thinks we are not so constrained, that our sexual desires can be brought into harmony with our reason in various ways. The sorts of desires the self-controlled need to restrain, or regret not being able to satisfy, either do not occur, or simply vanish as soon as the initially attractive sexual object is revealed as falling under a certain description (such as 'good grief, only *twelve!*' or 'murderer of my father' or 'philanderer on the make'). (Perhaps, given the caveats on 'Virtuous conduct gives pleasure to the lover of virtue' in Chapter 4, she should not claim that they can be brought into complete harmony, but she can admit the possibility of a few twinges of lust and regret without losing a robust distinction between temperance and (mere) self-control.)

Now, as I said, the parties to this disagreement (as I am imagining it) agree on a great deal, and a general way of capturing that great amount would be to say that they agree on all three of the theses I said made up 'Plato's requirement on the virtues'. Both believe that their candidate virtue *is* a virtue because it benefits its possessor (thesis (1)). Both believe that it is a virtue because its possession makes its possessor good *qua* human being (thesis (2)). And both believe (once again, as I imagined the debate) that these two features of their candidate virtue are closely related—in fact, as I described it, they both saw thesis (1) as just falling under thesis (2)— how could the candidate virtue fail to benefit its possessor if it makes its possessor well-endowed with respect to the first and third ends?

However, we can see in this disagreement the seed of a much larger and more threatening one. There is just the hint of a conflict between the ways in which self-control with respect to sex, as a character trait in human beings, conduces well to the first, second, and fourth ends, and the (perhaps) imaginable way in which licentiousness would conduce much better to the third, which raises the spectre of conflicts between the four ends breaking out between the first and third, on the one hand (which manifestly pertain to the benefit of the individual), and the second and fourth, on the other. The advocate of self-control settled his 'hint' of a conflict in part by allowing that, despite its irksome nature, self-control really did benefit its possessor, not only in relation to the first end, but also in relation to many characteristic enjoyments (i.e. those that reason can endorse) of human beings, as he conceives them to be. But what if he were more recalcitrant? What could ethical naturalism say to someone who maintained that, in the case of human beings (as, it might be thought, in the case of 'free-riding' wolves, or worker bees without stings, or infertile female cheetahs with, moreover, no reproductive instincts), the first and third, and the second and fourth, ends of naturalism just fall apart, thus severing the relation between thesis (1) and thesis (2)?

Now the parallels with the other animals are a mistake. In discussing the other animals, we noted a few ways in which, with respect to individual members of the species in question, the way or ways one was endowed might initially appear to conduce well to one or both of the first and third ends but less well, or even ill, to one or both of the others. But the overall evaluations of them as good or defective *x*s—with the consequent evaluation of them as living or failing to live good *x* lives—overruled that initial appearance by stressing the species' characteristic ways of going on and characteristic enjoyments or freedom from pain. The infertile female cheetah, free from pain as her life may be, is not well endowed with respect to *characteristic* freedom from pain, nor the free-riding wolf with respect to characteristic enjoyment of available food, nor the stingless worker bee with respect to the characteristic way of attaining its natural life span. So, as far as the other animals are concerned, the four ends of naturalism cannot fall apart; they are held together by what nature lays down as characteristic for the species (given, of course, the usual caveats about indeterminacy).

But, as has already been admitted, we do not have 'characteristic ways, etc.' laid down by nature, or at least, nothing like enough to guarantee that character traits which 'apparently' conduce well to two of the ends and ill to the others can always be dismissed as resulting in what is 'uncharacteristic'. So there really is a question, in our case, 'Mightn't the four ends fall apart? And where would the naturalistic criterion for virtue be then?' And the bold claim embodied in thesis (3) is, in effect, 'Don't worry, they can't. *Given* human nature, thesis (1) and thesis (2) *are* interrelated; given human nature, the four ends of naturalism cannot fall apart.' (Just as we can see a hint of the threat of serious conflict in the advocate of self-control with respect to sex, we can see the hint of the bold advocacy of thesis (3) in the advocate of real temperance. The former says, 'Well, I know there's a bit of a conflict between the conducing to the third end and the others, but overall, given the constraints nature imposes on us, self-control is a virtue.' The latter says, 'There isn't any conflict. *Given* human nature, as both sexual and rational, we can achieve harmony between our sexual desires and our reason and acquire a character trait that conduces without conflict to all four ends.')

According to thesis (3), human nature, quite generally, is such that we can develop character traits that meet the two criteria given in theses (1) and (2). 'We have the virtues neither by nor contrary to [our] nature,' Aristotle says, ' we are fitted by [our] nature to receive them.'[7] If we had the virtues by nature, then moral education would be unnecessary. If we had them contrary to nature, we would not enjoy their exercise at all, and other aspects of our nature would war against them even if we did enjoy their exercise. To say 'we are fitted by nature to receive them', by contrast, is to say that, having acquired them through the sort of moral education and self-improvement appropriate to rational social animals, we can enjoy their exercise and that other aspects of our morally educated, 'second', nature will not still contain recalcitrant aspects at war with our enjoyment of their exercise. They 'suit us', as I have heard Philippa Foot say. It does not just happen to be the case that those character traits which benefit their human possessor, enabling her to live a satisfying and fulfilling life, coincide with those character traits which are the good-making characteristics of human beings. They benefit her in this way *because* of her nature as a human being, the sort of rational social animal that human beings are.

Attractive (and traditional)[8] as such a view of human nature may

---

[7] *Nicomachean Ethics* 1103a24–6.

[8] See, for example, David Clowney, 'Virtues, Rules and the Foundations of Ethics' (1990), 61: 'Being good (that is acquiring and living in accord with the virtues) meets the needs of our nature, and therefore it must in general be good for us . . . virtues are "their own reward" (that is, it is fulfilling to have and exemplify them, no matter what results this brings). But practicing the virtues also tends toward the achievement of human potential and the living of a fulfilled life.' William Galston, 'Introduction' (1992), 3–4: 'As Aristotle suggests, our ethics reflects our emotions, our bodily constitution and our sociality not just our rational capacities. The human virtues then are doubly situated, and this duality is reflected in different ways of understanding them. If we look to human nature, we are led to view the virtues as intrinsic goods—dispositions that constitute our excellence or flourishing *qua*

be, it is not, of course, without its critics. The oldest objection to it in our tradition comes from Plato himself, put into the mouths of his characters Glaucon, Adimantus, and Thrasymachus in the *Republic*. Although nowadays a Thrasymachus 'figure' will often be used to represent the imagined view of the wicked mafioso drug baron challenging us to provide him with a motivating reason for being virtuous, this is not quite how the characters appear in Plato. They do not just dig in their toes over their personal values or desires; they advance a particular claim about human nature. The claim is that human nature is, biologically, so intrinsically egoistic that a 'conventional' moral upbringing which inculcates the virtues as second nature distorts and perverts it, producing defective human beings instead of good ones. According to such a picture, the third and fourth ends fall badly apart; the enjoyments reason can endorse are positively asocial or anti-social, and the character traits that benefit a human being (enabling her to get them) are ruthless injustice (and presumably, callousness, dishonesty, disloyalty, and so on).

But, as a claim about human nature, it is, I think, quite easily refuted, for if one granted their starting premise, the resulting idea that *good* human beings—human beings with character traits that fostered the four ends—could be as they envisage, is ludicrous. If to be a good, non-defective human being is to be endowed with those character traits that manifest themselves in seizing and enjoying whatever one wants, unconstrained by law and morality, and one's desires have not been enriched and amended by any of the training that begins the inculcation of the (real) virtues, then a collection of good human beings do not have any law or morality, do not give their children any kind of moral training—and indeed, clearly, do not bother about children at all, who, we must suppose, all die of neglect shortly after they are born. That 'man' is by nature an entirely self-centred egoist must surely be a view that could only come about through its proponents overlooking the fact that if their

---

human beings. If we look to human circumstances we tend to see the virtues as instrumental goods—that is, as dispositions that enable us to perform well the specific tasks presented by our situation.' J. Schneewind, 'The Misfortunes of Virtue' (1990), 43: 'Virtue is natural to humans not in the sense that it need not be learned or that it is easy to acquire, but in the sense that virtuous agents, individually as well as the community they compose, benefit from virtue. This fact indicates our social nature. Living alone and living without virtue are both harmful to us.'

mothers had not cared for them for many years in their infancy they would not have survived. The view also typically overlooks how much social co-operation has to be in place, held together not only by law and 'conventional' morality, but by loving parents bringing up their children to accept the morality as more than mere convention, in order for there to be the sorts of things its proponents fantasize about being free to enjoy.[9]

The idea that Plato's characters, as interpreted above, can represent the philosophical articulation of the views of the wicked of this world has always seemed to me a ludicrous one. True, in common with most if not all moral philosophers, I have no personal detailed knowledge of how the mind of anyone really wicked works, but, speaking from the same position of ignorance as the rest, I find it impossible to believe that they hold, even implicitly, *general* views about how human beings, as members of a species, ought to be in order to give full expression to their inborn nature. My bet is that most of them are totally indifferent to the goodness or badness of human beings and what it consists in, and to ethical judgements in general; they just aim for what they want and do what they want to do because they want it.

But there is, of course, another way of taking what the immoralist figures are maintaining which may, less implausibly, be regarded as the philosophical articulation of some wicked people. We can interpret Thrasymachus, and more obviously Nietzsche and Ayn Rand, as saying that, rather like hive bees, human beings fall, by nature, into two distinct groups, the weak and the strong (or the especially clever or talented or 'chosen by destiny'), whose members must be evaluated differently, as worker bees and the drones or queens are. Good weak human beings might, perhaps, have the virtues as we know them; but good strong human beings have something quite different, appropriate to their different nature, namely at least some character traits that occur on the standard list of the vices. And without much distortion we can, I think, see such views as also challenging the third thesis in maintaining that, with

---

[9] Speaking of the 'array of positions developed by Thrasymachus, Glaucon, and Adimantus, according to which justice [in the broad sense in which its concern is any right conduct in relation to others] is not a human virtue because the mutuality of human beings at their best is a mutuality of fear and exploitation', Sarah Broadie says, 'In the end, what is wrong with this view is not that it offends the moral sensibilities developed in us by upbringing, but that it could hold true only of beings who need no upbringing to be at their best.' *Ethics with Aristotle* (1991), 118.

respect to the strong, the end of characteristic enjoyments and the fourth end of the naturalism fall apart. The enjoyments of the strong are forms of self-realization or self-fulfilment which are, in some way, essentially solitary, and although they themselves may not be intrinsically anti-social, the character traits which benefit the strong, enabling them to enjoy self-realization, are. Self-realization calls for, again, injustice and callousness and perhaps other vices on the standard list as well.

Such views avoid the manifest fault of the first by recognizing, at least to some extent, that given the sorts of animals human beings are, the strong ones need to have the weak ones around, not only during the years in which they are emerging from infancy, but in order to maintain the society that, as rational social animals, they need to live in association with. Such views, if we take them seriously, cannot be refuted quickly. The only possible approach is to consider the details of each articulation and work out, in each case, where the implausibilities, incoherencies, inconsistencies, and just plain falsehoods lie.

This, clearly, would be a very lengthy task, but there is a small amount of relevant literature available.[10] An interesting feature of it is the way in which it promises to refigure our ethical outlook somewhat. Serious consideration of Nietzschean views does not leave the outlook unchanged, for we may find ourselves led to modify our concepts of, for instance, compassion and justice somewhat, and to take seriously (in a way naturalism has anticipated when it noted the division of labour amongst other animals) the fact that there are some exceptional individuals we commonly admire.[11] Quite aside from the question of what we should say about them if their admirability coincides with their possession of at least some of the vices (the Gaugin problem), there is the question of what we should say about them even if they are free from any such taint. Are they the *best* human beings, head and shoulders above all the rest of us, notwithstanding the fact that not even all the most virtuous (by the standard list) amongst us can aspire to being exceptional in

[10] See, in particular, Philippa Foot, 'Nietzsche: The Revaluation of Values' (1973) and 'Nietzsche's Immoralism' (1991); Neera K. Badhwar, 'Self-Interest and Virtue' (1997); Michael Slote, 'Virtue Ethics and Democratic Values' (1993); Christine Swanton, 'The Supposed Tension Between "Strength" and "Gentleness" Conceptions of the Virtues' (1997).
[11] Cf. Foot, 'Nietzsche's Immoralism'.

comparable ways? Or are they, like the best amongst the rest of us, unusually good *qua* human beings, though not in the standard way (supposing them to be not particularly well endowed with some of the virtues)? (And if so, does someone who is capable of being unusually good in either the standard or the non-standard way have reason to choose one way rather than the other?) Or are they (supposing them to be as well endowed as the best of the rest of us) unusually good *qua* human beings and *also* great artists, or leaders, or statesmen, or whatever? It seems to me that, at the moment, the ethical outlook we mostly share finds these questions unsettling, and thereby, perhaps, could do with a new plank or two.

In so far as serious consideration of Nietzsche's views might well lead to the improvement of our current ethical outlook I positively welcome it. But I do not see any signs, as yet, that it is bound to overturn the third thesis. Yet again, I emphasize the point that my aim is programmatic; of course Nietzschean views have not been disproved (from within our ethical outlook). As Foot continues to insist, there is much more work on Nietzsche himself still waiting to be done. But, although the existing attempts may be no more than first steps, we should, I think, be struck both by the fact that they make some advance, and also by the form it takes. Unsurprisingly, according to the line I have been presenting, the writers draw on a range of considerations. Some might count as available from the neutral point of view (can Nietzsche's account of the will to power count as plausible psychology? Can we not name great artists who were fair possessors of the virtues on the standard list?); some, in their careful unpicking of the concepts of 'strength' and 'independence' (as opposed to parasitism) appeal to some facts that may be, and others that may not. (Would Nietzsche and Rand recognize an example of someone whose compassion or charity expressed their strength rather than their *ressentiment* or hypocrisy? In both cases, it is hard to tell whether, with respect to a particular individual, they would insist on renaming the virtue in question, or ascribe the underlying motivation, or accept the counterexample but dismiss it as atypical.) Rarely, if ever, do we find a bare assertion of 'Well, we happen to value this and Nietzsche (or whoever) does not and there is nothing more to be said'. We find the usual philosophers' claims about inconsistencies and incoherencies and also appeals to the correct application of various virtue terms (or related terms) such as 'compassion', 'justice', 'strength', 'independence', and 'self-sufficiency', and to facts about human nature and how human life goes.

So although I concede that Nietzschean views present a problem for the third thesis, I do not think we yet have grounds for abandoning it, and thereby regarding ethical naturalism as doomed because, as far as the strong human beings are concerned, the third end would be at war with, at the very least, the fourth.

## THE SUPPOSED THREAT FROM DARWINISM

But, finally, there is a possible view of human nature that Bernard Williams has articulated which I think cannot be refuted, and unsurprisingly so, since it amounts to moral nihilism. Williams has introduced it in the context of his latest doubts about the naturalism project, and it is not clear to me whether he regards it, as I do, to amounting to moral nihilism. The view is, roughly, this: that in adding rationality to our social animality, nature has produced a sadly flawed and divided creature, an 'ill-assorted *bricolage* of powers and instincts', in Williams' words.[12]

From early on, Williams has expressed pessimism about the project of Aristotelian naturalism on the grounds that Aristotle's conception of nature, and thereby human nature, was normative, and that, in a scientific age, this is not a conception that we can take on board. In both *Morality* and *Ethics and the Limits of Philosophy* this was supported in ways that made it look very much like an objection that encapsulated some of those I have considered—that nowadays we hold no truck with nature as we find it, that we know we do not have characteristic ways of going on because we know so much about cultural variation, and so on. It also looked like an objection that encapsulated a more abstract one—that Aristotle's conception of nature is teleological, whereas our modern, scientific one is not. And all this looked as though it could be defused by claiming that the project was not to be conceived of as, in any ordinary understanding of the terms, either 'scientific' or 'foundational', by pointing out that the ethical evaluations the naturalism (we hoped) yielded were never supposed to be strictly analogous to the

[12] 'Replies', 199.

deliverances of biology/ethology. The project proceeds from within the ethical outlook, it is not just a branch of biology/ethology, etc.

Williams has now withdrawn his claim that the Aristotelian naturalism project 'requires a "top-down" derivation of ethical conclusions from a scientifically respectable account of human beings . . . I grant', he now says, 'that the enterprise may be understood in coherentist or hermeneutical terms. I also grant that we can understand Aristotle himself as having seen it in some such terms.'[13] But he still has doubts about the project, and rightly so, for there is a way in which Aristotle's conception of nature as normative has not been rendered innocuous by rejecting the idea that the project has to be, in a modern way, scientific.

He identified this as follows. Speaking of reasons against ethical naturalism, he says:

The second and more general reason lies not in the particular ways in which human beings may have evolved, but simply in the fact that they have evolved, and by natural selection. The idea of a naturalistic ethics was born of a deeply teleological outlook, and its best expression, in many ways, is still to be found in Aristotle's philosophy, a philosophy according to which there is inherent in each natural kind of thing an appropriate way for things of that kind to behave. On that view it must be the deepest desire—need?— purpose?—satisfaction?—of human beings to live in the way that is in this objective sense appropriate to them (the fact that modern words break up into these alternatives expresses the modern break-up of Aristotle's view). Other naturalistic views, Marxist and some which indeed call themselves 'evolutionary', have often proclaimed themselves free from any such picture, but it is basically very hard for them to avoid some appeal to an implicit teleology, an order in relation to which there could be an existence which would satisfy all the most basic human needs at once. The first and hardest lesson of Darwinism, that there is no such teleology at all, and that there is no orchestral score provided from anywhere according to which human beings have a special part to play, still has to find its way into ethical thought.[14]

One thing this passage draws to our attention is that the non-ethical evaluations of living things that I have outlined are 'Aristotelian' rather than Darwinian. They do, as I have been at pains to emphasize, rely on the idea that there is, in relation to each natural kind of thing, 'an appropriate (= characteristic) way for

[13] Ibid. 200.
[14] 'Evolution, Ethics, and the Representation Problem', 110.

things of that kind to behave' in relation to which they are evaluated as good or defective. The evaluations do not—as they might in a post-Darwinian age—evaluate members of species of living things simply as good, or not so good, or downright defective, as replicators of their genes.

It may well be, for all I know, that this form of evaluation will, as Darwinism informs our thought and talk more and more, just die out. I do not think one could say, simplistically, that Darwinism could prove it was 'all wrong'. It sets its own standards for what is right and wrong, and the most that Darwinism could do is show that, for whatever purposes we hitherto used those standards to identify the good and the defective, we would serve them better by setting Darwinian ones. It should be noted in this connection that what the 'Aristotelian' standards clearly do, whether we are always particularly interested in this or not, is identify healthy and unhealthy specimens of a kind, and if Darwinian standards are going to replace the 'Aristotelian' ones, rather than merely underwrite them, they will have to be more complicated than many philosophers standardly suppose. I have found in discussion that many people imagine that Darwinian evaluations would either rely solely on the second end (continuance of the species) or replace that, as the sole end, with 'replication of the individual's genes'. But human beings are not the only species in which the female members have a 'characteristic life expectancy' that extends well past the age in which they are replicating, or even nurturing, their genes. It is also true, so I am reliably informed, of elephants and whales, and there is some suggestion that it may also be true of some of the great apes. (Isn't it odd that we don't yet know!) But scientific ethologists are not considering giving up on the idea that there must be something defective about a female member of such a species who dies well before her allotted span for no external cause. On the contrary, they are trying to figure out whether, and if so how, the presence of these elderly females contributes to the good functioning of the social group and thereby to the continuance of its members and thereby, as an evolutionary strategy, to the replication of the elderly females' genes.

Be that as it may, while we have the Aristotelian form of evaluation, and it is reflected in the way we use such terms as 'good', 'defective', 'living well', etc. we should be conscious of what assumptions it embodies and whether they can be plausibly carried over to the human species. Does it embody the assumption that 'it must be the deepest desire, need, purpose or satisfaction' of individual *x*s 'to live in the way that is . . . appropriate to them'? Well, perhaps Aristotle himself thought something like that, but it does not seem to be a necessary feature of the evaluations as I have construed them, for we have noted that they do not, for instance, rule out the possibility that a defective *x* might do remarkably well as far as uncharacteristic individual survival and uncharacteristic freedom from pain and enjoyment is concerned. But what they do rule out is describing such an *x* as living well. Living well, for an *x*, just is living the sort of life good *x*s do live if nothing untoward and external to them intervenes, miserable and rotten though such a life may appear from a human perspective which values enjoyment, satisfaction, and freedom from pain

But therein, it might well be said, lies the significant difference between the ethical and the non-ethical evaluations. If the grammatical idea behind ethical naturalism is right, namely that our terms 'good', 'bad/defective', 'well' do not suddenly start being used in a totally new way when we start using them in relation to ourselves, then our concept of living *well*, or flourishing (or *eudaimonia*, when we use it in relation to ourselves), is connected to our evaluations of human beings as good or bad. But that concept, used in relation to ourselves, is indubitably *also* connected to *eudaimonia*, the Good Life that we all seek, the life that is of benefit to the individual whose life it is, as it appears in thesis (1). The other animals cannot form their own conceptions of living well, cannot say to themselves '*That's* the sort of life I want to live, the life in which . . .' and consciously aim to live it; they live as nature determines. We can.

And in so far as ethical naturalism assumes that, when it comes to us, its first and third, and its second and fourth, ends do not fall apart (the third thesis), it assumes that this *doubly* connected concept of living well or *eudaimonia* is a viable concept. With the other animals, there isn't an issue over whether their 'deepest desires' or whatever are satisfied by their living well, in the way laid down by nature; it is not for them to say, 'I am a rational being who can choose how I am to live and I choose *this* sort of life, not that; *this* would be living well, *eudaimonia*.' But with us there is.

So the Aristotelian conception of nature as normative has not been rendered innocuous by rejecting the idea that the naturalistic

project has to be 'scientific' when it comes to us. Although the non-
ethical evaluations can survive intact when we abandon the normative assumption about 'the nisus of each natural kind of thing
towards its perfection',[15] the ethical ones cannot. The naturalistic
concept of *eudaimonia*, of living well as a human being, namely, as
a rational social animal, just assumes that someone who is good *qua*
human being is truly well endowed with respect to the first and third
ends, as though human beings did, indeed, have a sort of 'inner
nisus' towards the virtues. It takes for granted, as Williams says 'a
strong view of the harmony among themselves of human capacities
and needs'. 'This assumption does,' he continues, 'seem to me more
plausible if you can help yourself to Aristotelian cosmology, than if
you regard it as an open question whether the evolutionary success
of humanity, in its extremely brief period of existence, may not rest
on a rather ill-assorted *bricolage* of powers and instincts.'[16]

However, at this point, we should remind ourselves of Chapter
8, where I maintained that the view that the virtues on the standard
list benefit their possessor is far from being an implausible view
(when considered from within the ethical outlook of the moderately
virtuous rather than that of the wicked). True, we could make it
'more plausible' to the immoralist if there were some (unimagin-
able) scientific, even cosmological, facts we could appeal to (just as
we could make it more plausible to him if we could avail ourselves
of some supernatural ones about the way God had organized the
world and our role in it). But we didn't even try, for to do so would,
yet again, be attempting to justify morality from the outside—as, in
a final vestige of his earlier view that ethical naturalism is supposed
to base itself on a 'scientifically respectable account of human
beings', Williams seems to be supposing we must do if we are aiming at 'plausibility'.

The view that the virtues on the standard list—all those social,
'other-regarding', virtues—benefit their possessor clearly embodies
the idea that human nature is harmonious no less than ethical naturalism, albeit in a different way. (Ethical naturalism embodies it
before it has said anything about which character traits *are* the
virtues just by assuming that there are some that conduce to all four
of the ends.) But just that fact, together with the age and nature of

---

[15] *Ethics and the Limits of Philosophy* (1985), 44.
[16] 'Replies', 199.

the debate over whether the virtues on the standard list benefit their possessor, should lead us to look with suspicion at Williams's suggestion that the idea that human nature is not harmonious 'still has to find itself into ethical thought'.

The suggestion is that this is a new idea—'the first and hardest lesson of Darwinism'. But it seems to me to be a very old one, as old as misanthropy and despair—as Williams himself suggests in another passage. The most plausible evolutionary stories currently available, he says, suggest that

> human beings are to some degree a mess, and that the rapid and immense development of symbolic and cultural capacities has left humans as beings for whom no form of life is likely to prove entirely satisfactory, *either individually or socially. Many of course have come to that conclusion before,* and those who have tried to reach a naturalistic morality which transcends it have had to read the historical record, or read beyond the historical record, in ways that seek to reveal a partly hidden human nature which is waiting to be realised or perfected. The evolutionary story, to the extent that it can now be understood (and to the much more modest extent to which I understand it myself) seems to me to give some support to the view that in this respect the historical story means much what it looks as though it means.[17]

Now I don't know about 'many' but I am sure that *some* people, long before Darwin, have looked at the dismal course of human history and reached the conclusion that human beings are just a mess. But, taken seriously, that conclusion amounts to despair, and, as I said above, moral nihilism.

If we really are, by nature, just a mess, then we are beings for whom no form of life is *likely* to prove satisfactory at *all*. Any individuals who flourish individually *and* socially are an extraordinary accident and so (please note) are those who flourish individually and anti-socially. Neither is *likely*, for given that we are just a mess, what is to be expected, what happens unless we are, individually, astonishingly lucky, is that we don't flourish at all, notwithstanding our rationality and our desire to do so. As social animals, we are likely to need to live together, as individuals we have our personal desires and projects; since we are rational and social some, but by no means all, of the latter are themselves likely to be social because of our upbringing; as rational, individual and social, we can

---

[17] 'Evolution, Ethics and the Representation Problem', 109 (my italics).

reconcile some of our conflicting desires and projects and abandon others as impossible without regret, but it is extremely unlikely that we can do this with all of them. Any human being who, at the end of her life, is able to look back and say, sincerely, 'That was satisfactory; I lived well', has been astonishingly lucky, and no inculcation of character traits, no supposedly rational plan of one's life or attempts at supposed self-improvement or supposed improvement of our societies can make anyone one whit more likely to be lucky; all such attempts are futile. There is no point in looking for a set of character traits that benefit their possessor, and no point in looking for a set of character traits which are the good-making characteristics of human beings. There aren't any.

Expressed in these terms, the view amounts to complete moral nihilism. (Note that even Kant and utilitarianism will be affected by this pessimism, since we cannot be required to adopt the happiness of others as an end, or its maximization, if happiness comes only through astonishing luck.) The belief that harmony *is* possible for human beings, that we have the virtues neither by nor contrary to nature, but are fitted by (our) nature to receive them, is, I think, an essential part of the ethical outlook even of the minimally virtuous—any of us who think that being right about ethics matters. We manifest it when we try to inculcate the virtues in our children. We manifest it when we try to make ourselves (as we think) better people and try to improve our own and other people's ethical views. We manifest it when we try to bring about social change. We manifest it by going in for ethical thought and talk at all.

So, taken seriously, the idea that we are just a mess is a particularly global form of moral scepticism, one which not only dismisses the whole ethical outlook of the (even minimally) virtuous as mere optimistic fantasy but simultaneously rejects the idea that practical rationality has anything substantial or long-term to do. (As I stressed above, if *we* human beings are a mess, by nature, then *I* am a mess, and there is no point even in my trying to live a satisfying life in my own, idiosyncratic, perhaps immoral way. I can exercise my practical rationality in keeping alive (just in case I might be one of the lucky few) and in securing short-term enjoyments and freedom from pain, but as for any more long-term ends, I might just as well throw dice to determine whether or not to go for them, and if so how.) As such it would be akin to other forms of global scepticism about, say, the possibility of scientific knowledge (based, as it is, on the non-scientifically validated assumption that nature is intelligible), or even the possibility of knowledge of the external world or other minds. And, as such, it would go well beyond the confines of this book into the very territory that I ruled out of consideration when I adopted McDowell's (and Quine's) picture of the Neurathian procedure as the appropriate one for the establishment of ethical (and scientific, and everyday, empirical) knowledge.

But, within the confines of this book, we might regard it as raising a question as part and parcel of our attempts to validate our ethical beliefs. Subjecting them, one by one, to critical reflection within our ethical outlook, we come upon *this* one, the belief that human beings are *not* by nature just a mess, but can, at best, through the correct moral education in their youth and then reflective, rational, self-modification, achieve a harmony that would enable us to live well, individually and socially. Subjecting *that* belief to critical scrutiny, within our ethical outlook, what do we find?

Well, as Williams rightly suggests, a rather dismal history for human beings. But also, as he rightly suggests, different ways of reading it. Yes, it 'can be read' as showing that human beings are just a mess; we know this because some human beings who cannot be described as completely crazy (for example, as reading the historical record as showing that the world will come to an end in the year 2000) have read it in exactly that way. But the point, I believe, that he has not acknowledged sufficiently, is that it can be read in another way—in the way in which all of us read it who think that our belief that human nature is, at best, harmonious, is justifiable.

Do we 'read the historical record, or read beyond the historical record, in ways that *seek to reveal* a partly hidden human nature which is waiting to be realised or perfected' (my italics)? Or do we, rather, read, and read beyond, the historical record and find our belief about the 'human nature which is waiting to be realised' confirmed? I would say that we did the latter. When our children, innocent, unphilosophical, moral sceptics that they are, ask us 'Why is it all so bad? How come so many human beings are leading and have led, such dreadful lives?' we are not merely driven to saying, 'Things could be much better; Aristotelian cosmology, or the existence of God, or Marxism, or whatever, assures us that human nature is such that this *must* be so. So we have to re-read the historical record in the light of that assumption, seeking to reveal it.' We can say, 'When we look, in detail, at *why* so many human beings

are leading, and have led, such dreadful lives, we see that occasionally this is sheer bad luck, but characteristically, it is because either
they, and/or their fellow and adjacent human beings, are defective
in their possession and exercise of the virtues on the standard list.'[18]

Now, for all that I share Williams's modest doubts about
whether, as a philosopher rather than a scientist, I understand the
evolutionary story (in its current state), I do find it impossible to see
how we could get from it to a scientifically guaranteed refutation of
the reading of human history that I have ascribed to our ethical outlook. Since the dawn of despair and misanthropy, there has been a
way of reading human history, and thereby the human condition,
which makes the pervasive lack of *eudaimonia* out to be the
inevitable product of our intrinsically flawed nature. And, all along,
there has been a contrary view which read things differently, as the
only-to-be-expected product of vices, which are not intrinsic to us,
but avoidable. We read it as arising from greed, injustice, callousness, selfishness, folly, intolerance, overweening ambition, licentiousness, cowardice—and the defect (which I think myself
Aristotle rightly identified as opposed to *megalopsuchia*, 'greatness
of soul') through which 'good men do nothing'. Of course such a
reading is not available from a neutral point of view. But what we
should be struck by is that it *is* available, from within the ethical
outlook, supported by a mass of details which cannot just be dismissed as mere myth-making nor shown to be such by some vague
appeal to Darwinism.

The fact, if it is a fact, that human nature is, at best, harmonious
is a highly contingent one. It is a contingent fact, if it is a fact, that
we can, individually, flourish or achieve *eudaimonia*, contingent
that we can do so in the same way as each other (i.e. in virtue of
possessing the same set of character traits), and contingent that we
can do so all together, not at each other's expense. If things had been
otherwise, ethics would not exist, or would be unimaginably different.

Atheists may find it hard to recognize the point nowadays, but
believing that human nature is harmonious is part of the virtue of

[18] I suppose that one of the reasons we find it so hard to come to terms with the
Holocaust is that pre-Nazi German society looks so like our own at the same period,
and we are forced to the unpalatable conclusion that if it happened there because of
lack of virtue in its members, we must have been similarly lacking and might have
gone the same way.

hope. Something at least very like it used to be called belief in (God's) Providence; to believe in Providence was part of the virtue of hope; to doubt it is to fall prey to the vice of despair. And that seems to me to be right. To view oneself and one's fellow human beings as, by nature, battlegrounds between passion and reason, or self-interest and sociality (or an unholy combination of both), so that there is no hope of human beings' living well, ever, however much theoretical and practical rationality we exercise now and hope to pass on to future generations, is a counsel of despair.

But hope, as a virtue, is not without its own validation. We could give it a sort of 'necessary condition of our practice' justification. The practice of the natural sciences, it might be said, has to be based on the non-scientifically validated assumption that nature is intelligible; if we suppose it is not, the whole practice collapses. And we know there is no refutation of scepticism about that assumption. But the practice is worth going in for, there is no practicable alternative for us, so we have to take the assumption on board. Analogously, the practice of ethical thought, as we know it, has to be based on the assumption that human beings, as a species, are capable of harmony, both within themselves and with each other. If we suppose they are not, the whole practice collapses. There is no refutation of scepticism about this assumption. But the practice is worth going in for, there is no practicable alternative for us, so we have to take the assumption on board.

Alternatively (or perhaps as well) we could stick with what we have—those facts about human nature and the way human life goes that support the claim that the virtues on the standard list benefit their possessor, and the reading of human history that ascribes our persisting failure to achieve *eudaimonia* in anything but very small patches to our vices. True, it is not easy to hold on to them sometimes; despair and misanthropy are temptations. But we should.

Keep hope alive.

# Bibliography

ALTHAM, J. E. J. and HARRISON, R. *World, Mind, and Ethics.* Cambridge: Cambridge University Press, 1995.

ANNAS, J. *An Introduction to Plato's Republic.* Oxford: Clarendon Press, 1981.

—— *The Morality of Happiness.* Oxford: Oxford University Press, 1993.

—— 'Virtue and Eudaimonism', *Social Philosophy and Policy* 15 (1998), 37–55.

ANSCOMBE, G. E. M. *Intention.* Oxford: Blackwell, 1963.

—— 'Modern Moral Philosophy' (1958), repr. in *Collected Philosophical Papers*, iii. 26–42. Minneapolis: University of Minnesota Press, 1981.

—— 'Practical Inference' (1974), repr. in R. Hursthouse, G. Lawrence, and W. Quinn (eds.), *Virtues and Reasons* (q.v.), 1–34.

ARISTOTLE. *Nicomachean Ethics*, tr. J. A. K. Thomson, rev. H. Tredennick. London: Penguin, 1976.

—— *Eudemian Ethics*, tr. M. Woods. Oxford: Clarendon Press, 1982.

ARPALY, N. and SCHROEDER, T. 'Praise, Blame and the Whole Self', *Philosophical Studies* 93 (1999), 161–88.

AUDI, R. 'Acting from Virtue', *Mind* 104 (1995), 449–71.

BADHWAR, N. K. 'The Limited Unity of Virtue', *Noûs* 30 (1996), 306–29.

—— 'Self-Interest and Virtue', *Social Philosophy and Policy* 14 (1997), 226–63.

BAIER, A. 'What do Women Want in a Moral Theory?', *Noûs* 19 (1985), 53–63

BARON, M. *Kantian Ethics Almost Without Apology.* Ithaca, N.Y.: Cornell University Press, 1995.

—— 'Varieties of Ethics of Virtue', *American Philosophical Quarterly* 22 (1985), 47–53.

—— PETTIT, P., and SLOTE, M. *Three Methods of Ethics.* Oxford: Blackwell, 1997.

BEAUCHAMP, T. L. and CHILDRESS, J. F. *Principles of Biomedical Ethics*, 4th edn. New York: Oxford University Press, 1994.

BLACKBURN, S. 'Dilemmas: Dithering, Plumping, and Grief', in H. E. Mason (ed.), *Moral Dilemmas and Moral Theory.* New York: Oxford University Press, 1996.

BLACKBURN, S. 'The Flight to Reality', in R. Hursthouse, G. Lawrence, and W. Quinn (eds.), *Virtues and Reasons* (q.v.), 127–39.

BLUM, L. *Friendship, Altruism and Morality*. Boston: Routledge & Kegan Paul, 1980.

BROADIE, S. *Ethics with Aristotle*. Oxford: Oxford University Press, 1991.

CLOWNEY, D. 'Virtues, Rules and the Foundations of Ethics', *Philosophia* 20 (1990), 49–68.

CONLY, S. 'Flourishing and the Failure of the Ethics of Virtue', in P. A. French, T. Uehling, and H. Wettstein (eds.), *Ethical Theory: Character and Virtue*, Midwest Studies in Philosophy 13, pp. 83–96. Notre Dame, Ind.: University of Notre Dame Press, 1988.

CRISP, R. 'Utilitarianism and the Life of Virtue', *Philosophical Quarterly* 42 (1992), 139–60.

—— (ed.). *How Should One Live?* Oxford: Clarendon Press (1996).

—— (ed.). J. S. Mill, *Utilitarianism* (Oxford Philosophical Texts). Oxford: Oxford University Press, 1998.

—— and SLOTE, M. (eds.) *Virtue Ethics*. Oxford: Oxford University Press, 1997.

DENT, N. J. H. *The Moral Psychology of the Virtues*. Cambridge: Cambridge University Press, 1975.

DRIVER, J. 'The Virtues and Human Nature', in R. Crisp (ed.), *How Should One Live?* (q.v.), 111–30.

DUPRÉ, J. *The Disorder of Things*. Cambridge, Mass.: Harvard University Press, 1993.

DUMMETT, M. *Truth and Other Enigmas*. London: Duckworth, 1978.

EVANS, J. D. G. (ed.). *Moral Philosophy and Contemporary Problems*, Royal Institute of Philosophy Lecture Series 22 (suppl. to *Philosophy*). Cambridge: Cambridge University Press, 1987.

ENGSTROM, S. and WHITING, J. (eds.). *Aristotle, Kant and the Stoics*. Cambridge: Cambridge University Press, 1996.

FLANAGAN, O. and RORTY, A. O. (eds.). *Identity, Character and Morality*. Cambridge, Mass.: MIT Press, 1990.

FOOT, P. 'Does Moral Subjectivism Rest on a Mistake?', *Oxford Journal of Legal Studies* 15 (1995), 1–14.

—— 'Euthanasia' (1977), repr. in *Virtues and Vices* (q.v.), 33–61.

—— 'Goodness and Choice' (1961), repr. in *Virtues and Vices* (q.v.), 132–47.

—— 'Moral Beliefs' (1959), repr. in *Virtues and Vices* (q.v.), 110–31.

—— 'Moral Realism and Moral Dilemma', *Journal of Philosophy* 80 (1983), 379–98.

—— 'Nietzsche: The Revaluation of Values' (1973), repr. in *Virtues and Vices* (q.v.), 81–95.

—— 'Nietzsche's Immoralism', *New York Review of Books* 38/11 (13 June 1991), 18–22.

Bibliography
269

—— 'Rationality and Virtue', in H. Pauer-Studer (ed.), *Norms, Values, and Society*, 205–16. Amsterdam: Kluwer, 1994.

—— 'Virtues and Vices', in *Virtues and Vices* (q.v.), 1–18.

—— *Virtues and Vices*. Oxford: Blackwell, 1978.

FRANKENA, W. *Ethics*. Prentice-Hall: Englewood Cliffs, N.J., 1973.

GALSTON, WILLIAM. 'Introduction', in J. W. Chapman and W. Galston (eds.), *Virtue. Nomos* 34 (1992), 1–14.

—— *Liberal Purposes: Goods, Virtues and Diversity in the Liberal State.* New York: Cambridge University Press, 1991.

GAUTHIER, D. *Moral Dealing*. Ithaca, N.Y.: Cornell University Press.

GEACH, P. T. 'Good and Evil', *Analysis* 17 (1956), 33–42.

—— *The Virtues*. Cambridge: Cambridge University Press, 1977.

GYLFASON, T. Introductory essay to *Njal's Saga*, trans. C. F. Bagerschmidt and L. M. Hollander. Chatham: Wordsworth Editions, 1998.

GLOVER, J. *Causing Death and Saving Lives*. London: Penguin, 1977.

HARE, R. M. *Moral Thinking*. Oxford: Oxford University Press, 1981.

HERMAN, B. *The Practice of Moral Judgement*. Cambridge, Mass.: Harvard University Press, 1993.

—— 'Making Room for Character', in S. Engstrom and J. Whiting (eds.), *Aristotle, Kant and the Stoics* (q.v.), 36–60.

HOOKER, B. 'Does Moral Virtue Constitute a Benefit to the Agent', in Crisp (ed.), *How Should One Live?* (q.v.), 141–55.

HUDSON, STEPHEN. *Human Character and Morality*. Boston: Routledge & Kegan Paul, 1986.

—— 'What is Morality all About?', *Philosophia* 20 (1990), 3–13.

HUME, D. *An Enquiry Concerning the Principles of Morals*, ed. L. A. Selby-Bigge. Oxford: Oxford University Press, 1902.

HURSTHOUSE, R. 'Acting and Feeling in Character: *Nicomachean Ethics* 3. i', *Oxford Studies in Ancient Philosophy* 6 (1988), 201–19.

—— 'After Hume's Justice', *Proceedings of the Aristotelian Society* 91 (1990–1), 229–45.

—— 'Applying Virtue Ethics', in Hursthouse, Lawrence, and Quinn (eds.), *Virtues and Reasons* (q.v.), 57–75.

—— *Aristotle: Ethics*, a booklet forming part of A292: *Greece 478–336 BC.* Milton Keynes: Open University Press, 1979.

—— *Beginning Lives*. Oxford: Blackwell, 1987.

—— 'Virtue Theory and Abortion', *Philosophy and Public Affairs* 20 (1991), 223–46.

—— Lawrence, G., and Quinn, W. (eds.). *Virtues and Reasons*. Oxford: Clarendon Press, 1995.

HUTCHINSON, D. S. *The Virtues of Aristotle*. London: Routledge & Kegan Paul, 1986.

IRWIN, T. Review of S. Broadie, *Ethics with Aristotle*, *Journal of Philosophy* 90 (1993), 323–9.

KANT, I. *The Doctrine of Virtue*, in *The Metaphysics of Morals*, trans. M. Gregor. Cambridge: Cambridge University Press, 1996.

—— *Groundwork of the Metaphysic of Morals*, trans. H. J. Paton. New York: Harper & Row, 1964.

KORSGAARD, CHRISTINE. 'From Duty and for the Sake of the Noble: Kant and Aristotle on the Morally Good Action', in S. Engstrom and J. Whiting (eds.), *Aristotle, Kant and the Stoics* (q.v.), 203–36.

LOUDEN, R. B. 'Kant's Virtue Ethics', *Philosophy* 61 (1986), 473–89.

McDOWELL, J. 'Deliberation and Moral Development in Aristotle's Ethics', in S. Engstrom and J. Whiting (eds.), *Aristotle, Kant and the Stoics* (q.v.), 19–35.

—— 'Two Sorts of Naturalism', in R. Hursthouse, G. Lawrence, and W. Quinn (eds.), *Virtues and Reasons* (q.v.), 149–79.

—— 'The Role of *Eudaimonia* in Aristotle's Ethics', in A. Rorty (ed.), *Essays on Aristotle's Ethics*, 359–76. Berkeley: University of California Press, 1980.

—— 'Virtue and Reason', *Monist* 62 (1979), 331–50.

MACKIE, J. L. *Ethics: Inventing Right and Wrong*. London: Penguin, 1977.

MARCUS, R. B. 'Moral Dilemmas and Consistency', *Journal of Philosophy* 77 (1980), 121–36.

MIDGELY, M. *Animals and Why They Matter*. Athens, Ga.: University of Georgia Press, 1984.

NUSSBAUM, M. C. 'Aristotelian Social Democracy', in R. Douglass, G. Mara, and H. Richardson (eds.), *Liberalism and the Good*, 203–52. New York: Routledge, 1990.

—— 'Aristotle on Human Nature and the Foundations of Ethics', in J. E. J. Altham and R. Harrison (eds.), *World, Mind, and Ethics* (q.v.), 86–131.

OAKLEY, J. 'Varieties of Virtue Ethics', *Ratio* 9 (1996), 128–52.

O'NEILL, O. 'Abstraction, Idealization and Ideology in Ethics', in J. D. G. Evans (ed.), *Moral Philosophy and Contemporary Problems*, Royal Institute of Philosophy Lecture Series 22 (suppl. to *Philosophy*), 55–70. Cambridge: Cambridge University Press, 1987.

—— 'Kant after Virtue', *Inquiry* 26 (1984), 387–405.

PECK, M. SCOTT. *The Road Less Travelled*. New York: Simon & Schuster, 1978.

PHILLIPS, D. Z. 'Does it Pay to be Good?', *Proceedings of the Aristotelian Society* 65 (1964–5), 45–60.

PINCOFFS, E. *Quandaries and Virtues*. Lawrence, Kan.: University of Kansas Press, 1986.

—— 'Quandary Ethics', *Mind* 80 (1971), 552–71.

QUINE, W. V. O. 'Identity, Ostension, and Hypostasis', repr. in *From a Logical Point of View*, 65–79. New York: Harper & Row, 1963.

REGAN, T. *The Case for Animal Rights*. London: Routledge, 1983.

SCHEFFLER, S. *Human Morality.* New York: Oxford University Press, 1992.

SCHNEEWIND, J. 'The Misfortunes of Virtue', *Ethics* 101 (1990), 42–63.

SINGER, P. *How Are We to Live?* Oxford: Oxford University Press, 1997.

SIMPSON, P. 'Contemporary Virtue Ethics and Aristotle', *Review of Metaphysics* 46 (1992), 503–24.

SLOTE, MICHAEL. 'Agent-Based Virtue Ethics', in P. French, T. Uehling, and H. Wettstein (eds.), *Moral Concepts.* Midwest Studies in Philosophy 20, pp. 83–101. Notre Dame, Ind.: University of Notre Dame Press, 1995.

—— *Goods and Virtues.* Oxford: Clarendon Press, 1983.

—— *From Morality to Virtue.* New York: Oxford University Press, 1992.

—— 'Virtue Ethics', in M. Baron, P. Pettit, and M. Slote, *Three Methods of Ethics* (q.v.), 000–00.

—— 'Virtue Ethics and Democratic Values', *Journal of Social Philosophy* 24 (1993), 5–37.

SOLOMON, D. 'Internal Objections to Virtue Ethics', in P. French, T. Uehling, and H. Wettstein (eds.), *Ethical Theory: Character and Virtue*, Midwest Studies in Philosophy 13, pp. 428–41. Notre Dame, Ind.: University of Notre Dame Press, 1988.

STATMAN, D. 'Introduction to Virtue Ethics', in D. Statman (ed.) *Virtue Ethics*, 2–41. Edinburgh: Edinburgh University Press, 1997.

STOCKER, M. 'The Schizophrenia of Modern Ethical Theories', *Journal of Philosophy* 14 (1976), 453–66.

STROUD, BARRY. 'The Charm of Naturalism', *Proceedings and Addresses of the American Philosophical Association* 70 (1996), 43–55.

SWANTON, C. 'Profiles of the Virtues', *Pacific Philosophical Quarterly* 76 (1995), 47–72.

—— 'The Supposed Tension Between "Strength" and "Gentleness" Conceptions of the Virtues', *Australasian Journal of Philosophy* 75 (1997), 497–510.

—— 'Virtue Ethics and the Problem of Indirection: A Pluralistic Value-Centred Approach', *Utilitas* 9 (1997), 167–81.

THOMAS, L. *Living Morally: A Psychology of Moral Character.* Philadelphia: Temple University Press, 1989.

THOMPSON, M. 'The Representation of Life', in R. Hursthouse, G. Lawrence, and W. Quinn (eds.), *Virtues and Reasons* (q.v.), 247–96.

THOMSON, J. J. 'A Defense of Abortion', *Philosophy and Public Affairs* 1 (1971), 47–66.

TRIANOSKY, G. V. 'Natural Affections and Responsibility for Character: A Critique of Kantian Views of the Virtues', in O. Flanagan and A. O. Rorty (eds.), *Identity, Character and Morality* (q.v.), 93–110.

—— 'What is Virtue Ethics all About?', *American Philosophical Quarterly* 27 (1990), 335–44.

WATSON, G. 'On the Primacy of Character', in O. Flanagan and A. O. Rorty (eds.), *Identity, Character and Morality* (q.v.), 449–83.
—— 'Virtues in Excess', *Philosophical Studies* 46 (1984), 57–74.
WIGGINS, DAVID. 'Eudaimonism and Realism in Aristotle's Ethics: A Reply to John McDowell', in R. Heinamen (ed.), *Aristotle and Moral Realism*, 219–31. London: UCL Press, 1995.
—— 'Truth, Invention and the Meaning of Life', *Proceedings of the British Academy*, 62 (1976), 331–78.
WILLIAMS, B. 'Acting as the Virtuous Person Acts', in R. Heinamen (ed.), *Aristotle and Moral Realism*, 13–23. London: UCL Press, 1995.
—— 'Ethics and the Fabric of the World' (1985), repr. in *Making Sense of Humanity*, 172–81.
—— *Ethics and the Limits of Philosophy.* London: Fontana/Collins, 1985.
—— 'Evolution, Ethics and the Representation Problem' (1983), repr. in *Making Sense of Humanity*, 100–10.
—— *Making Sense of Humanity.* Cambridge: Cambridge University Press, 1995.
—— 'Moral Luck', *Proceedings of the Aristotelian Society* suppl. vol. 50 (1976), 115–35.
—— *Morality.* New York: Harper & Row, 1972.
—— 'Morality and the Emotions' (1965), repr. in *Problems of the Self*, 207–29. Cambridge: Cambridge University Press, 1973.
—— 'Philosophy', in M. Finley (ed.), *The Legacy of Greece*, 202–55. Oxford: Oxford University Press, 1981.
—— 'Replies', in J. E. J. Altham and R. Harrison (eds.), *World, Mind, and Ethics* (q.v.), 185–224.
—— 'Saint-Just's Illusion' (1991), repr. in *Making Sense of Humanity*, 135–52.
—— *Utilitarianism For and Against*, with J. J. C. Smart. London: Cambridge University Press, 1973.
ZAGZEBSKI, L. *Virtues of the Mind.* New York: Cambridge University Press, 1996.

# Index

Printed in the United Kingdom
by Lightning Source UK Ltd.
105943UKS00001B/13